MANAGEMENT BY CROSS-TRAINING:

a business model for sustainable leadership, negotiation of organizational culture, participation, meaning, identity, vision, and innovation in the 21st century.

by

Clive S. Michelsen

First Edition

JAC International AB
Box 60 220
S-216 09 LIMHAMN Sweden
www.mmc.st / www.cross-training.eu
info@cross-training.eu

© Clive Michelsen, 2008

Cover & Layout: Clive Michelsen
Written by: Clive Michelsen

Printed by: Book Surge, Charleston, S.C. USA 2007

Library of Congress Control Number: 2009902580

ISBN-10:   91-975326-5-7
ISBN-13:   978-91-975326-5-5
EAN: 9789197532655

Special thanks go to Rexam
and their insightful and visionary leaders in Fosie, Sweden:

Claes Bjäreholt, Plant Manager,

Ulf Larsson, Human Resources Manager,

Katarina Bergh, Assistant Human Resources Manager

Henrik Lidman, Production Manager,

Stefan Anderson, Assistant Production Manager

Niklas Andreasson, QA Manager,

Maria Rutholm, Supply Chain Manager, and Rexam's

six motivated shift managers (Stefan, Bengt, Mikael, Ulf, Christer, & Inaet),

and to

Bengt Andersson at (3) Screen

Contents

Preface

Section *1* Cross-Training Management Philosophy and Theory
Chapter

Section *2* Cross-Training System Analysis & Identification
Chapter

preface   **Management by Cross-Training**

Management by Cross-Training is a tool used by management to frame cultural practices within the organization. The main purpose is to produce mutually beneficial and competitive advantages from within the organization and individual. This book provide managers and leaders with the resources necessary to empower employees to negotiate a favorable outcome in regard to understanding one's working environment, participation, innovation, efficacy and identity. Management by Cross-Training comprises a number of disciplines from engineering and strategic planning to psychology and ergonomics with special emphasis on motivation and participatory teamwork through competency development. The book consists of fourteen chapters covering managerial and leadership principles, systems identification, knowledge and process understanding, change, company culture and the economics of Cross-Training.

In order to be competitive in the new environment, organizations should aspire to create their competitive advantages from within, individual by individual. Buying a distribution system or a patent is no longer viable in the new global economy. This strategy has in the past forged corporate giants, individualistic greed, and identities foreign to corporate synergy. Today, many of these corporate giants lack an organizational culture which strives after innovation, creativity, and development, but instead they have become lethargic dinosaurs infected with the complacency virus.

Too many corporations are infected with undefined organizational cultures allowing the complacency virus to incubate and affect, ethics, vision, participation, workplace knowledge and mutually beneficial philosophies. These are the foundations of competitive advantage and a democratic society which we all so treasure.

Realizing the importance of workplace knowledge, process understanding, vision, identity and individual well-being, this model emphasizes leadership traits necessary to forge a sustainable organizational culture which can support and enhance these fundamentals. This book introduces managers, leaders, consultants, strategists, graduate MBA students as well as business and psychology majors to the complexities surrounding ethical and sustainable management in the 21st century.

The fourteen chapters take the reader through a roller-coaster of disciplines, skills, and tools necessary to empower creative and innovative organizational cultures in a competitive environment. Section one (chapter 1,2,3 & 4) deals with management and leadership, motivation, health, and behavior analysis. Section two (chapters 5,6,7, 8 & 9) covers systems identification, ergonomics, process, standard operating procedures and knowledge. Section three (chapters 10, 11 & 12) discusses the negotiation of individual change, strategy and structural change and organizational culture. Section four (chapters 13 & 14) looks at the economics of Cross-Training and how to work with corporate "Stars." The appendix section includes a number of assessment tests and a practical approach guide to understanding process.

This book will explain the theory behind Management by Cross-Training and the techniques used to enhance on-the-job-training (OJT), education, and quality control methods that will help to improve employee motivation, knowledge, participation and ability to multi-task in team environments. It also introduces the readers to: "The Process Theory of Perpetual Motivation Positioning" (PMP), process, the complacency virus, knowledge, identity, participation and lots more.

As with most books of this nature, and because Management by Cross-Training covers so many disciplines its full effect will not become evident until you have read all the chapters. It is the combination these disciplines and the ambiguous nature of implementing a multi-dimensional process approach to organizational culture that requires a view of the 'forest and the tress.' Leadership skills require the ability to feel and live your organization's pulse through signals, participation and vision.

Clive Michelsen

Section *1*   *Cross-Training Management*
Philosophy and Theory

Management by Cross-Training comprises a number of disciplines from engineering and strategic planning to psychology and ergonomics with special emphasis on motivation and participatory teamwork through competency development. This section incorporates four chapters which look at the philosophy of management in relation to Cross-Training with emphasis on sustainable and ethical management through mutually beneficial obligations.

Chapter one Leadership and Management in Cross-Training takes a look at management and leadership, how these roles differ, and common duties that are overlooked today.

Chapter two *The C-T Equation (PMP + CD + R = IDP)* looks at a number of key leadership traits which inspire the Innovative Development Process (IDP) through enhancing employee motivation, competency development, participation, rotation, and teamwork balanced by "Perpetual Motivation Positioning."

Chapter three *A Matter of Health* discusses various cuases of stress, anxiety and defense mechanisms found in the workplace and provides managers with a number of signals that they should be looking for. The chapter also delves into the complacency virus, the façade jam, and long-term induced physical & psychological injuries.

Chapter four addresses *Behavioral Analysis and Management* (BAM) and its process of understanding, preventing, promoting and trust in relation to Cross-Training. The Complacency Gap Analysis is introduced along with other leadership techniques used to facilitate signals identified in the previous chapter.

chapter *1*   *Leadership & Management in Cross-Training*

We begin this book by reflecting on the roles and duties of the manager and the leader. Whether, they are wearing both of these hats or not, their responsibilities are different. Their roles, responsibilities, obligations, and commitment to both the individual and organization will become more evident as you progress through this book. Furthermore, this chapter addresses the sustainable and ethical expectations demanded by internal and external stakeholders.

Are *persons of responsibility* leaders or managers or both, and what is the difference between leadership and management? What dissimilarities are evident in management and leadership styles, and how can these roles be clarified to minimize the disparity between these objectives?

This chapter will attempt to address the unique differences between these two very different roles and to shed light onto the forgotten roles of management.

*Webster defines **leadership** as "**1**. the position or guidance of a leader **2**. the ability to lead **3**. the leaders of a group," and leader as "a person or thing that leads; directing, commanding, or guiding head, as of a group or activity." They define **manager** as "a person who manages; esp., **a**) one who manages a business, institution, etc. **b**) one who manages affairs or expenditures, as of a household, a client (an entertainer or athlete), an athletic team, etc. **c**) Baseball the person in overall charge of a team and the strategy in games." **Management** is defined as "**1**. the act, art, or manner of managing, or handling, controlling, directing, etc. **2**. skillful managing; careful, tactful treatment **3**. skill in managing; executive ability **4**. **a**) the persons or person managing a business, institution, etc. **b**) such persons collectively, regarded as a distinct social group with special interests, characteristic economic views, etc." **Responsible***

> *is defined, "***1***. Expected or obliged to account (for some-thing, to someone); answerable; accountable ***2***. involving accountability, obligation, or duties ***3***. that can be charged with being the cause, agent, or source of something ***4***. able to distinguish between right and wrong and to think and act rationally, and hence accountable for one's behavior ***5***. readily assuming obligations, duties, etc.; dependable; reli-able..."* **Responsibility** *is defined as "condition, quality, fact, or instance of being responsible; obligation, accountability, dependability, etc."*[1]

Therefore, *persons of responsibility* can be leaders and/or managers. Distinct and separate in nature their roles and key responsibilities are all too forgotten in today's competitive climate. To prevent role dilution and contradiction I will address the matter of leadership and management separately. Unfortunately like most jobs in today's fast moving global environment, leaders and managers find it difficult fulfill all of their duties effectively.

This global economic paradigm along with threats from the external envi-ronment, rapid growth, complacency, and the ambiguousness of management and leadership responsibilities is the leading cause of tension and conflict with-in organizations. To provide these positions with more clarity and to further define their roles I will begin with management's role as its policies paths the strategic road-map for leaders to follow. This strategic road-map includes the policies that support departmental goals and objectives, organizational vision and company culture that leaders are required to implement.

If you manage your car well with regular service, change the oil, oil-filter, air-filter, spark plugs, drive sensibly and fill-up with the right gasoline the chances are that your car will serve you well. The same goes for management of an orga-nization. It too needs check-ups, a service plan and adjustments on a continual basis. If your car starts to leak oil, then just cleaning up the oil leak from the ground will not resolve the problem of the oil leak.

The Role of Management and the Manager

There are seven major responsibilities of management and they are:

1. to constantly insure that the organization is functionally and economically sound through the effective production of goods and/or services by all ethical and sustainable means available,

2. to frequently update and improve processes and operating structures within the organization through good management practices and statistical controls,

3. to provide a working climate that is mutually beneficial to all stakeholders (employees, stockholders &customers) with vision and core values,

4. to foster an organizational culture with vision and dialog, open communication channels between all stakeholders and partners (employees, union, leaders, stockholders, and customers),

5. to endorse and support a learning and flexible organization using "Perpetual Motivation Positioning" (PMP: chapter 2) and PROCESS (chapter 7),

6. to underwrite guidelines that foster the health of the employees and good ethical behavior in relation to one another, the company, its stockholders and customers,

7. to root out departmental stagnation, greed enhances and other inconsistencies in management.

Top management is solely responsible for the procedural guidelines necessary for a healthy organization (employees, goals, culture, product, equipment, plant and the balance sheet), what it produces, how it produces, and the ethical standards of its managers and employees. If something goes wrong then it is top management that is accountable.

7 Golden Responsibilities of Management

- Managing a sound organization
- Managing process structure through statistical controls
- Mutually beneficial management
- Managing organizational culture & vision
- Managing a learning organization
- Managing health and ethical behavior
- Management of cancers in the organization

Fig. 1.1. The seven golden responsibilities of senior management. The purpose for these rules is to create a stable environment fostering efficacy, growth, innovation and team-work.

(1) Managing a sound organization

Management should constantly insure that the organization is functionally and economically sound through the effective production of goods and/or services by all sustainable and ethical means available. This golden rule has really two parts. The first relying on the function of sound economics by providing attainable financial goals, not dictated by short-term quarterly reports or the stock market but rather by manageable realistic and sustainable means. The second part emphasizes the use of ethics in obtaining these goals through social, environmental and ergonomic means acceptable. For example, if you are producing at a set of standards (Environmental protection Agency, International Standards Organization, Occupational Safety and Health Administration, and others) in the USA then these standards should be reproduced and maintained elsewhere. Otherwise your ethical standards are in question and management should be held accountable if a failure occurs in the production process (Union Carbide spill in India in the 80's). Not only does this show poor ethical standards but it also shows inconsistency in management.

(2) Managing process structure through statistical controls

The second rule is basic management practice and derives from engineering disciplines. It requires proper understanding of the landscape, process, and workflow environment (the flow of the product or service from start to finish). Management should direct operative staff to frequently create, if necessary, update and improve processes and operating procedures within the organization.

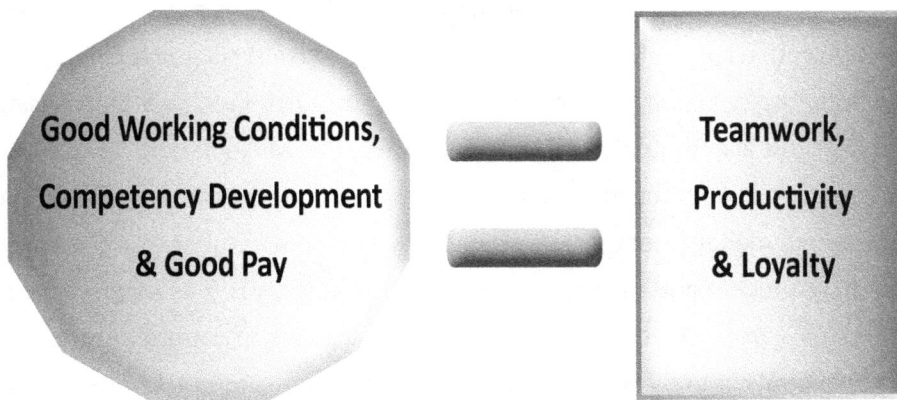

Good Working Conditions, Competency Development & Good Pay = **Teamwork, Productivity & Loyalty**

Fig. 1.2. Management should always strive to achieve good working condition, high competency levels, and good pay as it produces a mutually beneficial relationship between the company and its employees. This relationship is a requirement for good teamwork, productivity and loyalty ingredients necessary for long-term objectives.

These procedures are living instruments and vigilant monitoring of these structural informational tools should be made a priority. These processes should be linked to statistical controls taken from measurements at various control points throughout product/service flow. These can be maintained and monitored manually or electronically.

(3) Mutually beneficial management

Just as a legal contract needs to be mutually beneficial for it to be legal so should the relationship between management and the various stakeholders too. Management should ensure that a working climate is available to all employees within the organization not just the top of the hierarchy. Good working conditions, competency development and good pay equals teamwork, productivity and loyalty which is mutually beneficial. Stockholders and other stakeholders should also receive a mutually beneficial deal along with the customer. It is a balance and that is why we need good managers.

(4) Managing organizational culture and vision

Management has a duty to foster an organizational culture which includes open communication channels (laterally and vertically) with all stakeholders and partners (employees, union, leaders, stockholders, and customers), and focuses on openness but also mutual respect, loyalty, trust and willingness to solve problems no matter how drastic. As management set the stage for organizational culture it is management's responsibility to implement this culture through governing process and in real practice. Communication is a key ingredient in motivation and teamwork and if management is weak in communication the organizational culture will suffer through segmentation and isolationism resulting in a loss of trust and loyalty. Management must be willing to participate in the solution with weekly walkabouts, be willing to take responsibility for wrong decisions, and other anomalies in management. By this I don't mean just walking through the departments but actually taking time to sit down and chat with personnel and if work cannot stop for any reason be willing to pitch in and help while talking. If there is one aspect in which most managers are lacking it is this.

(5) Managing a learning organization

Management should endorse and support a learning organization where all personnel can develop their skills, improve their ability to multi-task and to accept change and flexibility without duress. This is a long-term and strategic management tool which produces results; however, it does take time and commitment from all parties. The educational process should always begin with the individual and their specific duties; thereafter, spreading throughout departments, divisions and the entire organization like a spider's web. As the teams and departments become trained you'll notice a change in participant's motivation and participation. The economic and ethical consequence of competency development or helping employees to help themselves is staggering and will be presented in chapter seventeen.

(6) Managing health and ethical behavior

Management should commit to a healthy organization and they are directly responsible for the health and wellbeing of all persons within the greater environment of the organization. Management should underwrite guidelines that foster the good employee health and ethical behavior in relation to one another, the company, its stockholders and customers. Health is both physical and psychological in nature. If a machine breaks down you either have to fix it or you have to replace it. It is obvious that by scheduling regular maintenance and replacement of parts the machine will last a lot longer. It is therefore obvious that the psychological and physical wellbeing of the employee needs attention too.

Multitasking personnel with frequent rotational schedules will help to alleviate undue physical demands placed upon them. Psychological health is also affected by lack of stimulus, low self-esteem, other stresses and defense mechanisms related to work and the individuals' private life. Therefore management needs to create and support directives to insure that the operative leaders' monitor and adjust the demands of the working environment to meet this. Remuneration is not sufficient to ethically justify abuse of an individual's psychological and physical health and a commitment to ethics is therefore essential. As with all working environments some jobs are more physically and/or mentally demanding and can cause great strain or long-term stress overtime. Therefore, management should be looking for alternative ways to ease the physical and mental stresses placed upon the individual by continually re-evaluating the workflow process, equipment and procedures. Quick solutions such as moving production to a third world country to reduce macro problems associated with cost instead of looking at the micro conditions which effect those costs are not ethically conducive to the long-term health of the corporation.

Sweeping leadership and management responsibilities under the carpet to alleviate cost demands by not addressing the issues at hand is quite frankly poor management—not to mention the image and message it sends to employees. Corporate culture and behavior should include ethical standards and these standards begin with boardrooms, management, leaders and union representatives.

An example of one such company that practices this is Rexam in Fosie Sweden. Their human resources manager Mr. Ulf Larsson treats his employees with an ethical approach far beyond standards seen in other industrial production companies. Although the plant has reduced its workforce by more than one third in the past 15 years, production has increased year after year. Mr. Larsson's his ethical approach to his employees' wellbeing justifies that ethical behavior should be a part of all organizations.

Management should also realize that ethical behavior becomes part of the organizational culture and is forged by their example. If they rape the corporate balance sheet with outrageous bonuses and other perks how can they expect other not to follow suit or to even respect their leadership? Would you pay a cleaner a bonus if he/she cleaned poorly? Ethics therefore includes one's ability to be consistent with the skills to balance individual expectations and demands, and the competency to lead by example in order to meet competition while maintaining employee health and motivation.

(7) Management of cancers in the organization

Management has the responsibility to prevent, fix and/or root out whenever possible all illnesses within the organization, three of which (stagnation, greed, and inconsistency) will be discussed here in short.

Individual and/or departmental stagnation is an infection which affects about 80% of the working environment sometime during their working career. Excluding mechanical or structural deficiencies, individual output/participation follows a trend from the introduction phase (2 weeks) to the growth phase (1-24 months) to maturity phase (18-52 months) and finally the stagnation phase (36-96 months). Productivity/participation tends to decrease during the maturity phase, see page 18, and management need to act or put processes into place to inhibit this from happening.

Contrary to other economic models, I do not believe in motivation through bonuses or in form of extra remunerations packages for management or employees. Pay should be set for the position, market expectations and the output expected and agreed upon from day one. If employees do not produce as agreed then they should be encouraged to do so, counseled and cautioned if appropriate. If goals are not met then management should take responsibility and take appropriate action to correct the discrepancy/ies. Management should not seed the illness of greed. It only encourages short-term quarterly management practices, see chapter 4, back-stabbing and individualistic antisocial activity/ies. It is counter-productive and directly affects the organization's stability, long-term employment (high turnover), teamwork, loyalty and fosters ill feelings amongst other employees.

Inconsistencies in management are also the responsibility of management. Inconsistencies exist due to the lack of guidelines, direction and/or proper leadership in following established guidelines. If motorists decided to ignore the traffic signals, what would be the outcome at most heavily used intersections?

Management needs to cutout some of the ambiguity, or gray, in the organization. Achieving gray objectives is not the easiest way to go about managing an organization or motivating employees.

The Role of the Leader and Leadership

Management's role is to create the guidelines for a mutually beneficial agreement between the various groups (internal and external) within the organization such as, employees, customers, stockholders and other stakeholders. Naturally, this can be accomplished using some leadership skills; nevertheless, the leaders (shift managers, team leaders, department managers, supervisors and union) are responsible for implementing management's guidelines and to adjust these guidelines with management's approval in order to best produce the expected results. Leadership is a pendulum in balance that needs to be in balance between management's expected goals and personnel's achievable productive ability. Leaders' are therefore expected to use the following seven leadership traits:

1. to have a hands on approach,
2. to produce maximum effective production results safely and by taking and requiring responsibility through delegation and other methods,
3. to set short-term goals (daily, weekly and monthly),
4. to balance the use of resources to meet the internal/external demands (need based management) through flexibility and rotation,
5. to motivate, encourage participation, innovation and creativity,
6. to continually improve staff knowledge and workflow synergy, awareness, and
7. to practice open communication and reduce stresses and defense mechanisms.

7 Leadership Traits

- Hands-on-approach
- Maximum effective production
  (safely & with responsibility)
- Set short-term goals
- Balance resources
  (rotation & flexibility)
- Motivate and encourage: participation,
  innovation and creativity
- Improve staff knowledge and workflow
  synergy awareness
- Open communication and reduction of
  stresses and defense mechanisms

Fig. 1.2. The seven golden leadership traits for leaders with responsibility. These traits will help to keep order whilst at the same time creating guidelines to work from and more. Furthermore, they create a stable leader environment fostering efficacy, growth, innovation and team-work.

(1) A hands-on-approach

Participatory leadership is a good way to describe "a hands on approach" as it suggests just that. A leader is close to the action and participates in all facets of operations. Problem solvers at the root, they take care of all issues related to the workflow process and any and all conflicts before they grow into problems by understanding the effects of polarization, individual and group dramatics, personal attacks, we-them attitudes, and act as the change agent by promoting improvements, ergonomic understanding and teamwork.

Leaders are jack-of-all-trades and pitch in when necessary, they need to understand the functions and processes of their entire working environment and are role-models for all to follow. If leaders are willing to get on their knees and pitch-in then their staff will be inspired and follow. Participatory leadership is an important catalyst to success and well-being. As the old saying goes, "what you put in is what you get out".

(2) Maximum effective production (safely & with responsibility)

As soon as one hears the words maximum effective production results one suspects that an accountant has been in the picture somewhere, well this is not always the case. Naturally, a company must be competitive and therefore it needs to stem off competition by producing its products/services more reliably, quicker, and less expensive than competitors. Obviously producing in this context means design, production, logistics, marketing, and so on.

It is the leader's task to insure that production is as optimal as possible and to eliminate or correct, when possible, all ineffective workflow processes. Therefore, effective production requires a LEAN philosophy with a leader that can drive production delegate tasks, to encourage participation and ownership, and to make employees accountable for their actions when completing such tasks. It is important that the leader not delegate tasks above an individual employee's ability, and if so, the leader should take full responsibility if something goes astray. Clearly, all tasks should be in accordance with national acceptable safety standards, such as OSHA. Sustainable leadership is built on taking responsibility for your employees.

(3) Set short-term goals (daily, weekly and monthly)

Obviously, we are not all hard-core athletes and not everyone can run and win a 10 000 meter race either; on the other hand, we can all participate and complete the race whether we walk, jog or even divide up the 10 000 meter race into 100 x 100 meter walks. At this point, participation is vital, how we do it is irrelevant, it is the reward of achieving a set goal that is satisfying. This accomplishment, or the anticipation of accomplishing, provides situational control resulting in improved motivation further participation. McClelland, Atkinson, and Alderfer et al., theories on motivation found that how well individuals are motivated depends upon their various achievement needs, see motivation in chapter two.

In Cross-Training, the leader is charged with creating achievable daily, weekly, and monthly goals for all members of his/her team. Naturally, these goals should include production, personal development, educational (internal and external), process innovation, and reevaluation of current duties, communication strategies and many others. Keeping your staff active through short-term goals is vital to good leadership. Clearly, some goals can be assigned on an individual basis, in pair, or even newly created teams or task groups; however, it is important to remember that teamwork starts with the individual.

> *If your boat sunk and you are required to tread water for say eight hours, which is an almost impossible feat I might add, and if you knew when the boat sank that you would have to tread water for the next eight hours, most people would begin their ordeal with huge trepidation, even though they knew there would eventually be saved, not due the situation at hand but the task ahead of them. They would be overwhelmed by negative thoughts of failure, an almost fatalist start to the long task ahead. Many people would give up after just five to ten minutes, when their muscles started to build lactic acid and begin to hurt.*

> *By changing the ordeal from a long impossible task to small tasks which are both attainable and constructive of say ten minutes/waves/swells each the ordeal becomes a little easier. Keeping the mind focused on trying to find solutions like float-ing on your back, or taking off your long pants and tying a knot at the bottom of the legs and filling the legs up with air and using the pants as a life jacket (a trick learned in the US Navy), or looking for debris that could be used hang on. Naturally, the task of treading water becomes less horrific in small bits rather than all at once.*

Leadership is the ability to adjust and create achievable goals for your employ-ees and to acknowledge it when they have accomplished them.

(4) Balance use of resources (need based management with individual ability to rotate and to be flexible)

Need-based management was originally developed for the computer engineer-ing sector to build program solutions for changing variables. Need-based man-agement in Cross-Training has to do with the individual employee's ability to multi-task in a number of environments throughout their working life cycle.

It is obvious that one is not expected to out-perform or produce at full ca-pacity from the age of 20 until retirement at 65 years. Neither is one expected to be entirely participatory during all of those 45 years. Nevertheless, a good leader will utilize his staff well by balancing his/her resources to harness maxi-mum benefit, see Perpetual Motivation Positioning in chapter two.

I have seen many examples of long-term induced Tunnel-Vision Syndrome as a management consultant. Tunnel-Vision Syndrome, occurs during the la-tent stages of the complacency period (see positional work-cycle stages Fig. 1.4; chapter 4, 2. prevent; and chapter 13, Complacency Gap Analysis) and affects one's ability to think outside of the box, participate openly, create and innovate. Balancing resources therefore requires a fluid team that can meet the internal/

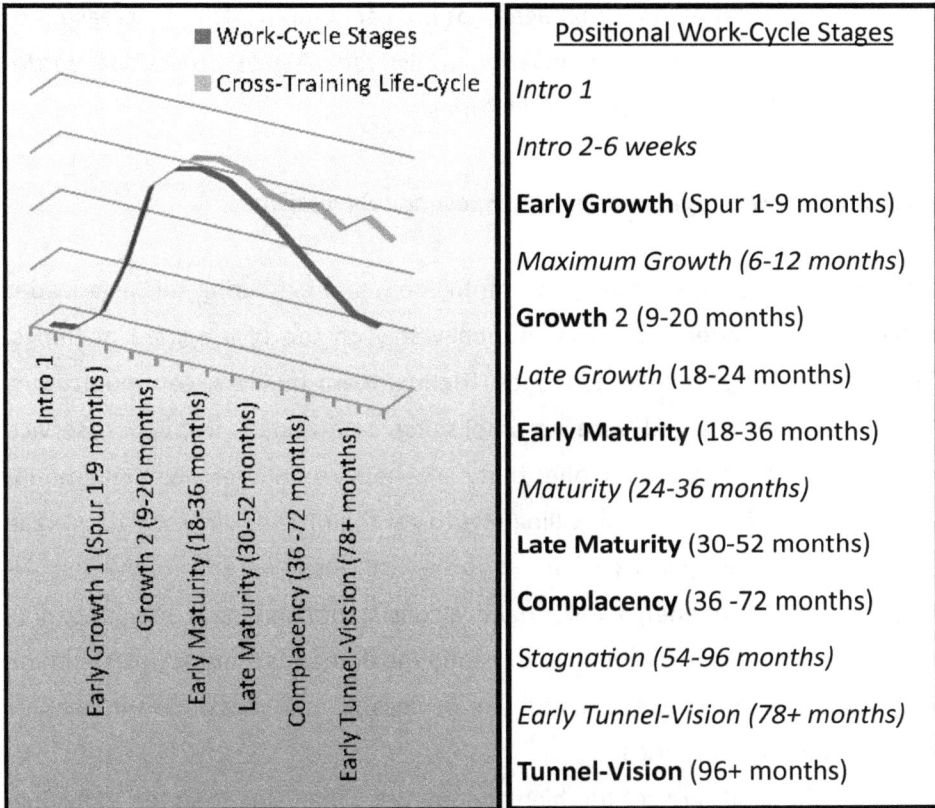

Work-Cycle Stages — Cross-Training Life-Cycle	Positional Work-Cycle Stages
	Intro 1
	Intro 2-6 weeks
	Early Growth (Spur 1-9 months)
	Maximum Growth (6-12 months)
	Growth 2 (9-20 months)
	Late Growth (18-24 months)
	Early Maturity (18-36 months)
	Maturity (24-36 months)
	Late Maturity (30-52 months)
	Complacency (36 -72 months)
	Stagnation (54-96 months)
	Early Tunnel-Vision (78+ months)
	Tunnel-Vision (96+ months)

Fig. 1.4. Positional Work-Cycle Stages for industrial jobs. This example shows the six key stages related to, participation, productivity and willingness to take responsibility (PPR) during an employee's working career.

Willingness to learn and participation increases rapidly through the growth stage, and fol-lowed closely by productivity and responsibility taking phases through the late maturity stage. Thereafter PPR decreases during the late maturity and complacency stages and stagnating with tunnel-vision. Cross-Training's key is to introduce additional duties, rotations and assignments during the late maturity stage thus keeping productivity levels at their highest. Naturally, this might require a number of adjustments during the employee's working career. As always, there are exceptions to the rule, some employees move rapidly into the stagnation stage whereas some others never do and remain productive for their entire careers.

external demands through flexibility and rotation. Not only is this good for the company but it is healthy for the individual employee as it supports long-term physical and psychological health by reducing stress signals, defense mecha-nisms, and other work related injuries, see chapter three.

As a result, need-based management is a very helpful tool to increase productivity, participation and innovation whilst reducing or preventing bottle-necking, physical and psychological injuries.

(5) Motivate, encourage participation, innovation & creativity

Nothing comes free, especially not motivation, and extracting this as a leader is hard work. Leaders have to continually stay on top of a myriad of things. They are parents, confidants, judges, friends, team builders, communicators, and motivators charged with accomplishing determined production/service goals optimally. They are the ones that make heavy work seem light and mono-tone work fun. Through their willingness to get their hands dirty and to partake when needed their participation has to be both inspiring and motivating. Always vigilant, full of energy and proactive consistent handling is integral to success. Therefore, leaders have to understand the demands that they place on the individual and that these demands are achievable, see motivation in chapter two for additional theories.

If the demands are set too high and are not achievable then the individual and/or team will experience additional stress which in turn will lead to a rise in defense mechanisms and frustration with lower motivation and productivity as a result. On the other hand, if the goals are set too low and additional duties not assigned, a monotone and passive atmosphere will naturally decrease participation and production/service levels too.

Leaders should not show favoritism in anyway publicly. Consistent treatment of all personnel is by far the most important trait in motivational leadership. If you have to reprimand or congratulate an individual then that should be done behind closed doors. Never do this in front of other team members as it will only cause them to question impartiality or favoritism. Equally, you should never reprimand an individual in front of other team members as it will directly affect the morale and subsequently teamwork and motivation. However, you can collectively congratulate a team for good work. Delegation, empowerment, and education are additional tools used to encourage participation, creativity, and innovative process reviews. Rewarding individuals and/or teams through appraisals, recognition, promotion, extra leave/time-off, and increased basic pay are also good motivation tools. Conversely, incongruent objectives, broken promises, poor communication techniques, and inconsistencies in leadership will de-motivate employees.

(6) Improve staff knowledge & workflow synergy awareness

There are many similarities between leadership and a football coach. A football coach needs to insure that he prepares his/her players to meet the demands of the game. They need to be physically and psychologically fit and needs to be continually updated in regard to the changing game plan, plays, position re-sponsibilities and flexibility. Naturally, players will also be required to operate in other positions within the team, and to understand and anticipate the conse-quences of their actions/moves and how they affect the other team members.

The sixth leadership trait insures that all team members understand the various stages of the workflow process within their working environment and are familiar with the responsibilities for each position. This is a key to innovative and creative thinking and will eventually lead to suggestions for improvement or betterment of services. Not only will this lead to improvements but it helps the individual to understand that for every action there is a reaction. By this I mean, how the individual's attention to detail, quality control efforts, and effi-cacy will directly affect the workflow at the position receiving the product/ser-vice from the individual. If you do a poor job your teammate and/or customer will have to correct it. If you do a good job the product or service flows without impediment.

Knowledge provides the individual the ability and courage to think outside of the box and to anticipate the consequences of their actions; thereby, it is the first step towards taking responsibility.

Cross-Training is about competency development and empowering the individual to take responsibility for their working environment. Initially, leadership is required to create an environment conducive to learning thereby enhancing the individual's ability to participate fully.

(7) Open communication & reduce stresses and defense mechanisms

It is impossible for a leader to lead with good communication techniques. Poor communicators are usually destined to fail in at least four of the seven leadership traits above. In order to create goals, motivate and educate, build trust, discuss changes and improvements, enter into dialogs and combat illnesses of the organization one needs to communicate. Not only should a leader communicate concisely but they should do it consistently and respectfully to all members within the organizations no matter what position they might have.

Information dissemination is a critical element in leadership. The leader needs to practice horizontal communication at all times. Open dialog and feedback is essential for the leader so that he/she unequivocally knows that the message has been understood correctly, confirmed and acknowledged. Miscommunication is the most common cause for failure, conflict, office politics, façade building and poor team work.

Communication is about collaboration and collaboration generates involvement or participation. When individuals and a group are allowed to contribute with ideas, creativity and innovative solutions they feel part of the solution and find it easier to take responsibility for their actions. Therefore, knowledge leads to communication which leads to team work reducing undue stresses and defense mechanisms, see chapter three.

In conclusion, there is a distinct difference in the roles between that of the manager/management and the leader/leadership. Naturally, top management will have to practice some form of leadership too as they will have to leader their middle, line, section and shift managers. However, middle, line, section and shift managers are therefore expected to bear the brunt of the leadership by implementing management's policies with a hands on approach by producing maximum effective production results, safely, with responsibility, and by delegation and other methods, through the setting of short term goals, proper use of resources which are flexible, rotatable, and are motivated, encouraged to participate, and innovate while at the same time improving staff knowledge and workflow synergy awareness by practicing open communication.

Now, if that is not a daunting task I do not know what is? Obviously, if we want to be more competitive in the future "the forgotten role of the manager" needs to be addressed. These roles are separate and distinct.

chapter 2   **The C-T Equation**
(PMP + CD + R = IDP)

The C-T Equation (Perpetual Motivation Positioning + Competency Development + Rotation = Innovation Development Process) and is one of the fundamental components crossing management and leadership boundaries. As you proceed through this book, a number of these models will repeat themselves in other contexts and will suffice to justify their use is your overall leadership style.

Motivation

Motivation and how to motivate employees has been a bane in the side of psychologists and businessmen for centuries. However, in recent times we have become more adept in dissecting various motivational causes.

Basically there are a number of accepted theories on the market today from drive reduction to affective-arousal through need, cognitive and unconscious theories and other concepts such as reward and reinforcement, intrinsic and extrinsic and even self-control.

The author's process of "Perpetual Motivational Positioning" is based upon a combination of theories and claims that it is impossible to set motivation policy by running a comb over an organization and treating all individuals by the same motivational method. As David McClelland, Nadler, and the author claim, workers are not solely motivated by money and that this one-sided approach will only extinguish individual intrinsic motivators. The author believes that balance and continual adjustment of various motivators is the key.

Abraham Maslow's Hierarchy of Needs points out that individuals have wants and needs. Needs are stronger so unsatisfied needs will influence a person's behavior. These needs are listed in importance and the theory states that the lower level of needs need to be satisfied before one can move up to the

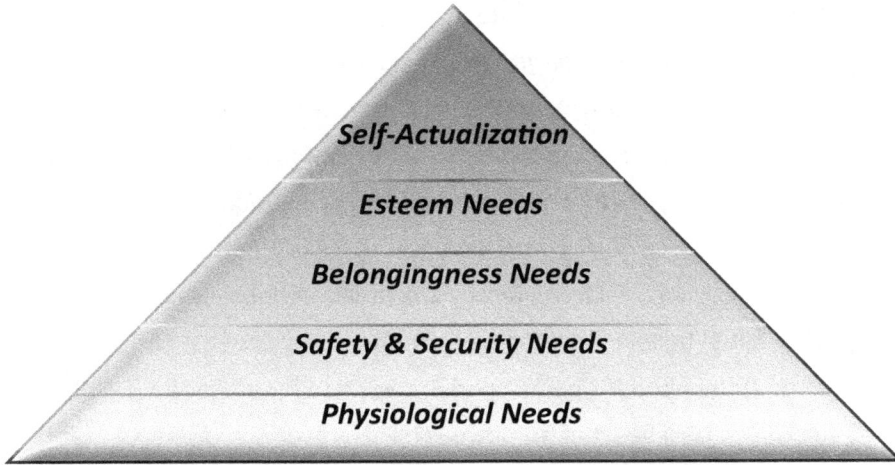

Fig. 2.1. Pyramid representing Maslow's Hierarchy of Needs. The theory of motivation states that people are motivated to meet these five types of needs. These five basic needs are ranked into a hierarchy. Once the lower level is achieved, the person moves up to the next.

next level. The levels, from lowest to highest, are: physiological, safety & security, social, self-esteem and finally self-actualization (Fig. 2.1).

In many circumstances, behavior is motivated by an urge to satisfy one's own needs whether those needs are self-serving or not. **Fredrick Herzberg** believed (Herzberg et al., 1959) that motivation is enhanced by maximizing the motivators or Satisfiers at work and minimizing the Dissatisfiers or maintenance factors (Fig. 2.2). Employees rated aspects associated with work. The results showed that the **Satisfiers** were the motivating factors related to job perfor-

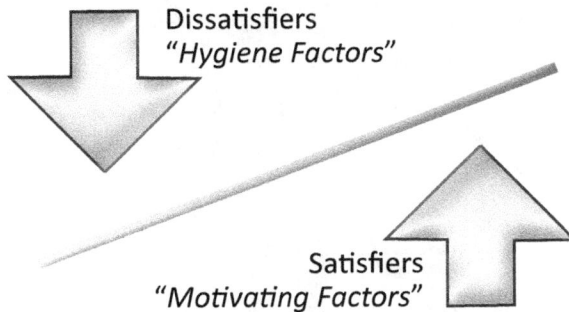

Dissatisfiers
"Hygiene Factors"

Satisfiers
"Motivating Factors"

Fig. 2.2. Herzberg's motivational theory stems from his two-factor theory, which suggests that work satisfaction and dissatisfaction arise from two different sets of factors.

mance and substance and they include such aspects as *recognition, responsibil-ity, advancement*, and *personal growth*. **Dissatisfiers** or "hygiene" factors on the other hand did not motivate employees if present but demotivated them if absent and were connected to the *policies* or *administrative rules* within the company's framework, their *salary*, and *working conditions, supervision* and overall *effectiveness*.

Other associative aspects studied by **David McClelland** (McClelland et al., 1961, 1962 & 1963) believe that people have three basic needs: 1) the need for achievement, 2) the need for power, and 3) the need for affiliation (Fig. 2.3.).

John Atkinson believes that employees have a reservoir of energy that they can draw from in times of need (Atkinson et al., 1983). This hidden energy is released depending upon:

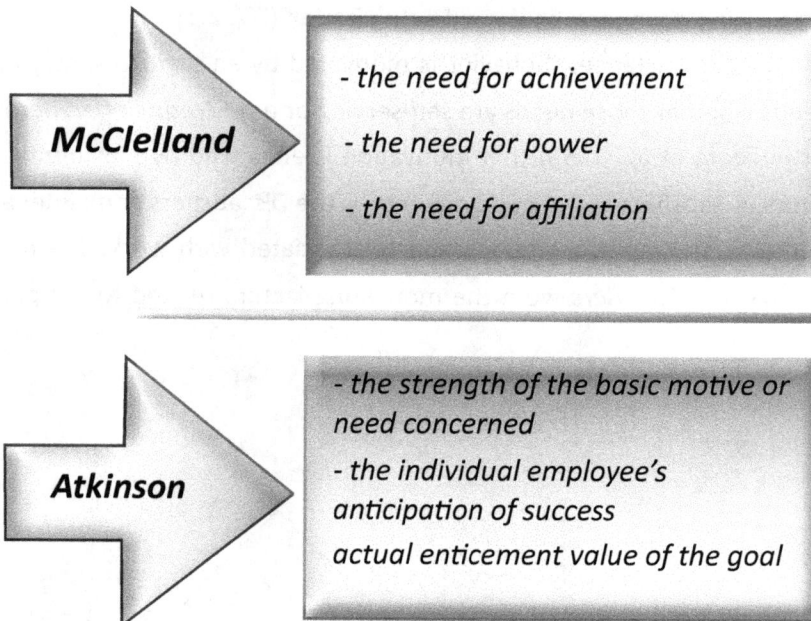

McClelland
- *the need for achievement*
- *the need for power*
- *the need for affiliation*

Atkinson
- *the strength of the basic motive or need concerned*
- *the individual employee's anticipation of success*
- *actual enticement value of the goal*

Fig. 2.3. McClelland's & Atkinson's theories on motivation. McClelland found that how well indi-viduals are motivated depended upon a strong need for achievement and the desire to succeed or excel in competitive situations. Atkinson's model suggests that performance and behavior are related to the strength of the need, and that the anticipation of achieving the goal, along with the incentive value, are the driving forces behind motivation.

1) the strength of the basic motive/need concerned,

2) the individual employee's anticipation of success, and

3) the actual enticement value of the goal (Fig. 2.3).

A good example of this can be a course at high school. If you remember the courses that you liked the most, were they not the courses that you did the most preparation for, and were they not the courses with the best grades, and did you not have a more social atmosphere both internally and externally around those classes as a result of increased motivation?

As discussed earlier, Maslow alleged that motivation is a function of meeting a hierarchy of needs and that a person will try to fulfill the most powerful level first. The most basic level is physiological (food, shelter, etc.), then safety and security, followed by belongingness (to be part of the social company), esteem needs, and lastly self-actualization needs. The content theory of motivation tries to shed light on the behavior that drives people to act in certain ways whilst trying to satisfy their innermost needs (Fig. 2.4).

Layton Alderfer agreed with Maslow in many ways; nevertheless, in his ***ERG theory*** (Alderfer et al., 1969 & 1972) he had just three levels of needs levels: Existence needs, Relatedness needs, and Growth needs. (Fig. 2.5). More impor-

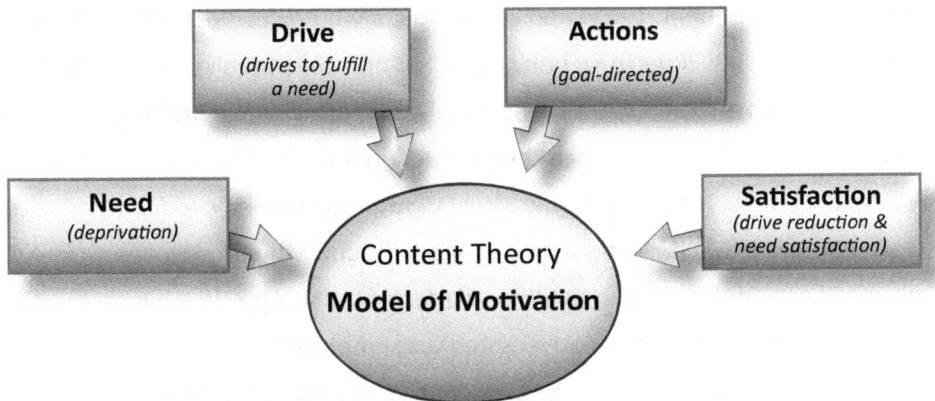

Fig. 2.4. Content theories of motivation concentrate on the various needs that motivate behavior.

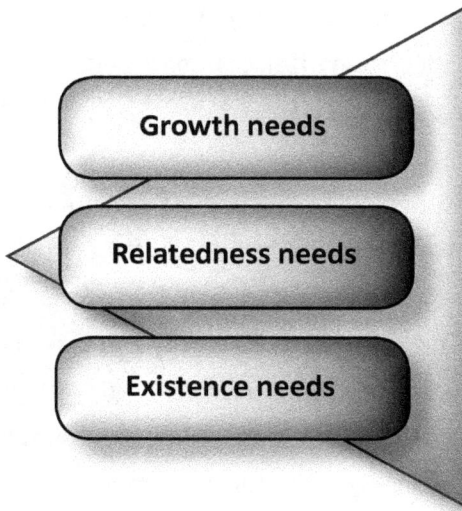

Fig. 2.5. ERG Theory. Alderfer believed that needs existed in only three
categories: Existence needs (basic
needs as addressed by Maslow plus the
fundamental needs in the workplace
such as basic benefits, coffee etc.),
Relatedness needs (the social company
or interpersonal relations) and lastly,
Growth needs (creativity, personal
development and productive influence
over the process).

tant was that he believed that when the higher needs were frustrated the lower needs would return, whereas, Maslow claimed that once a need was satisfied that need disappeared altogether.

Studies conducted in, amongst others, Western Electric's Hawthorne plant near Chicago between 1924-1933 by **Elton Mayo** (1880-1949) were ground-breaking in thought. Mayo was known for his 'Human Relations Model' and the 'Hawthorne Effect' and other studies. The **'Human Relations Model'** found that repetitive tasks and boredom actually reduces motivation whilst social contact and greater decision making abilities helped to create and sustain motivation. The 'Hawthorne Effect' suggested that workers who received special attention, in various forms, will perform better just because they received that attention. Similarly, Mayo also showed that by simply increasing the lightning on the factory floor he could also increase the production output. (Mayo et al., 1953).

McGregor, in his research into the **'Human Resources Model'** (McGregor et al., 1960 & 1967) believed that managers grouped their employees into two groups of assumptions. **'The Traditional Method'**, **Theory X**, he advocates holds that work is distasteful to employees and that employees can only be motivated by force, money or praise. On the other hand, he suggests in **Theory Y** that employees are intrinsically motivated to work and to do a good job (Fig. 2.6).

Theory X

People dislike work

Although necessary try to avoid work when possible

Work as secondary so more benefits and motivation are needed

Theory Y

Work is natural as play

People want to work and get satisfaction from work

Have the capacity to get and seek responsibility, creativity & innovation from the organization

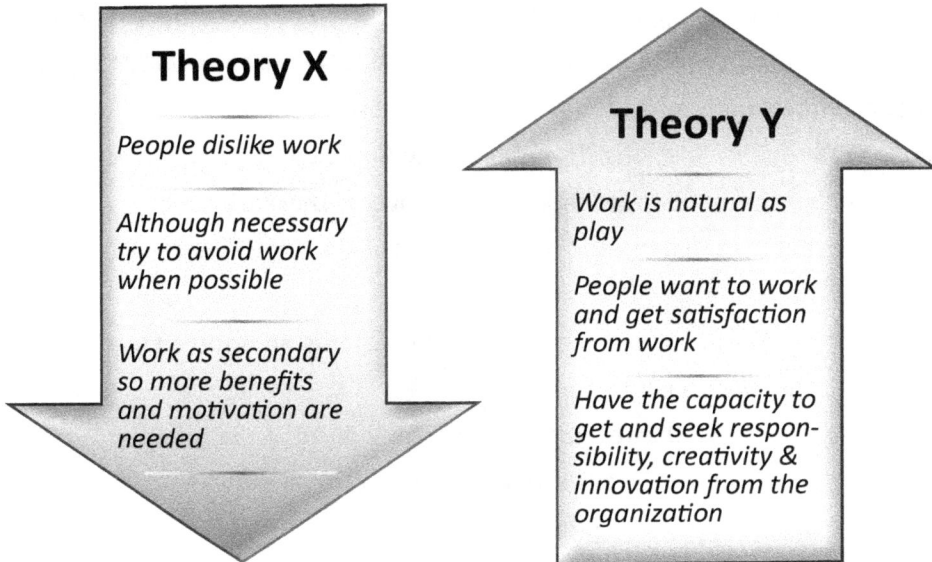

Fig. 2.6. Theory X & Y suggests that there are two types of employees X&Y and in order to motivate each type you would need two different approaches to do so. There are a lot of similarities between Theory Y and the Complacency Stage in the Positional Work-Cycle.

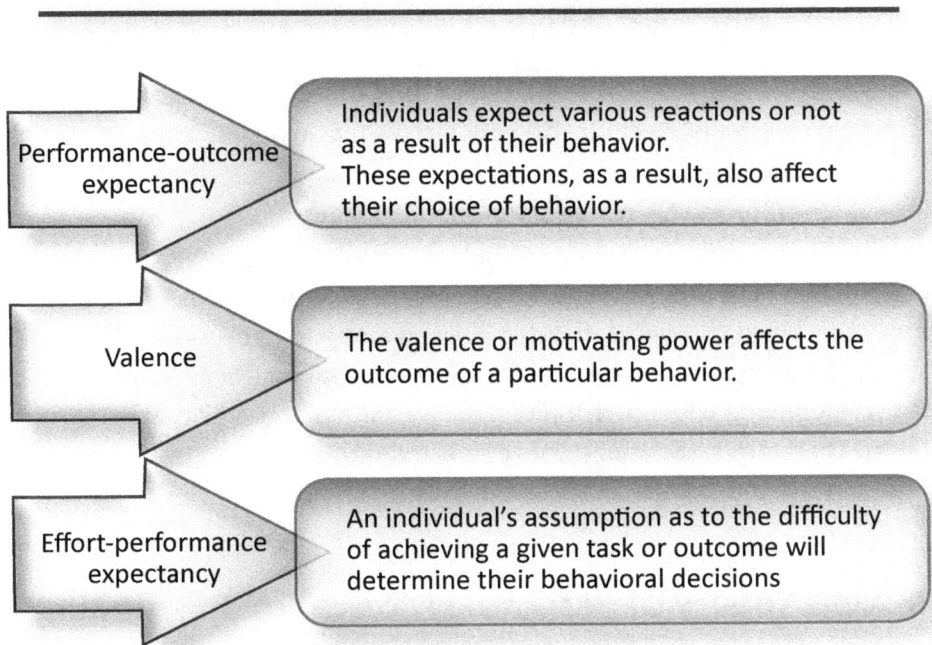

Performance-outcome expectancy

Individuals expect various reactions or not as a result of their behavior.
These expectations, as a result, also affect their choice of behavior.

Valence

The valence or motivating power affects the outcome of a particular behavior.

Effort-performance expectancy

An individual's assumption as to the difficulty of achieving a given task or outcome will determine their behavioral decisions

Fig. 2.7. The Expectancy Approach is a process theory of motivation and focuses on the thought processes made by the individual and the various decisions on how to behave concerning their degree of performance, specific role and/or degree of responsibility.

There is another approach to motivation called '***The Expectancy Approach***' or '***Expectancy Valence Approach***' (Nadler et al., 1977). ***David Nadler*** suggests that all employees and all situations are not alike. Like the author, fluid situations require fluid solutions. The Expectancy Approach (Fig. 2.7) suggests that there is no single best way to motivate employees. There are four assumption's in their hypothesis of behavior in organizations:

1) the individual and organizations behavior is determined by a combination of factors;

2) the needs, desires and goals of the individual are different;

3) individual behavior in an organization is a conscious decision;

4) the individual's expectations for a given outcome will determine the behavior of the individual.

Self-Determination Theory (Deci et al., 1985) suggests that intrinsic motivation drives individual behavior, and that this behavior has a propensity to grow and develop as a result of active encouragement from the existing environment. According to ***Edward Deci***, the primary factors that motivate are relatedness, autonomy, feedback and competence.

Goal-Setting Theory (Locke and Latham, 2002) is a cognitive theory and suggests that there is a connection between goal-setting, self-regulation and job satisfaction. Fundamentally, ***Edwin Locke***'s and ***Gary Latham***'s theory stems from goal specificity (clearly defined goals) which has to be achievable (moderate in difficulty, not too easy as the reward in accomplishing the goal would be lessened), and within reach (accessibility and time feasibility from start to finish). Therefore associations between work satisfaction and goal-setting are directly related to the expectancy theory (Fig. 2.8).

Process Theory of Perpetual Motivation Positioning

Process Theory of Perpetual Motivation Positioning (Michelsen, 2007) is a product of seven elements combining a number of motivational theories such

Self-Regulation	SMART Goal-Setting
Planning: *steps, strategy, obstacles, goal-setting.*	**S = Specific:** *goal specific (time and task).*
Monitoring: *observing, monitoring and measuring progress toward accomplishing set goals.*	**M = Measurable:** *monitoring progress and rewarding achieved goals.*
Evaluating: *grading progress and assessing outcome.*	**A = Achievable:** *creating achievable goals as unachievable goals are very demotivating.*
Reinforcing: *recognition of success by reward and reflection by self-regulation, task orientation and resource development (skills & abilities).*	**R = Resourced:** *invest in resources needed to accomplish tasks.*
	T = Time-based: *realistic short- and long-term goals.*

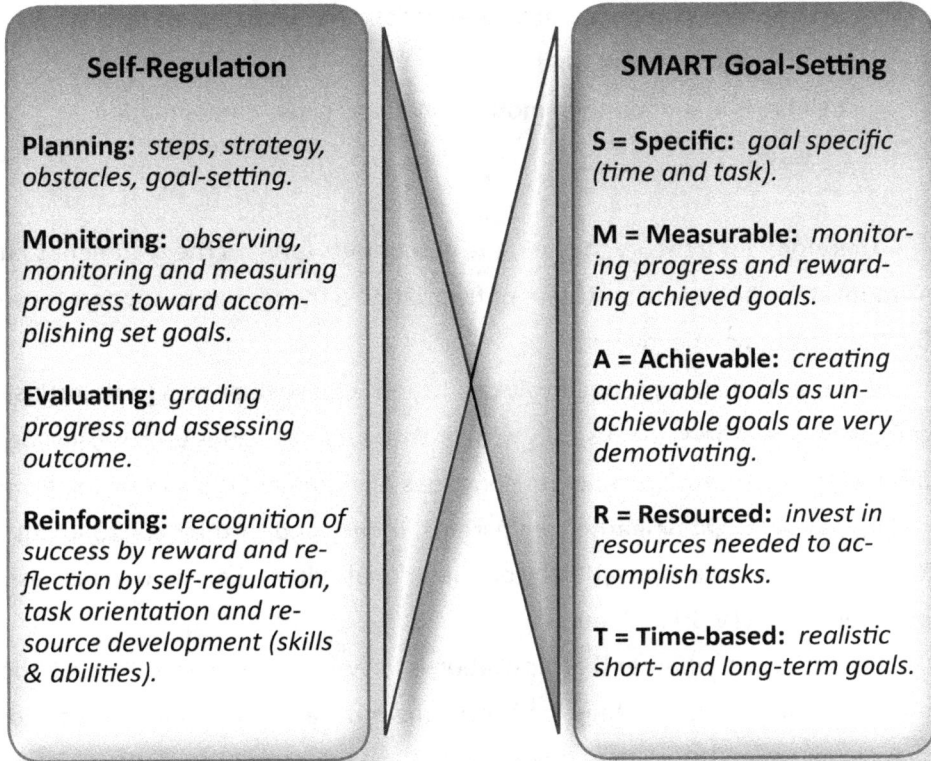

Fig. 2.8. Self-Regulation and Smart Goal Setting are very similar in nature and are cognitive processes of planning, monitoring, evaluating, and reinforcement. As self-regulation has shown to produce work satisfaction, SMART Goal-Setting should produce comparable results.

as: Need-based, Affective-Arousal, Cognitive, Unconscious, and Pseudoscientific Controlling. Simply, the author believes that there is no single solution to the theory of motivation because:

1) life is in continual motion,
2) there are many uncontrollable variables (perceived or actual) at any given time,
3) human nature is abstract and conditioned to react to reality or to perception as a reality,
4) human behavior is contextual and conditional upon variables (perceived or actual),

    5) lack-of or abundance-of awareness or ignorance of oneself or
        ones environment, and

    6) if life is in motion then motivation at any given time/situation
        is too.

Therefore, for a theory to work, the author puts forward the argument that as motivation is in a constant state of fluctuation a theory has to support those fluctuations to be effective.

Some individuals can cognitively create and achieve their own goals intrinsically. Whereas others, extrinsically with or without a conscious process, just figure things out through instinct (unconscious environmental conditioning from childhood, as taught or learnt from parents, friends and/or their environment). This can also include motivation by organizational culture, i.e., sports, business, entertainment (TV & Film), etc.

Nevertheless, whether this motivation is instinct, learned or controlled, the manager/leader is responsible for finding the motivational formula for each of their employees. The author theorizes that the variables (demands, expectations, needs, etc.) facing the individual, at any given time, are in a state of flux and therefore instable. The formula therefore has to be in continuous movement to meet this fluctuating landscape, which affects the individual. For that reason, the author believes that in order to maximize potential motivation the manager/leader has to perpetually adjust one or all of the seven motivators to coincide with the changing environment. The seven motivating keys for Perpetual Motivation Positioning are: Self-Expectancy, Physiological, External Demand, Social, Education, Transparency and Self-Esteem (Figs. 2.9. & 2.10.).

Self-Expectancy is the individual's own expectations, perceived or realistic or unrealistic in nature, and his/her knowledge, skills, ability, and competence to achieve the related task/goal for a given situation. They are normative (perceptive) or subjective for each task/goal/situation both in the workplace and in private life. This can include an expected satisfaction/reward for achieving individual behavior. Not knowing oneself and poor planning will result in tension, conflict and can cause defense mechanisms or stress.

Process Theory of **Perpetual Motivation Positioning** (**PMP**)

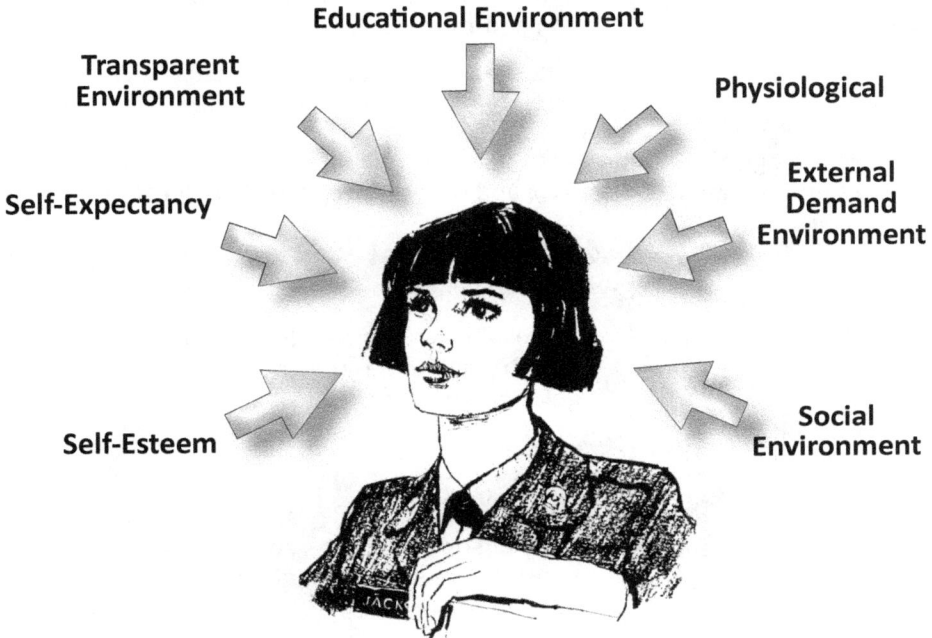

Fig. 2.9. The author's Process Theory of Perpetual Motivation Positioning (PMP) is based upon seven fluid variables facing the individual which can affect any specific situation. As the circumstances change, so does the ability to achieve all seven variables. The individual's motivational level increases with each of the motivational criteria. These criteria are achieved either subconsciously (with a manager's help) or consciously through personal appraisal and goal setting.

Physiological Environment is similar to that of Maslow, however, it includes both his first and second tiers. All the basic biological human needs such as sleep, security, thirst, hunger, health, and safety including safety from poverty, safety at the workplace, employment, protection of resources, protection of the family and morality. Balancing biological demands (sleep, eat, play, fitness, weight, lifestyle, and hygiene) with work related demands. Protection of resources includes poor environmental conditions such as lack of clean air and disease-free water, and other causes of ill-health.

External Demand Environment is both achievable and non-achievable demands set by external entities (working associates, boss, company, family, friends, etc.) which can affect the individual's ability and level of control. These

Self-Expectancy → Individual goals for a given situation or task including actual or perceived ability, satisfaction and/or reward.

Physiological Environment → Safety, security, hunger, sleep, eat, work, play, and health (fitness, weight, lifestyle).

External Demand Environment → Achievable and non-achievable demands set by external entities (partner, boss, company, government, etc.).

Social Environment → Being part of a team, group, family and knowing that someone cares about what happens to you. A sense of belongingness.

Educational Environment → Competence (knowledge, skills and ability) to cope with a given situation or the experience and capacity to find a solution, solve a situation or goal. Helps to create identity.

Transparent Environment → Openness and trust. The ability to communicate without repute or fear of reprimand. Free from façade building and isolationist activities.

Self-Esteem → An individual's belief and self-appraisal of his/her own worth and what other think. The need for respect and the need for self-respect.

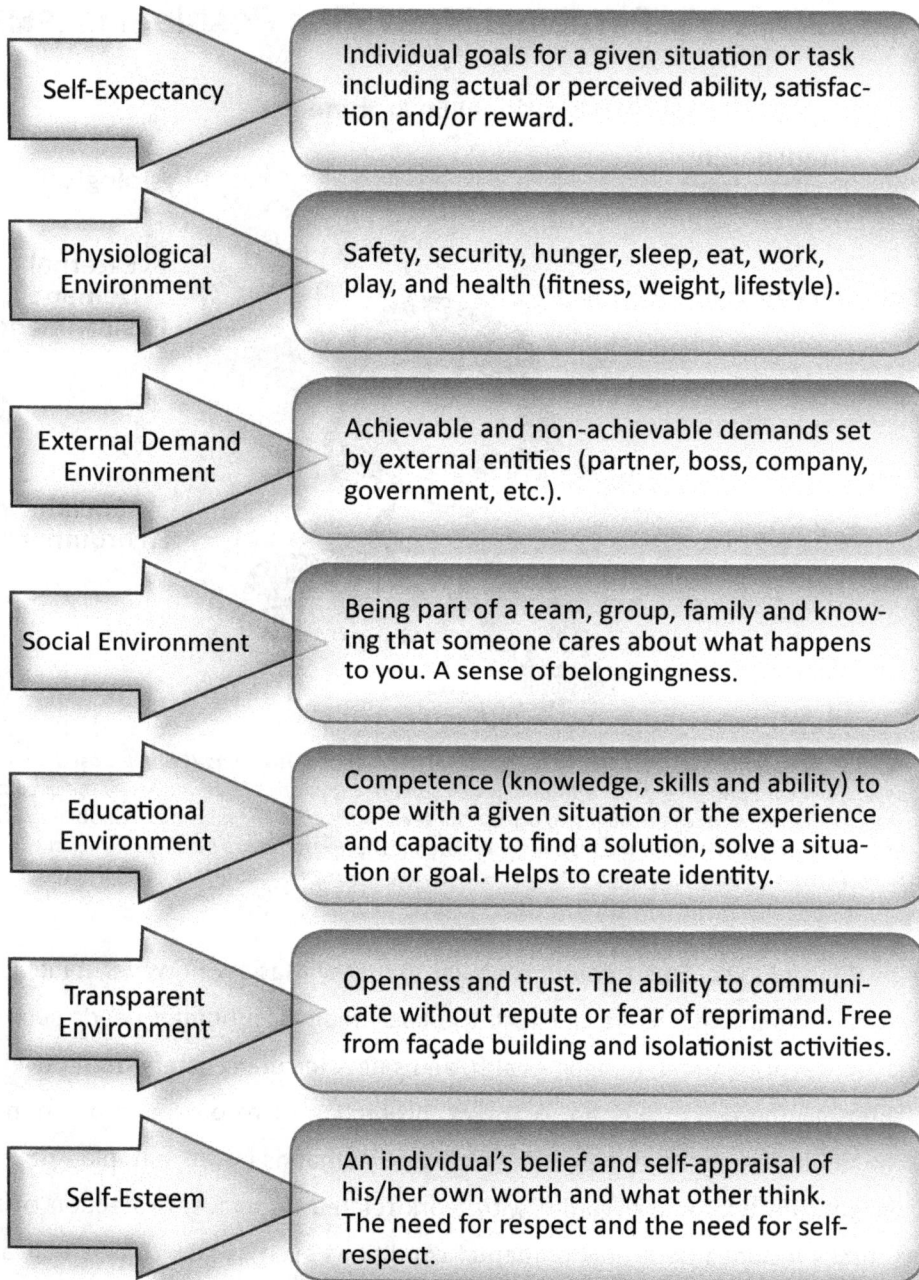

Fig. 2.10. The author's Process Theory of Perpetual Motivation Positioning (PMP) is based upon seven fluid variables facing the individual at any given point in time. Maximum benefit (IDP Fig. 2.18,) can be expected once fulfillment of all criteria is achieved. Naturally, employees will be able to produce and interact without achieving all of these; however, it is in the best interest to all parties if "employee-actualization" of PMP can be achieved.

demands can be both perceived and actual and can include other demand aspects as participation level, responsibility, authority, and how theses demands reflect on coworkers the boss and the organization. Consistency in rules—what is and what is not accepted, i.e. if the rules are inconsistent and keep changing without due participation this will cause tension and conflict. Naturally, PMP balance and motivation will be affected.

Social Environment is not only belongingness but identity, form and being part of a team, group, and family. Knowing that someone is concerned about your wellbeing, has your back, and is willing to stand up for you in times of need. The social environment can also include identity in the form of colleagues with a common respect for one another (not in the knowledge context). Although social status and climbing is considered by many to be a motivating factor, the author believes that this "snobbery or egocentric" attitude is more negative than positive and emerges through deficiencies in ones self-esteem and or true educational environment. Participating and fulfilling individual social responsibilities within the team/group/family are also important as a lack of this will cause guilt and tension.

Educational Environment is competence, see chapter 9, and one's command or control over development within the changing environment. This environment includes knowledge, skills, ability and the competency to fulfill objectives which can be perceived or real. As life is in continual movement so must one educational environment and it should be conducive to learning and individual competency development (tacit and explicit), including participatory activities such as communication, storytelling and decision making skills. Improved knowledge and experience will help the individual to cope in various situations and provide him/her with the experience and capacity necessary to work effectively or to find a solution if one is not

at hand. This environment must meet the needs of the external demand environment and the self-expectancy environments otherwise tension and conflict will arise. This should include flexibility in one's knowledge, skills and ability and adaptability to the changing environment, throughout one's career. Adequate competence (task, job, or professional field) is fundamental to teamwork, innovation and creativity; conversely, a lack of competence has a tendency to cause loss of identity, insecurity, isolationism and façade building.

Transparent Environment about openness and trust. If your educational, social, self-expectancy, external demand, self-esteem, physiological environments are lacking or out of balance then your transparent environment never function. This environment is responsible for implementing individual defense mechanisms and will directly affect the effect of tacit and explicit knowledge transfer, belongingness, and self-expectancy. This environment also includes the willingness and/or ability to take chances, take calculated risks and to conduct fearless speech (Foucault, 2001). This includes ability to be who you are and to be what you stand for; moreover, having the stability to accept others for who they are and what they stand for.

Self-Esteem is an individual's belief and self-appraisal of his/her own worth, what others think of them, and the perception of what others think of them. Respect from others and being able to respect oneself. If one does not respect oneself then respecting others and participating in a team environment is extremely difficult.

Education and perception of one's education, mutual respect, open communication, fairness in delegation, participation, belongingness, achieving expected demands/goals (mirco and macro), teamwork, and satisfaction through reward and/or acknowledgement are all good self-esteem builders and provide confidence motivation and willingness to take responsibility.

All seven motivational positions are critical to management policy and leadership implementation. Naturally, the Process Theory of Perpetual Motivation Positioning (Figs. 2.9. & 2.10.) is a theory for business managers and leaders and is part and parcel of a complete Cross-Training program.

As Cross-Training focuses on adult competency development, motivation and self-regulation, which are in continual flux, so too must the motivational denominators. Consequently, the leader is needs to monitor and adjust the parameters and variables facing and affecting the individual and the changing environment in order to maximize the potential of PMP.

Corollary, employee's performance is, by product, the sum of their universal environment. Motivation is therefore a consequence thereof—however. If performance is, related to knowledge and knowledge is the key to flexibility. Knowledge, flexibility and motivation therefore produce transparency and communication. Naturally, safety follows and façades drop, and the ability to function in a changing environment become much easier.

C-T Equation *(PMP* $^{perpetual\ motivation\ positioning}$ *+ CD* $^{competency\ de-}$ ^{velopment} *+ R* ^{rotation} *= IDP* $^{innovation\ development\ process}$ *)*

In aiming to achieve the C-T Equation managers and leaders should naturally be consistent in their ability to develop the employees understanding of their working environment, to empower employees to take responsibility, to communicate effectively, be able to define goals, to rotate and be rotated, to reward employees for good work, and to reprimand for less than adequate performance.

Taking Responsibility, Communication & Competency Development

During the growth and maturity stages of the "Positional Work-Cycle" empirical evidence has shown that employees are more willing to take responsibility for tasks because:

1) they want to fit-in and be part of the team

2) their tasks are new and interesting

3) they want to impress their new boss.

4) their seven motivational factors (PMP)

As time progresses and individual positions become routine, an individual's willingness to take responsibility and to participate diminishes. This decline is rapid during the complacency stage and almost ceases to exist in the latency part of that phase which I call *"tunnel-vision syndrome."* Therefore, appreciation for the seven motivators in PMP and the problematic changes in personal behavior is critical to good management and leadership.

> Webster defines **accountable** as *"1. obliged to account for one's acts; responsible 2. Capable of being accounted for; explainable 3. implies liability for which one may be called to account [he will be held accountable for anything he may say]"*. They define **responsible** as *"1. expected or obliged to account (for something, to someone); answerable; accountable 2. involving accountability, obligation, or duties [a responsible position] 3. that can be charged with being the cause, agent, or source of something [the moisture that is responsible for the rust] 4. able to distinguish between right and wrong and to think and act rationally, and hence accountable for one's behavior 5. a) readily assuming obligations, duties, etc.; dependable; reliable b) able to pay debts or meet business obligations 6. Applies to one who has been delegated some duty or responsibility by one in authority and who is subject to penalty in case of default [he is responsible for making out reports]"*. Webster defines **answerable** as *"implies a legal or moral obligation for which one must answer to someone in judgment"*.

Naturally, management should look at ways to increase participation and address any causes that might reduce an individual's willingness to take responsibility and accountability. The five most common causes for this reduction are:

1) perceived goal/s is too difficult to achieve

2) perceived reprimand for failure to attain established goal/s

3) poor delegation (wrong person for wrong job, time constraints and other demand pressures)

4) perceived or lack of knowledge to accomplish the goal

5) poor communication, lack of encouragement and lackluster follow-up, guidance and adjustment if necessary

6) perceived reward insufficient (lack of team spirit, motivation and direction)

All of the above problems directly relate to organizational policy and poor leadership; for that reason, efforts to lead prospective individuals to take responsibility require that they know what is expected and how they are going to be measured. Learn about their PMP needs and provide the necessary training and supervisory assistance to accomplish the established goals. Practice open communication and recognize good performance and correcting and/or eliminating poor performance.

However, by planning correctly, establishing adequate controls with feedback reports, evaluations, adjustment for any deviations, and if necessary, construction of a new action plan, many problematic issues can be resolved in a proactive manner even though some are reactive in nature. This encourages participation and a willingness to take responsibility.

Communication

Cross-Training is about communication and people. People are different, and for this reason, the design and delivery of a message (Fig.2.11.) is vital if you want to achieve the intended perception of the message from conception.

Communication is not about you. It is about the recipient of the message and it is about the recipient's comprehension of the communicated subject matter. It is not as simple as one might think especially when communicating a motivating or reprimanding message. One should take great care in planning the delivery of message as it can directly affect the recipient's ability to comprehend and accomplish the directed and desired task. Naturally, poor communication will also affect goals, motivation and participation.

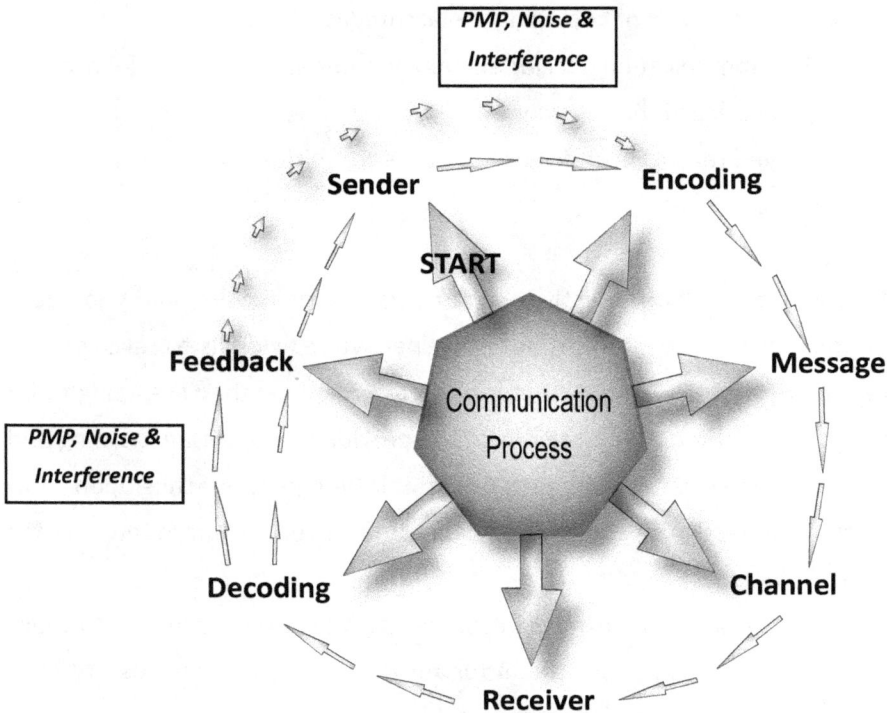

Fig. 2.11. Shows the seven basic stages found in the communication channel. These are: the
Sender *(source of the message);* ***Encoding*** *(translation of information into a series of symbols for communication to the intended recipient);* ***Message*** *(The encoded information sent by the sender to the receiver);* ***Channel****, the medium in which the communication is sent between a sender and a receiver (written, verbal, body language, etc...);* ***Receiver*** *(The individual whose senses perceive the sender's message);* ***Decoding*** *(The interpretation and translation of the message into meaningful information perceived by the receiver);* ***Feedback*** *(a repeat of the communication process that occurs when the receiver expresses his or her reaction to the sender's message).*
PMP, Noise & Interference *PMP represents the recipient's motivation state in relation to Perpetual Motivation Positioning which can affect encoding of the message; Noise and Interference is anything that confuses, disturbs, diminishes, or interferes with communication which can affect encoding or decoding of the message.*

Not only, is the content of the message important, but how you communicate the content in the message will also play a vital role in its success.

Group communication or presenting a new idea can take various forms. Most people are in one of three zones (Hoff, 1992): the Blue, the red, or the gray. Good presenters will be able to cross-over from zone to zone depending upon

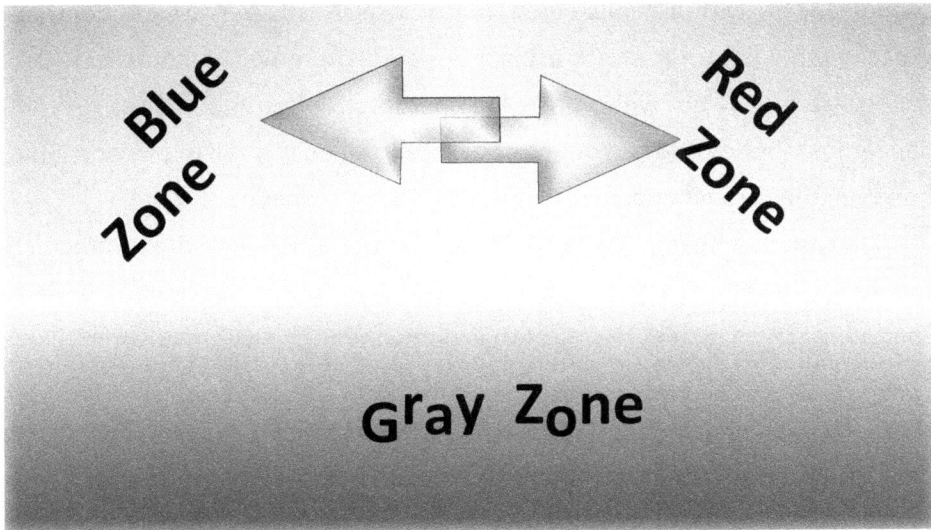

Fig. 2.12. Adapted from Ron Hoff's 1992 "I can see you naked" book, shows the three communication zone styles that are used to motivate, lead and manage a variety of situation at work. The Blue Zone is analytical, logical and pragmatic in style. The Red Zone is emotional, charismatic and instinctive used as a motivational style. The Gray Zone is an accommodating, compromising and noncommittal approach which can be used more in conflict resolution rather than inspirational or directional.

the subject matter and the recipients. There are gradients to each of the three zones. The Red Zone can range from scarlet to pink, and the Blue Zone from midnight to eggshell, but the Gray Zone is just gray and dull. Naturally, a good presenter will be able to fluctuate or cross-over between the Red and Blue Zones (Fig. 2.12).

Characteristics represented by the Blue Zone are analytical, logical, pragmatic, thoughtful, rational, restrained, intellectual, and deliberate. Characteristics represented by the Red Zone are emotional, driven, surprising, instinctive, charismatic, creative, impulsive, and daring. Unsurprisingly, characteristics found in the Gray Zone are cautious, traditional, accommodating, compromising, predictable, neutral, noncommittal, ambivalent, and boring.

Blue Zoners work well in strategic planning, goal setting, and boardroom-like situations as well as during evaluations, reprimands and process, workflow analysis situations. Red Zoners elicit a feeling of participation, motivation and connectedness with a hands-on-approach style. A let's get the job done approach with a pat on the back using more emotion rather than intellect. Gray Zoners are usually not welcome in the boardroom or on the floor as they are dangerously boring and can put most people to sleep in a relatively short time; however, they are functional in conflict resolution scenarios.

The situation, team, and individual will dictate which zone the communicator will use in order to achieve the best results. No matter what style you use to communicate, that style should always be two-way or horizontal communication.

Two-way communication or ***horizontal communication*** on a level playing field is by far the most effective way to communicate. Closed one-sided communication only produces one clear result, the message was transmitted; however, was it received, interpreted, and understood correctly and does it equate into realistic terms in regard to the recipient's expectations, demands and perceptions? What is quite certain is that without proper feedback your management and leadership will suffer.

In addition to the communication cycle (Fig. 2.11.) there are tips that can improve your communication style in Cross-Training (Fig. 2.13). They include:

1) Posing open-ended instead of closed questions related to the subject matter of concern. This allows the receivers to participate in the discussion, whilst producing a sense that their opinion is worthwhile.

2) Listen more and allow others to communicate. Naturally, your vigilance and guidance is vital to productivity.

3) Allow for detail and dissection as it can produce creativity in feedback.

4) Encourage others, using non-verbal behavior, to partake with their thoughts too.

5) Stimulate their mental participation with thought provoking questions.

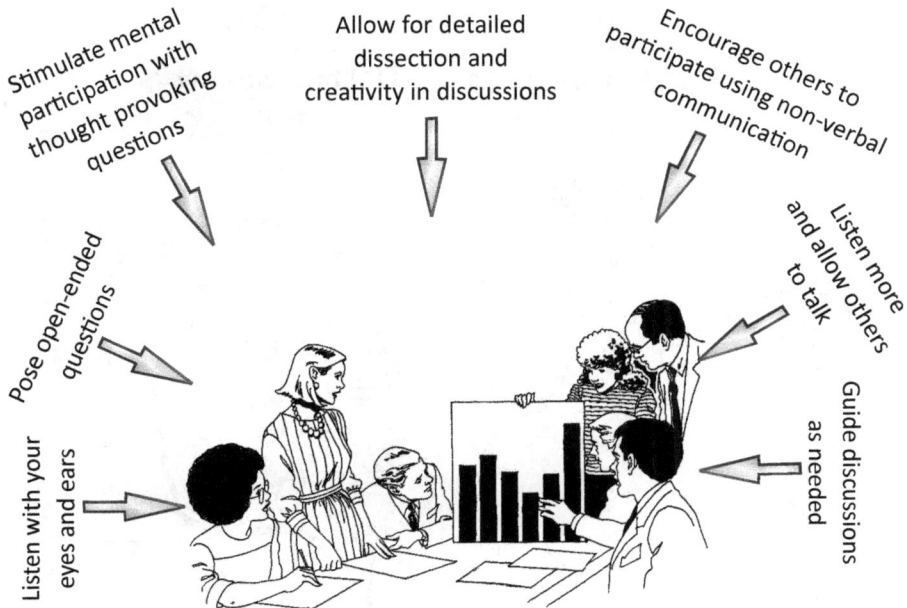

Two-way / Horizontal Communication

Fig. 2.13. Shows a number of ways to practice two-way / horizontal communication while conducting Cross-Training. Open communication channels are vital to the success of goals and aids in the prevention of façade and isolationist tendencies. It also assists in building knowledge and self-esteem through participation and teamwork.

6) Listen with your eyes and ears. This will help you to ascertain and/or confirm various aspects of the conversation.

Individual communication or coaching is also vital to the Cross-Training process as participation, taking responsibility, teamwork all start with the individual. The individual is, or should be, in control of his/her own behavior; therefore, if you want to change, improve or motivate certain actions then this is where you need to focus. Obviously, group dynamics and other factors can also affect behavior, but it is the individual's willingness to partake in a given task which can be improved through coaching. Do not try to change your colleague, change yourself as participation and taking responsibility begins with the individual.

(3) Analyzing

(4) Interviewing

(2) Observing

(5) Consensus

(1) Listening

(6) Feedback

Individual Communication/Coaching

Fig. 2.14. Shows the six key factors used in individual communication or coaching in Cross-Training namely: listening, observing, analyzing, interviewing, consensus, and giving feedback. Examples of open-ended questions are: Can you explain it for me? What do you think went wrong? What do think about it? Who do you think we should talk to about it? Why do you think that we should do it this way? How do you feel? Can you come up with some alternatives to think about? Examples of some closed-ended questions are: Do you know what is expected of you? When will you be finished? Are you prepared to volunteer for this project next week? Who is responsible for this problem?

Coaching in Cross-Training is focused on proactive teamwork, reinforcement, belongingness and support. There are six key factors (Minor, 1995) namely: listening, observing, analyzing, interviewing, consensus, and giving feedback (Fig. 2.14).

Listening involves paying attention to the individual by making eye contact, eliminating as many distractions as possible, displaying an open and relaxed body language. Ask open-ended questions, rephrase and confirm with additional open-ended questions. Pay attention to all non-verbal signals and try to create a relaxing situation. Remember it is about the individual.

Observing involves just that. Observe the employees and wait for them to indicate that they need help or can take responsibility for the discussion. Look, listen, watch, and if necessary, use non-verbal-communication to prompt a reply. Try to identify changes in performance, and observe them in various situations and in their operating environment. This information can help with discussions related to competency development in Cross-Training, and to reinforce good behavior, effective teamwork and façade prevention tactics.

Analyzing involves using your ability to determine the root cause of a problem by questioning what or why until you arrive at the core of the cause (what is the real cause of the oil leak?). Look at all the possibilities such as skill/knowledge deficiency, lack of motivation, PMP status, boredom or personal issues. Try to identify their preferred learning method (school, reading, practical, on-the-job training, etc...).

Interviewing involves creating a personable style that puts the individual at ease and not in an interrogating atmosphere or on the defense. Use questions related to the individual's skills, perception of their skills/knowledge, their values, their team members and personal achievements at home and in the workplace. Carefully design your questions prior to the interview and ask both open-ended and closed-ended questions that best fit the situation. Use appropriate verbal and non-verbal language that supports your interview. Do not use over complicated language.

Consensus involves an agreement between you and the individual as to what, when, how, and other important PMP issues. It is a partnership of genuine respect including all expectations, goals, commitments related to work and personal issues. Most coaches will try to stay away from personal matters; however, I feel this is an integral part of an individual and if there is a personal matter of great concern facing the individual, this matter will usually find its way into the working environment either through reduced productivity, motivation and/or teamwork. Establish a plan for personal development, and goal-setting for the individual and for that of the team.

Feedback involves candid coaching techniques where openness is vital to a constructive outcome. Here you can discuss competency skills and knowledge in relation to their position and Cross-Training. Correlate this learned information and be specific about the individual's own subjective perceptions and those observed by you. Discuss behavior and deportment; however, take care not to overload the individual thereby creating a stressful situation and/or putting the individual into a defensive state. Behavioral discussions should be limited to matters that the individual can do something about. Keep it personal by saying "I" and not "the team has noticed" or "everyone feels", etc... Avoid labeling the individual and describe situations rather than making judgments. Keep your message simple and specific. Remember, it is about the individual and his/her development.

Competency Development

What makes individuals act or react a certain way? Is it genes, education, environment, good luck, bad luck or a combination of all? If you look at any given working environment, you will find that ALL tasks require a certain competency level. Competency development, as in Cross-Training, is a management philosophy built on providing a competent multi-task-oriented workforce, see chapter nine for more detail on knowledge, skills, ability, and competency. This is accomplished through task competency development where individuals are trained for a multiple of tasks within their working environment. Obviously, the objective is to insure that tasks are completed consistently in the most efficacious manner possible, in a motivated and participatory way, saving time, money, and resources whilst minimizing physical and psychological injuries. Furthermore, Cross-Training requires that each individual can effectively perform at least two lateral and subordinate positions and one senior position in order to comprehend and appreciate the impact that their and other positions have on the workflow process.

> *Webster defines **competency** as "a meeting, agreement **1**. Sufficient means*
> *for a modest livelihood **2**. Condition or quality of being competent; ability;*

fitness; specif., legal capability, power, or jurisdiction." They define **competent** *as "***1***. Well qualified; capable; fit* **2***. Sufficient; adequate* **3***. Permissible or properly belonging (with to)* **4***. Law legally qualified, authorized, or fit." They also define* **development** *as "***1***. A developing or being developed* **2***. A step or stage in growth, advancement, etc.* **3***. An event or happening* **4***. A thing that is developed; specif." and the definition of* **develop** *is "***(I.)1***. To cause to grow gradually in some way; cause to become gradually fuller, larger, better, etc.; esp., 1 to build up or expand (a business, industry, etc.)* **2***. To make stronger or more effective; strengthen* **3***. To bring (something latent or hypothetical) into activity or reality* **4***. To cause (one's personality, a bud, etc.) to unfold or evolve gradually* **(II.)** *to show or work out by degrees; reveal; disclose; esp.,* **1***. To make (a theme or plot) known gradually* **2***. To explain more clearly; enlarge upon."*

There are a number of computer programs such as SAP, which integrate a PA/HR function by providing competency information for individuals and tasks. This is good so far, however, it goes further by grading or ranking the competency level (novice—1, experienced beginner—2, practitioner—3, knowledgeable practitioner—4, expert—5) for the individual. The author does not agree with this for a number of reasons.

1) It creates a social hierarchy related to competency,
2) It can create isolationist tendencies or grouping,
3) It negates the quality of the training. You are either qualified or not, and
4) It lacks synergic integration, innovative long-term development strategies, and focuses more on the now, quick-fix solution.

Although there are nine phases to the Cross-Training process, there are four major steps which focus on explicit and tacit understanding in relation to ones landscape, workflow and processes, they are:

Step 1 introduction overview,
Step 2 theory phase,
Step 3, the practical phase,

Step 4, affirmation of learned tasks and readjustment/redesign if
   necessary.

All positions have a theoretical explanation and a practical aspect behind
the process. In order for an organization to take advantage of this, a variety of
educational or competency development programs need to be designed.

The educational design phase is where both the macro-tasks (job description) and the micro-tasks (specific tasks) and their position constraints are analyzed. Commonly there are four distinct task forms sorted into actual position
skills required (Fig. 2.15). These are based upon formal educational requirements from certifying authorities. These can also include demands from the
company's established internal quality controls.

Registered & Certified Positions (RCP) are the most complicated of these
consists of formal registered and certificated position-skills. These skills are cer-

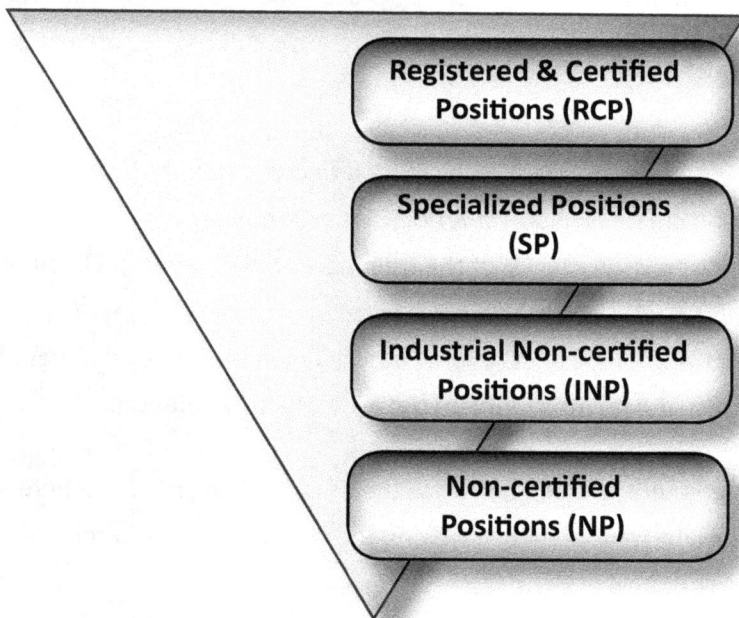

Fig. 2.15. The illustration shows the four educational position designs for Cross-Training. These
designs are Registered & Certified Positions (RCP), Specialized Positions (SP), Industrial Non-certified Positions (INP), and Non-certified Positions (NP). Also shown by the upside down triangle,
as the requirement for certification and specialization diminish so do the educational constraints
thereto.

tified through external means such as the government or a higher education facility. These positions include doctors, nurses, teachers, accountants, technicians, etc., and their responsibilities demand both an internal and external educational design, rotation, continual renewal, knowledge, skills, ability, competence, and process awareness, see chapter nine for more detail on knowledge.

Specialized Positions (SP) are internal quality control demands from the company itself. Although many university-educated personnel could find themselves within this category, there are *no state or government-required certification and registration requirements* demanded for this category. The company's own quality control functions could demand specific competency requirements (could be both internal or external in design) which are required to conduct specialized or specific tasks, for example, an engineer, plumber, teacher, marketing, etc. Their positions require knowledge, skills, ability, competence and process understanding.

Industrial Non-certified Positions (INP) are positions and tasks which are controlled solely by the company or organization. They are positions governed by the company's own quality control keys and SOPs. These positions can require little explicit knowledge but tacit knowledge, in the form of cross-training and on-the-job-training, with focus on process, skills, and ability, internal certifications and/or specializations. Positions could include machine operators and others.

Non-certified Positions (NP) are positions that require no specialized training or internal certifications. A general, non-technical, sales team is a good example. The educational design of the NPs differ slightly from the other three categories due to the fact that a decisional tree process is used for specific types of sales positions and are incorporated into SOPs. Other positions within this category can include facility maintenance and other service related positions. Major focus is on process understanding and ability to perform tasks well.

As a result, the educational design, in most cases, adapts to the four educational design positions and the specific skills needed for each task (Fig. 2.16). Again, the key factor in competency development is the individual. If he/she is

RCP	SP	INP	NP
• Knowledge, Skills, Ability, Competence, and Process Awareness	• Knowledge, Skills, Ability, Competence, and Process Awareness	• Tacit Knowledge, Ability, and Process Competence	• Tacit Knowledge, Ability, and Process Competence
• Organizational and Departmental Objectives	• Departmental Objectives	• Job Description	• Job Description Specific Responsibilities
• Job Description Regulatory & Certification Requirements	• Job Description	• Specific Job Responsibilities	• Work Flow Chart
• Landscape and Workflow Understanding	• Specific Job Responsibilities	• Specific Workflow Charts	• Decision Tree
• Required Specific Certified Education from an External Source	• Specific Workflow Charts	• Task definitions & SOPs	• Other Job Related Tasks and Safety Responsibilities
• Other Job Related Tasks and Safety Responsibilities	• Specialized Education from an External Source	• Other Job Related Tasks and Safety Responsibilities	
	• Task definition & SOPs		
	• Other Job Related Tasks and Safety Responsibilities		

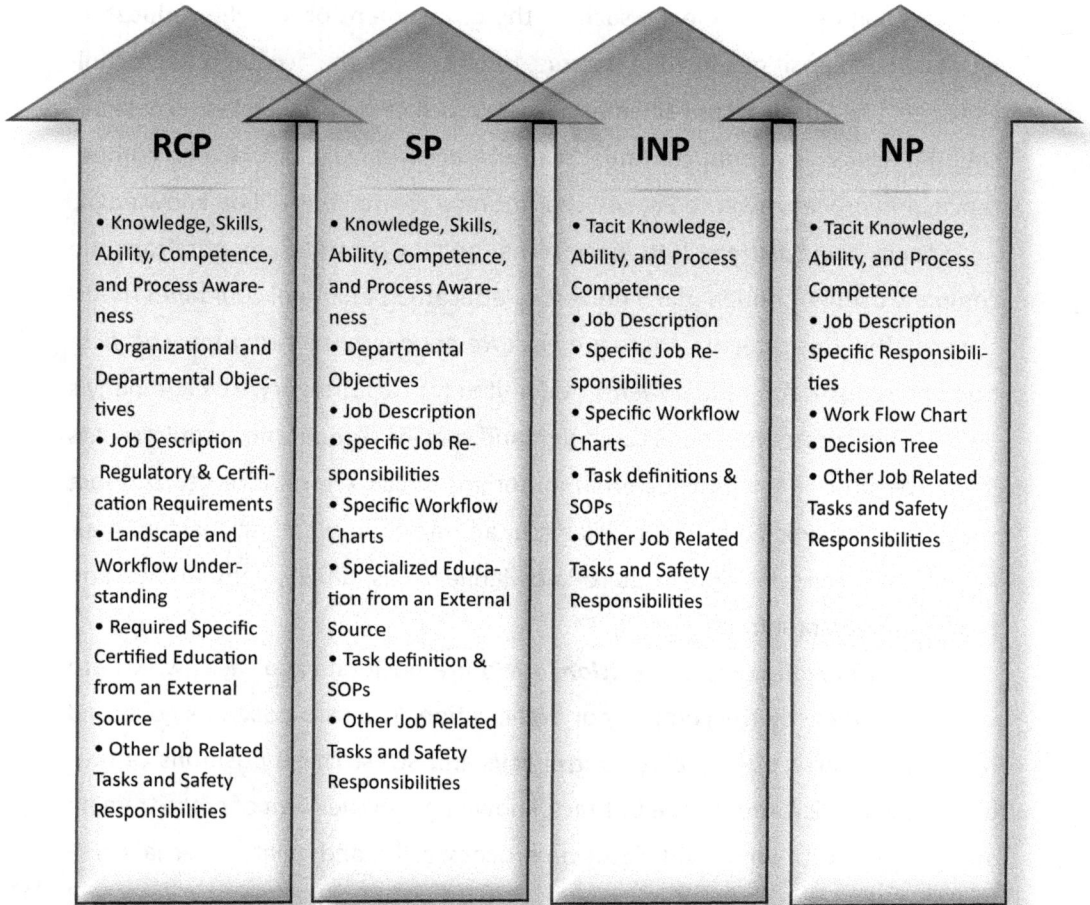

Fig. 2.16. The illustration shows the four educational constraints in the design process for Registered & Certified Positions (RCP), Specialized Positions (SP), Industrial Non-certified Positions (INP), and Non-certified Positions (NP). RCP & SP positions can, in some cases, require additional education from external educational entities that have the sole authority to certify. However, this does not preclude all tasks for RCP, SP, INP, & NP positions that might require an internal company certification for specific tasks. Nor does it preclude rotational assignments once certain objectives have been accomplished. Obviously various development strategies from formal to (OJT) On-the-Job Training is used to meet the competency needs of the individual and position.

not educated with the correct skills and know-how for their job requirements, does not understand the significance of their role within the landscape, workflow, and process their motivation and productivity will suffer. It is therefore important to communicate team effort, understanding, and participation through proper leadership and company policy. Job specifics and workflow knowledge is instrumental for the individual to control his/her environment and for Cross-Training to be successful.

Competency development can also include a base *"**psychometric test**"* evaluation to aid the leader in discussions with the individual. Naturally, our objective is to maximize the potential of each employee through all means available. Sometimes insight or even stimulus can be provided through a simple "psychometric test." Although these tests are helpful and give you some very realistic evaluations they should never be your only tool. They are aids and can never replace good leadership instinct.

Peripheral Demand Competency is another issue that can help to prevent *tunnel-vision syndrome*. Not only is the PA/HR manager responsible for insuring that staff are equipped to implement the mission but they are also responsible for realizing the significance of market demands placed on the company. Together with R&D and the marketing department, management need to understand these external demands. A good example of this is Ford's inability to realize the need for eco-friendly alternative energy cars in their Volvo brand. They took a short-term strategy by focusing a major part of their production on SUVs. As reported on Swedish television (SVT1) Ford halted all environmental energy alternative driven vehicle development research. Now five years later (2008) after losing the competitive advantage, that they once had, selling Jaguar and Land Rover, and in the wake of high gasoline prices, they have to re-evaluate their position; moreover, it looks like Volvo might be sold to the Chinese. A little Cross-Training might do wonders for the management of Ford.

Innovation, Creativity & Participation

The author's Management by Cross-Training theory suggests that knowledge is one of the key indicators to motivation and participation. Moreover, it is the perceived and subjective security gained from one's strength in knowledge that produces willingness to communicate, openness and flexibility. Accordingly, I have found that employees that are less transparent (due to the lack of PMP or

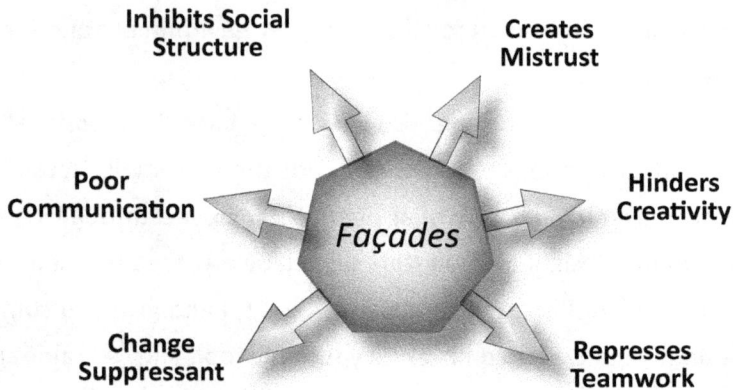

Fig. 2.17. Façades can occur from the result of a lack of knowledge. They are destructive and all efforts to prevent their formation should be taken. They hamper teamwork, development, openness, change, efficiency, creativity and eventually lead to complacency and tunnel-vision syndrome effect.

knowledge for a given task) tend to produce façades which are hindering -co-coon-like working environments which, in most cases, are resistant to change, are low morale, and are poor in communication (Fig. 2.17). Greater knowledge will lead to more transparency and open-communication. Consequentially this will increase flexibility and elevate employee self-esteem and a willingness to participate in creative activities.

Theory of ***Innovative Development PROCESS (IDP)*** contributes, in a major part, to the thinking behind Cross-Training (Fig. 2.18). ***IDP*** is a profound combination of synergy emerging from a balanced PMP and the understanding of one's working environment (chapter 5, systems identification; chapter 7, process, chapter 8, SOPs; and, chapter 9, knowledge). This combination along with rotation help to negotiate the reification of identity and participation, and organizational culture (chapters 10, 11, & 12) leading to creative and innovative development. Management policy, organizational culture, and leadership traits outlined in these chapters are therefore instrumental. The seven derivatives are:

Productivity increases with improved competency levels and improved understanding of the production/service processes, per unit of input versus out-

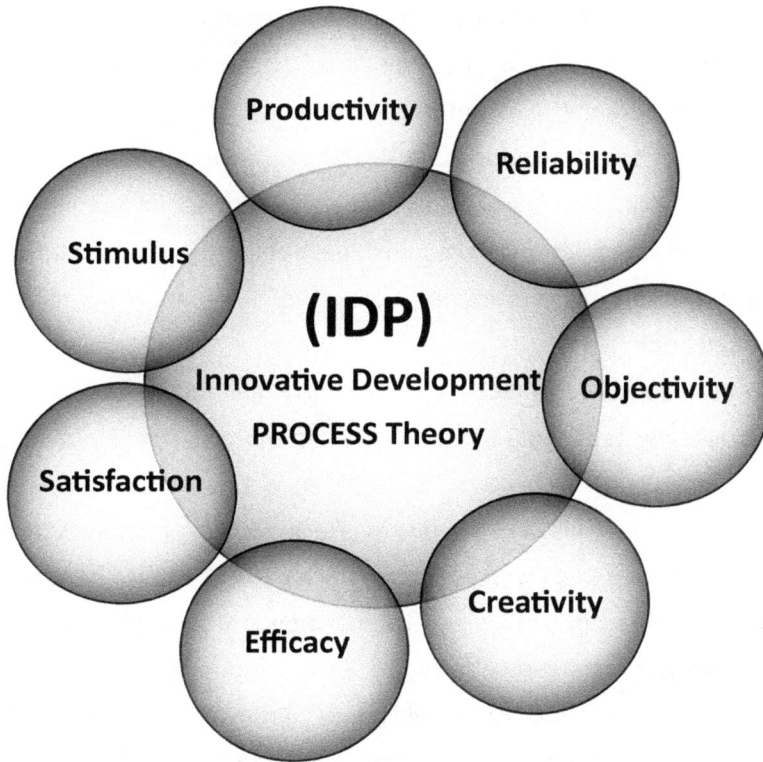

Fig. 2.18. IDP or Innovative Development PROCESS Theory with its seven derivatives is the product of a good competency development program, a balanced Perpetual Motivation Positioning (PMP), and sufficient internal and external rotation. The two provide the impetus to IDP through enhanced job security, motivation, flexibility and synergic understanding of the working environment.

put, are understood more comprehensively. Naturally, the more one understands the processes the easier it is to improve processes and to find solutions to possible problems. Productivity is typically measured as a ratio of input per labor-hour divided by output (Jorgenson & Griliches, 1967).

Reliability or taking responsibility and participation, see chapter 11, is enhanced through competency development. As one's ability and understanding of tasks improves, so does consistency which leads to enhanced self-confidence in relation to the task at hand. This increase in self-confidence and consistency creates a willingness to accept greater responsibility for a specific task or a series of learned tasks. As these competencies increase so does the reliability of the individual.

Objectivity or focus and goal recognition enhances through greater understanding of one's working environment and the processes therein. As the individual competency level improves so does the ability to be self-reliant. Self-reliance or self-expectancy is a key to goal generation and individual drive. As knowledge increases so does the ability to set and achieve goals. This increased capability gives the individual a chance to see "outside of the box" or the bigger picture thereby raising the bar standards in relation to established goals.

Creativity is achieved as a result of improved control and understanding of one's environment. By being able to meet expectations, and the demands of the established tasks, consistently with confidence a natural development of creativity emerges. This in turn leads to critical thinking outside of the box. This becomes a self-generating process which naturally has to be supported through rotation and encouraged by management and good leadership. Unfortunately, if management policy does not support, creativity the process will end here and motivation will be lost. Entertaining creativity should therefore be a priority for management policy and as a leadership tool.

Efficacy rides on the back of creativity, and is also generated by achievement of self-reliance and achieving established and individually developed goals. However, here the individual questions and seeks answers to improve processes both within the immediate workflow environment and adjacent areas too. Obviously, this leads to even greater understanding and can produce some revolutionary changes improving productivity, efficiency and even the landscape. Leaders should promote and encourage suggestions of this type.

Satisfaction or self-actualization naturally follows as the individual has more control over his/her environment, can meet the demands of the position and achieve the established goals. Satisfaction creates an openness which in turn produces a climate where criticism is seen as proactive and not negative. The willingness to accept change, teamwork, and to share is also prevalent. Satisfaction enhances the feeling of togetherness and success for a job well done.

Stimulus is motivation. Employees are motivated through satisfaction and achievement. This becomes self-generating as long the environment continues to offer potential. However, motivation can be lost due to a lack of renewable goals. Management should therefore be diligent in renewing and adjusting individual, and team responsibilities to support competency development and growth through Perpetual Motivation Positioning.

Flexibility, Rotation & Team Dynamics

Good leadership requires discipline and consistency, good team-dynamics requires flexibility, rotation and rejuvenation, which in turn, requires the right amount of hands-on-control, motivation, correction and promotion of self-control. Cross-Training provides all of these ingredients and much more.

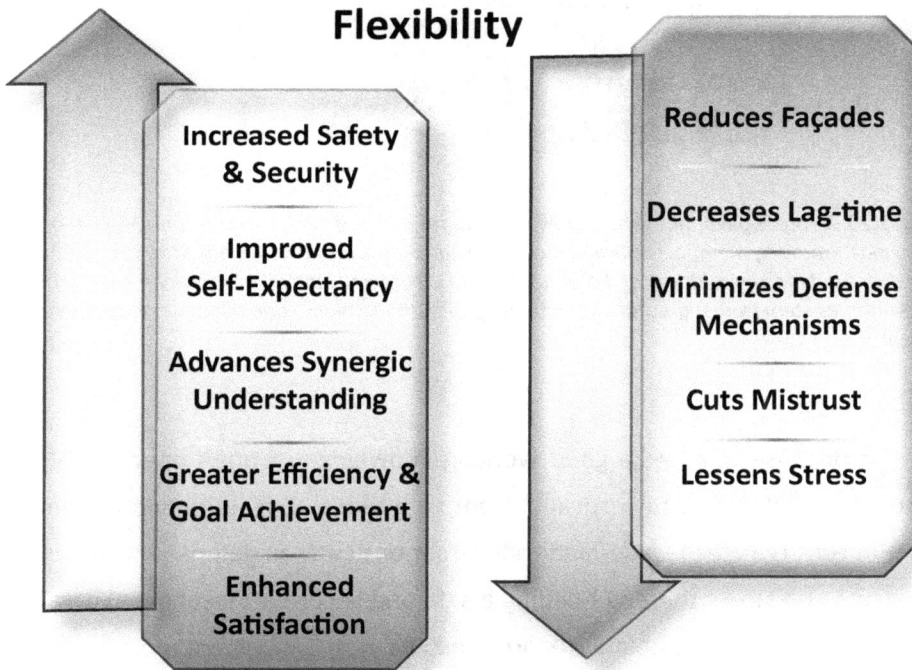

Flexibility

Increased Safety & Security

Improved Self-Expectancy

Advances Synergic Understanding

Greater Efficiency & Goal Achievement

Enhanced Satisfaction

Reduces Façades

Decreases Lag-time

Minimizes Defense Mechanisms

Cuts Mistrust

Lessens Stress

Fig. 2.19. Flexibility reduces illnesses related to stagnant workplaces and improves teamwork in a changing environment. Cross-Training helps to improve flexibility though competency development which is a combination of both didactic and practical experience. This combination helps the individual to understand both the micro-working demands within their environment thereby more readily willing to accept change.

Rotational Workforce

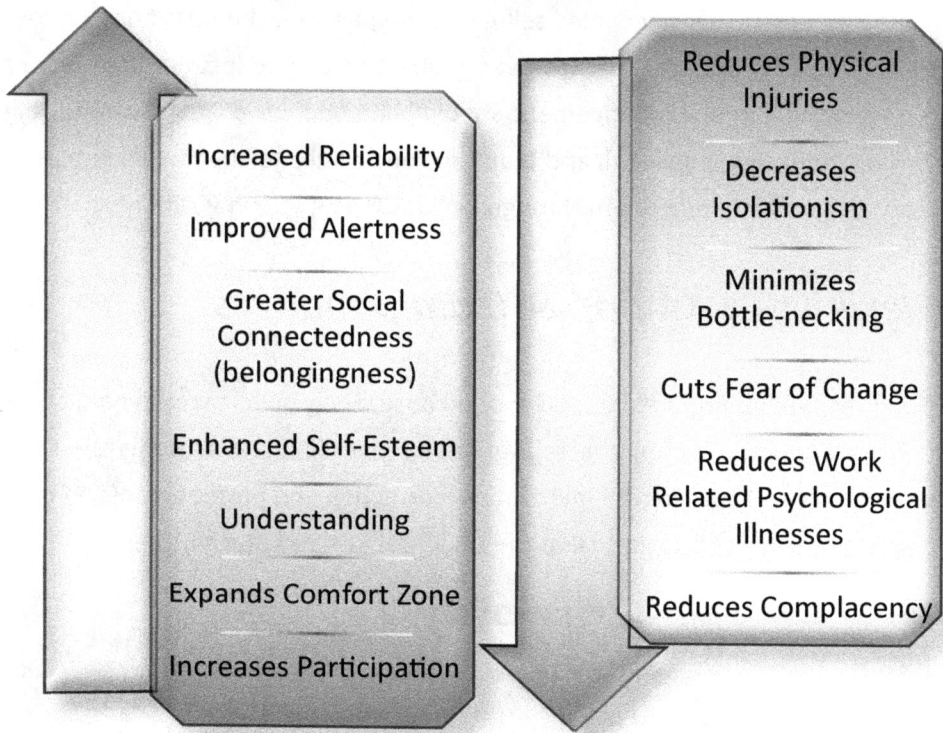

Increased Reliability

Improved Alertness

Greater Social Connectedness (belongingness)

Enhanced Self-Esteem

Understanding

Expands Comfort Zone

Increases Participation

Reduces Physical Injuries

Decreases Isolationism

Minimizes Bottle-necking

Cuts Fear of Change

Reduces Work Related Psychological Illnesses

Reduces Complacency

Fig. 2.20. A rotating workforce has many advantages over a stationary environment. First or foremost, rotating members take less-sick days than non-rotating members. They are positive to their working environment and are more apt to create and innovate to solve problems. These advantages stem from a greater understanding of both the macro and micro working environment.

As discussed earlier, a good working knowledge of one's operational environment (laterally and vertically) leads to a sense of security and openness. This in turn reduces façade-hindering situations such as defense mechanisms, mistrust and stress thereby building a safe and secure atmosphere. There are many benefits to a flexible workforce such as synergic understanding, quicker solutions, reduced lag-time, greater efficiency and improved self-expectancy, goal achievement and satisfaction. (Fig. 2.19).

Rotation leads to increased understanding of both the micro- and macro-working environment. Rotation also reduces both long-term physical and psychological injuries in the workplace. Rotation decreases isolationist tendencies and provides stimulus through a changing-environment; increases reliability, as one is no longer afraid of change; improves alertness, through a more active environment; enhances creativity, by having the ability to see things from another perspective; self-esteem improves, with one's capability; increased social connectedness (belongingness), through frequent interaction and improved communication (Fig. 2.20). Furthermore, a flexible, rotating team can reduce any bottle-necking as the leader can practice need-based management through a voluntary and participatory means rather than by requirement.

Leaders cannot do it all. Naturally, their success is measured by their results and their ability to delegate and motivate their team to achieve the established goals. It takes a team to produce a product or service but it takes a dynamic team to do it efficaciously in a motivated manner whilst sustaining quality, under budget and with time to spare.

Three basic types of rotations There are three basic types of rotational forms supporting competency development (Fig. 2.21). These are short-term rotations, long-term rotations, and roaming rotations.

Short-term rotations focus on improving employee positional workflow understanding while at the same time providing, stimulus and reducing the impact long-term physical and psychological injuries associated with the execution of monotone duties. Short-term rotations can span a vast area and encompass non-certified positions (NP), industrial non-certified positions (INP) related to assembly lines and industry. They also include national and community services such as the fire department, police force, customer service positions and even the delivery of primary care.

Long-term rotations focus on improving managerial, supervisory, specialized position (SP), and registered & certified position (RCP). Why to you suppose that most multi-national corporations have a manager trainee program? Some of these programs have two three or even five steps. During each stage, the trainees' are exposed to another aspect or operation within the corporation. Each step increases their understanding of the corporation, its strategy and culture. However, most programs stop there. Cross-Training managers, supervisors,

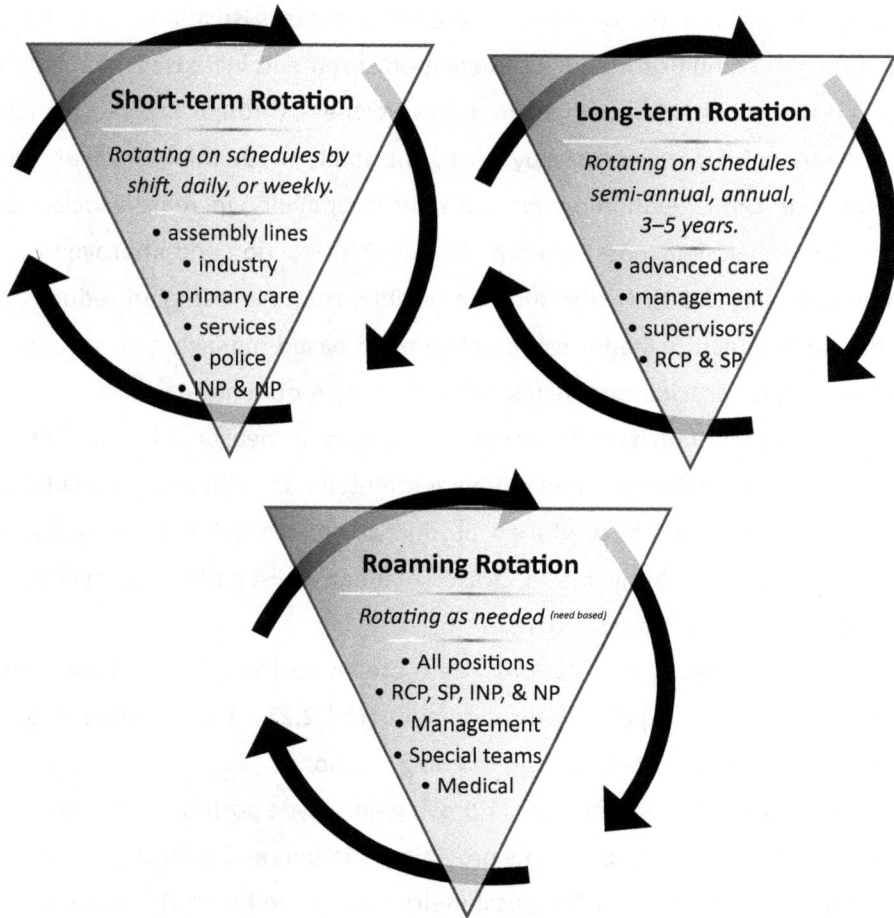

Fig. 2.21. The three basic rotation types found in Cross-Training are important as they are instruments to enhance understanding of ones working environment, help to balance PMP and are application tools for spreading organizational culture, tacit and explicit learning instruments and assist in need based management.

RCPs and SPs should be continual as the corporate world in not static. Balancing the internal and external demands placed on the corporations require flexible, up-to-date managers that are IDP advocates and process owners of organizational culture. If managers and leaders cannot practice this philosophy, they cannot expect anyone else too. Manager, leaders, supervisors, RCPs and SPs can also get the complacency virus. Due to the nature of these positions, long-term rotations can usually last for six months, twelve months and even three to five years for continental or international assignments. Another important reason is that management styles, leading organizational culture, methods and routines will develop more rapidly with the integration and rotation of key personnel.

Roaming rotations focus on need based management and multi-taking employees. Naturally, all employees within these rotational groups need to be prepared to meet the demands of the changing environment. A number of hospitals use roaming teams to alleviate bottle-necking and other medical emergencies. The police use SWOT members and task forces to tackle unexpected situations. Large corporations can use an individual or individuals with development experience to enhance focus groups and to stimulate working teams. Roamers or those participating in roaming rotations are usually manned by, doers, fixers and implementers.

Team Dynamics is synergy in a team. A dynamic team is the product of a balanced PMP, IDP, flexibility, rotation, and trust. Logically, trust stems from PMP via transparency (open communication) and is an essential aspect of motivation and thereby influencing team performance, commitment to one another and trust. Obviously, any inconsistencies in leadership will be detrimental to commitment and trust. Policy cannot instill commitment, nor can it be required or demanded, it is self-generating through PMP, flexibility, rotation and good on-hands-leadership. It is a common fact that people increase their commitment or participation to a team and/or goal as their permissible contribution increases. As this permissible input to a goal/team increases so it creates a sense of responsibility, ownership and belongingness, thereby stimulating other members of the team too. Knowledge is naturally a ley ingredient.

Individual and team goals are a necessary function for good team-dynamics. Perpetual Motivation Positioning provides the individual with continual feedback and guidance from their leader concerning their personal development, commitment and contribution to the team. The team also receives continual feedback and adjustment of their goals. Establishing goals (micro, macro, short- and long-term) are therefore critical to team dynamics. Logically, if you establish goals you need to create a structure to measure these goals. Without proper measurements in place, the reward of achieving said goals will be lost thereby affecting motivation and possibly even participation.

It is given that a goal needs to include some kind of performance criteria. As you would expect, achieving a goal without performance or quality criteria would be a moot point because the effect of the expectant reward (satisfaction and/or acknowledgement) is less.

Team and individual goals and standards (quality and performance) therefore need to be established (Maddux and Wingfield, 2003). Establishing these measurements should be done together with the responsible individuals first and thereafter with the team. The reason for this is to prevent creation of unrealistic demands.

Goals

Goals are statements of objectives or results that have to be met or achieved. They are:

1) They can include certain resources (funds, materials and personnel) that the organization is willing to entrust in realizing the objective or goal,
2) Expectations and conditions that will exist after completion of the desired goal,
3) A time frame in which the goal or objective has to be completed.

Standards are the quality performance criteria expressed as qualitative or quantitative for both the product/service and personnel. They are:

1) Safety standards as set by OSHA, HACCP and others,
2) Production rates such as output per work/hour, etc.,
3) Acceptable manufacturing or production (service) tolerances,
4) Breakage, defects and other quality control standards,
5) Attendance or participation minimum and maximum.

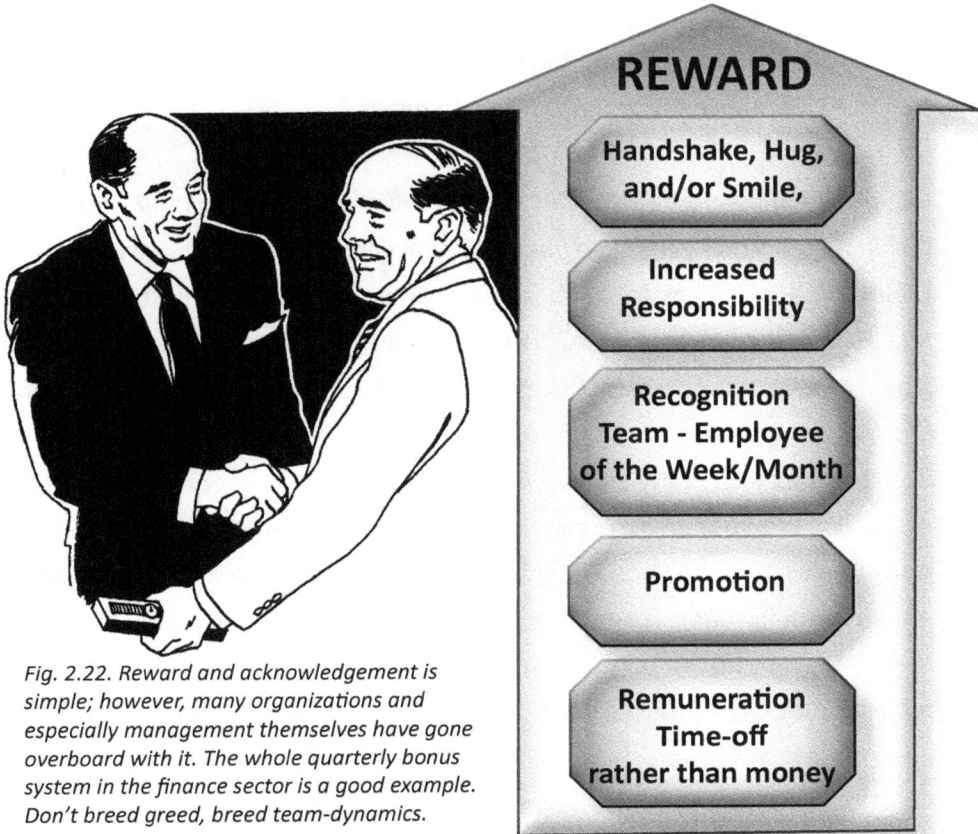

REWARD

Handshake, Hug, and/or Smile,

Increased Responsibility

Recognition Team - Employee of the Week/Month

Promotion

Remuneration Time-off rather than money

Fig. 2.22. Reward and acknowledgement is simple; however, many organizations and especially management themselves have gone overboard with it. The whole quarterly bonus system in the finance sector is a good example. Don't breed greed, breed team-dynamics.

Team dynamics is also about entrusting task specific and criteria development responsibilities to the team itself. Naturally, the supervisor or leader is updated continually, and adjustments to the goals, made as needed. Team members can help to design checkpoints and other control functions. They can prepare actions and decisional steps for various tasks and even specify whom or to what extent participation is needed at each point in the process.

Obviously, other philosophies such LEAN, SIX Sigma and other company quality control tools should also be taken into consideration. These are incorporated into the SOPs or Standard Operating Procedures, which will be addressed in more detail in section 2, chapter 8.

Good Cross-Training is also about delegation and giving the individual and team space to participate and learn. Notwithstanding good leadership, reinforce and assistance in problem solving as needed.

Reward, Problem Solving, Conflict and Reprimand in Cross-Training Good leadership requires that you acknowledge employees and teams when they achieve their goals. Recognition for a-job-well-done is both motivating for the individual and team and good for their self-esteem. It can be in the form of a handshake, a hug, a smile, words, increased responsibility, recognition (team of the month, employee of the week, etc.), promotion and lastly, and least of all, remuneration (Fig. 2.22.). As I have stated before, pay your employees properly from the beginning. Money, money, money only leads to more money and greed, and removes focus. Everyone benefits from positive feedback, use it instead. Showing appreciation for effort is a leadership trait that will promote good work rather than demote it. Do not reward or dwell on an absolute obvious or minor task as it will reduce the significance and sincerity of genuine appreciation and might even reduce motivation.

Along with the proactive team-dynamic activities, the leader may have to serve in a reactive role once in a while. As reality has it, there are always problems that require a solution and conflicts between members that need to be resolved. There are seven steps to solving problems (Maddux and Wingfield, 2003). They are:

Step 1. State what the real problem appears to be. In many instances, the real problem only comes to the surface once all the facts have been collected and analyzed. A subjective approach is always a good start because it can be confirmed or corrected later.

Step 2. Gather information such as opinion, facts or feelings. Who, what, when, where and how did the problem occur. If costs or damages are needed then the necessary information needed to estimate or calculate them should be used.

Step 3. Restate the problem. After gathering of the facts, you will be in a better position to understand the problem.

Step 4. Identify alternative solutions. Gather as many solutions to solve the problem as possible. Identify the risks and benefits when looking for solutions.

Step 5. Evaluate alternatives. Look for the best solution. Assess the various risks, costs, benefits associated to the problem and the solution.

Step 6. Implement the decision and decide on how to report the effect of the solution.

Step 7. Evaluate the results. Consider what were the actual costs, who implemented the solution and how was it received. What was the outcome? Is the problem solved or are additional actions needed?

Naturally, solving a problem is a process and this process is a team effort. Each member of the team should try to participate to solve the problem as constructively and as efficiently as possible. Open communication is vital and each person's experience could help to solve the problem. A good leader will allow individuals/groups to voice their opinions, if they so wish, and not to arbitrarily overrule them without due consideration.

Individual corrective action in less than optimal situations is another matter (Fig. 2.23.). This is done behind closed doors and **never in front of other team members**. This is the quickest way to de-motivate individuals and a team. When reprimanding someone you need to be concise and to the point. Always be consistent. If it is not acceptable for one then it is not acceptable for anyone. Good leadership requires that you do not show favoritism. Evaluate the cause of the problem together with the individual to be reprimanded. Discuss the best method to correct the action or behavior and decide on a preventive measure to inhibit a repeat in the future. Give the person a chance to state his/her side of the story. Listen to every word contentedly and try to understand it from his/her point of view, needs and objectives. Make a decision and stick to it. Reprimand by stating your view either verbally or in writing and affirm that you do

REPRIMANDING

Conduct Discussions Behind Closed Doors

Do Not Show Favoritism
(Good for one good for all)

Always Consistent

Decide on a Method to Correct and Inhibit Repeat

Always Concise

End with a Positive Statement
(Behavior, teamwork or contribution)

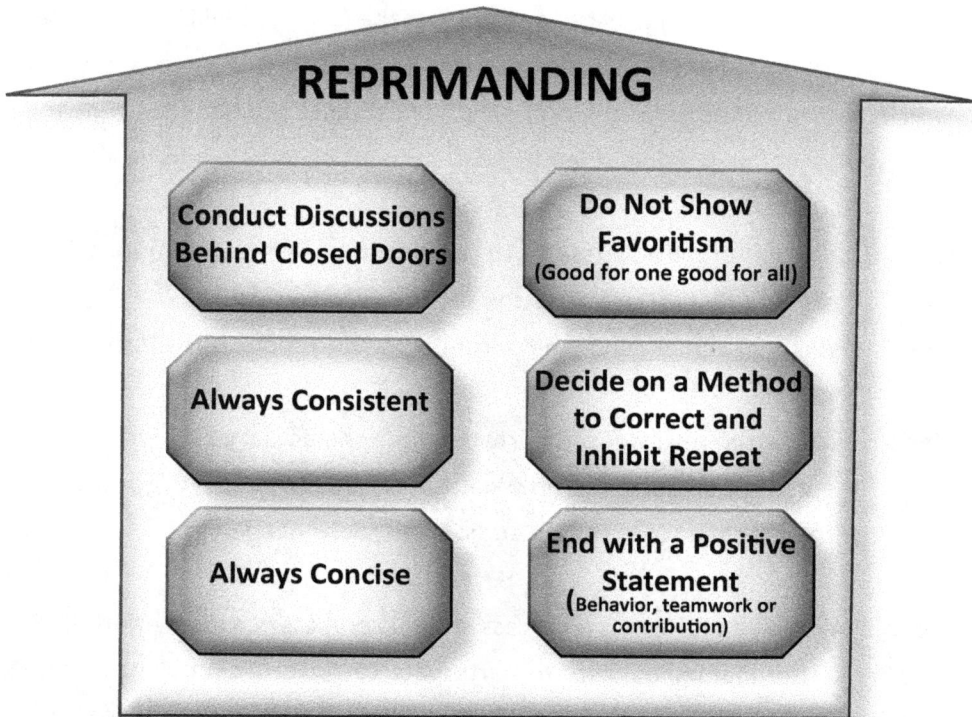

Fig. 2.23. Reprimanding is not an easy job, not even for the most experienced manager or leader. Nevertheless, sometimes one has to. The session should be conducted in privacy, behind closed doors. If the union has to be present then see to it. Listen to the individual's point of view and consider all angles. Be consistent, concise and do not show favoritism. Decide on corrective action and a plan together to prevent the incident from happening again. Always end with a positive statement about participation, contribution and/or teamwork. Make sure that you document the incident.

not want to see them for this problem again, as you now have a plan to correct this from happening again. Leadership with no conviction will not work. End the discussion with something positive about their behavior, teamwork, contribution and say how much you enjoy working with them.

Solving a conflict between team members should not occur if the correct policies, responsibilities and guidelines for each task is known. Nevertheless, conflict does sometimes raise its head. In analyzing the causes the leader should look at the differences in the individual's (PMP) motivation position and consider the individual needs, objectives and values. These differences can be perceived or real and present themselves in actions, words, situations and/or perceived motives. They can be due to unrealistic demands, expected or perceived. The conflict can even be due to one's belief that the other is not collaborating, participating or compromising concerning allocated tasks or work-share, or individual obligations. In resolving the conflict the leader should analyze the problem and decide on a course that best unravels the situation. The leader can decide one of five styles: avoidance, accommodating, win/lose, compromising or problem solving (Maddux and Wingfield, 2003).

> **1) *Avoidance*** is used because the differences are too minor or too large to fix. An attempt might make the precarious situation worse and could even damage relationships.
>
> **2) *Accommodating*** or agreeable is used because it is not worth risking general harmony within the team or even a relationship.
>
> **3) *Win/Lose*** is a little confrontational and is only used when one part is absolutely right and is both ethically and professional justified. Any other decision would only prove to be inconsistent.
>
> **4) *Compromising*** is used when all parties have a pretty good argument and no one person or idea is perfect. It ends up being a give and take scenario.
>
> **5) *Problem solving*** as in the "7 steps", page 67.

chapter *3* *A Matter of Health*

You might wonder why a whole chapter on health is included within a book on the philosophy of management? Well, with the onslaught of globalization, increased competition, and the necessity to meet these new challenges, our work environments are continually inundated with new efficacy and productivity maximizing strategies, change, and new product development. Naturally, there are consequences attached to these demands. An ever hectic working climate causes a number of stress-related side-effects or illnesses which affect the individual, process and productivity. For this reason, and obviously for ethical reasons too, leaders and managers need to be able to understand and recognize these stresses. Reducing such causes and minimizing all subsequent effects is therefore critical. PMP & Cross-Training is about maximizing employee potential through competency development, rotation, and change, whilst minimizing physical, psychosocial (psychological development in and interaction with a social environment) and psychological work-related injuries through team-dynamics and balance.

If employees are asked to sign an employment contract before accepting a position which states "In consideration for a job and *pay, the organization reserves the right to break you physically or psychologically or even both...*" How many employees do you think would sign up for the job? Furthermore, if you replied in thought, *"they need the money so they'll take the job,"* that's unethical and you should rethink your role as a manager or leader, and maybe even see a psychiatrist.

Just as a beam can snap with too much stress so can a person. There is no economic or business model which advocates abuse of employees; on the contrary, the EU-OSHA estimates that work-related stress costs the European Union around €20 Billion annually or nearly 3% of the budget (European Agency for Safety and Health at Work, 2002). They define work-related stress as *"The experience of stress arises from an imbalance between the perceived demands of the environment and the perceived resources available to the individual to cope with those demands."*

The European Agency for Safety and Health at Work have identified a number of issues related to health in the workplace and subsequently created an annual awareness campaign to highlight a safer, healthier, and more productive workplace. According the EU-OSHA fact sheet, (osha.europe.eu, 2008):

> *"every three-and-a-half minutes, somebody in the E.U. dies from work-related causes. This means almost 167,000 deaths a year as a result of either work-related accidents (7,500) or diseases (159,500)."* In the same report they state, *"Every four-and-a-half seconds, a worker in the EU is involved in an accident that forces him/her to stay at home for at least three working days. The number of accidents at work causing three or more days of absence is huge, with over 7 million every year."*

To combat this identified problem, the EU-OSHA began an awareness campaign, directed towards its member states, to highlight these issues. These campaigns started in 2000 with:

2000) Turn your back on musculoskeletal disorders

2001) Success is no accident

2002) Working on stress

2003) Dangerous substances, handle with care

2004) Building in safety

2005) Stop that noise

2006) Young people

2007) Lighten the load, Musculoskeletal disorders (MSDs)

2008) Risk Assessment The Health Workplace: Good for you –
    Good for business

Management by Cross-Training is about reducing the stresses at work by empowering employees with knowledge, encouragement and participation, not only now, but during their entire working careers. This naturally includes ergonomic and occupational health and safety issues too. Management should therefore strive to enhance the working environment using ergonomics, PMP, IDP, and rotation thereby reducing or preventing, through a partnership, psychological, psychosocial and physical workplace injuries.

Stress & Stress Signals

The author believes that STRESS is the common root cause denominator in all three, physical, psychological and psychosocial workplace injuries, and that with PMP, Cross-Training, and common sense, managers and leaders can prevent a vast majority of the stresses from emerging. Obviously, reviews of the processes, workflow, routines and environmental conditions will minimize exposure or prevent extended exposure.

Hans Selye presented his *"General Adaptation Syndrome"* in 1936 where he explains the harmful effects of stress and individual responses thereto. *Selye* divided these responses into three stages *Alarm*, *Resistance* and *Exhaustion* (Selye, 1950).

The *Alarm Stage* is activated when the body/mind identifies or perceives a threat. This threat results in the activation of the hypothalamic-pituitary-adrenal axis (HPA or HTPA Axis). A series of stimulants are sent from the brain (hypothalamic and pituitary) to the adrenal gland, above the kidneys, which excretes a number of hormones such as cortisol , epinephrine, and norepinephrine resulting in the fight or flight response we are all so familiar with. The second stage is the *Adaptation Stage* where the body tries to adapt to the heightened state. Naturally, if this continues for extended periods of time the third stage of exhaustion sets in. The *Exhaustion Stage* is due to depletion and is a result of the body being unable to maintain normal bodily functions at the newly adopted or heightened stage.

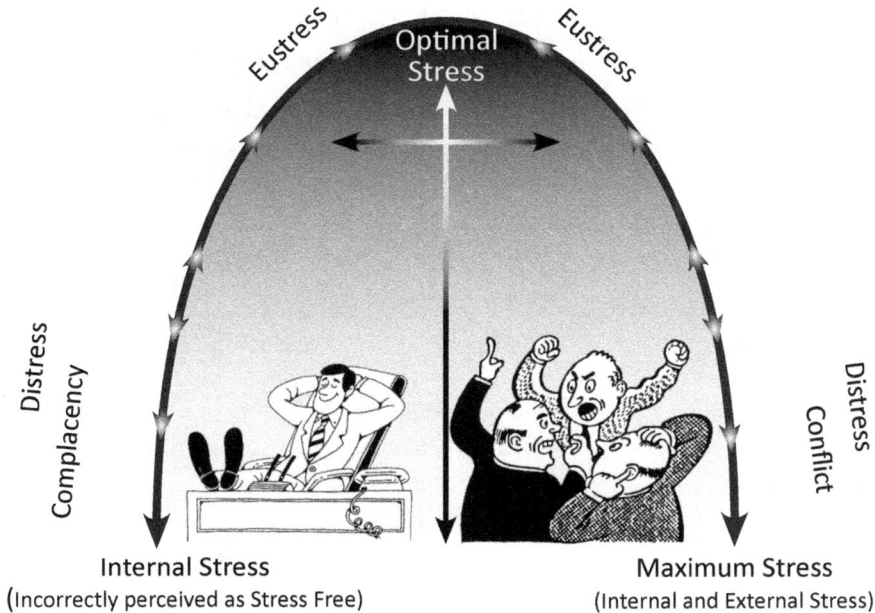

Fig. 3.1. An adapted illustration showing Eustress versus Distress using Lazorous's performance stress curve and PMP. He argues that we cannot always avoid stress, in verity, we should not. His theory suggests that a small amount of stress is beneficial as it gives us our competitive advantage. The illustration suggests that in performance related matters it is advantageous with small amounts of stress. In addition, the author believes that complacency leads to stress as a result of inequities in one's PMP. This is caused by not fulfilling one's External Demands and Self-Expectancy potential and sub-conscious guilt related to one's non-fulfillment and lack participation in the Social Environment which subsequently leads to poor Self-Esteem and increased internal stress.

Another theory introduced by Lazorous suggests that stress can be good. **Eustress** and **Distress** is a model which he divided stress into two camps, *good stress* or Eustress and *bad stress* or Distress (Lazorous, 1974). In Lazorous's model he suggests that the Eustress actually enhances physical and mental function, whereas, Distress is caused by a persistent inability to adapt or cope which leads to anxiety, withdrawal and even depression. He believes that any disparity is balanced between to the result of the individual's expectations, resources to cope with the situation or demand and personal experience, whether or not, it is real or perceived. Therefore, his model suggests that a cognitive process of appraisal determines whether or not the situation is of threat and signifies the level of performance. His performance stress curve (Fig. 3.1.) illustrates this balance.

Finding the balance therefore is critical. Dr. Thomas Holmes and Dr. Richard Rahe introduced a stress scale called the **Holmes and Rahe Stress Scale** (Holmes and Rahe, 1967) after examining over 5000 medical journals in the early 1960s. They found that a positive 0.1 correlation (Rahe and Athur, 1978) sup-

Holmes and Rahe Stress Scale

Life Event	Points	Life Event	Points
Death of a spouse	100	Trouble with in-laws	29
Divorce	73	Outstanding personal achievement	28
Marital separation	65	Spouse starts or stops work	26
Imprisonment	63	Begin or end school	26
Death of a close family member	63	Change in living conditions	25
Personal injury or illness	53	Revision of personal habits	24
Marriage	50	Trouble with boss	23
Dismissal from work	47	Change in working hours/conditions	20
Marital reconciliation	45	Change in residence	20
Retirement	45	Change in schools	20
Change in health of family member	44	Change in recreation	19
Pregnancy	40	Change in church activities	19
Sexual difficulties	39	Change in social activities	18
Gain a new family member	39	Minor mortgage or loan	17
Business readjustment	39	Change in sleeping habits	16
Change in financial state	38	Change in no. of family reunions	15
Change in frequency of arguments	35	Change in eating habits	15
Major mortgage	32	Vacation	13
Foreclosure of mortgage or loan	30	Christmas	12
Change in responsibilities at work	29	Minor violation of law	11
Child leaving home	29	**Total Points (1 year):**	_____

Fig. 3.2. *The Holmes and Rahe Stress Scale assesses and measures a number of "Life Change Units" for an individual for specific events over a year. The final score gives a rough estimate of how much stress the individual received. Naturally some individuals take stress differently; however, the leader and manager should take into account various stresses that could affect the health and well-being of the employee. Obviously, job demands and tasks should be adjusted to minimize high stress scores.* **Scores: under 150** *had a* **slight risk of illness; 150-299+** *had a* **moderate risk of illness** *(30% less than highest); and* **300+** *points meant that one was at* **risk of illness**.

ported and validated a link between stress and illness (Fig. 3.2.). It is important to keep in mind that lifestyles and conditions today are not the same as those in the 1960s, their scale, although validated in many subsequent studies, should only be used to raise *red flags* and to give the manager/leader additional information for consideration and/or action if needed.

Long-Term Induced Physical and Psychological Injuries

The American Institute of Stress (AIS) lists the 50 most common signs of stress (Fig. 3.3.). AIS makes a point in stipulating that stress is subjective and that it differs from person to person. Some people might find a certain thing stressful while others might find the same thing pleasurable. Logic, communication and some empathy is therefore prescribed.

Stress related to basic muscular and skeletal disorders/injuries in the workplace are rather obvious to comprehend. Their causes usually derive from a number of situations and/or tasks such as:

1) Lifting incorrectly or carrying articles which are too heavy
2) Repetitive tasks using the same muscles or affecting the same skeletal areas for prolonged time frames
3) Standing or sitting in the same position for extended periods
4) Eye strain from long-drawn-out period in front of a computer or television screen
5) Age, genetic predispositions (arthritis, osteoarthritis, etc.) and prior related or unrelated injuries.
6) Poor planning of time, resources, and demand expectations.

Job demands over time in combination with age are major factors affecting stress. It is natural, that as we age we lose some of our physical and even mental abilities over time. Unfortunately, we sometimes forget to take this into consideration when planning demands and responsibilities. This laps, lack of

American Institute of Stress (www.stress.org) 50 Most Common Signs of Stress	
1. Frequent headaches, jaw clenching or pain	26. Insomnia, nightmares, disturbing dreams
2. Gritting, grinding teeth	27. Difficulty concentrating, racing thoughts
3. Stuttering or stammering	28. Trouble learning new information
4. Tremors, trembling of lips, hands	29. Forgetfulness, disorganization, confusion
5. Neck ache, back pain, muscle spasms	30. Difficulty in making decisions
6. Light headed, faintness, dizziness	31. Feeling overloaded or overwhelmed
7. Ringing, buzzing or "popping sounds	32. Frequent crying spells or suicidal thoughts
8. Frequent blushing, sweating	33. Feelings of loneliness or worthlessness
9. Cold or sweaty hands, feet	34. Little interest in appearance, punctuality
10. Dry mouth, problems swallowing	35. Nervous habits, fidgeting, feet tapping
11. Frequent colds, infections, herpes sores	36. Increased frustration, irritability, edginess
12. Rashes, itching, hives, "goose bumps"	37. Overreaction to petty annoyances
13. Unexplained or frequent "allergy 'attacks'	38. Increased number of minor accidents
14. Heartburn, stomach pain, nausea	39. Obsessive or compulsive behavior
15. Excess belching, flatulence	40. Reduced work efficiency or productivity
16. Constipation, diarrhea	41. Lies or excuses to cover up poor work
17. Difficulty breathing, sighing	42. Rapid or mumbled speech
18. Sudden attacks of panic	43. Excessive defensiveness or suspiciousness
19. Chest pain, palpitations	44. Problems in communication, sharing
20. Frequent urination	45. Social withdrawal and isolation
21. Poor sexual desire or performance	46. Constant tiredness, weakness, fatigue
22. Excess anxiety, worry, guilt, nervousness	47. Frequent use of over-the-counter drugs
23. Increased anger, frustration, hostility	48. Weight gain or loss without diet
24. Depression, frequent or wild mood swings	49. Increased smoking, alcohol or drug use
25. Increased or decreased appetite	50. Excessive gambling or impulse buying

Fig. 3.3. The American Institute of Stress is a non-profit organization established in 1978 at the request of Han Selye, the founder and guru of Stress understanding shows their 50 most common symptoms of stress. The AIS states that stress is America's number one health problem and TIME magazine called it "The Epidemic of the Eighties."

realization or even denial can become very stressful for all parties concerned. If workplace routines, rotation and other assignments are not readily reviewed to meet these changing conditions, stress will inevitably increase, leading rise to isolationist, protectionist and other defense mechanisms. The frustration

Fig. 3.4. Some physical symptoms of chronic stress can be life threatening such as cancer, high blood pressure and even heart disease. Other less life-threatening physical signs include insomnia, constant fatigue, digestive disorders, overeating and many more. Understanding these symptoms is vital for the leader. He/she should try to prevent them by balancing work related demands to that of the individual, whilst at the same time, improving on the employees PMP and IDP.

(stress) related to these physical demands clearly affects our psychosocial and psychological well-being.

Psychological stresses affect our psychosocial behavior and our adaptability. This in turn inhibits teamwork, productivity and even physical health. The European Agency for Safety and Health at Work state, *"Stress arises from an Imbalance between the perceived demands of the environment and the perceived resources available to the individual"* naturally, this includes both mental and physical, perceived and actual ability too.

If not remedied these perceived or actual imbalances can cause an individual to go into conflict with others, withdraw or even isolate him/herself. This isolationist behavior draws attention, criticism, conflict and sometimes even mobbing from the remaining coworkers.

The World Health Organization describes **harassment** as an increasing world-wide problem which is of concern (WHO, Raising Awareness of Psychological Harassment at Work, 2003). Harassment can be a serious problem in many workplaces and should be dealt with before it gets out of control. Leaders should quell harassment by correcting the underlying causes, whether they are perceived or actual, educational, physical or mental capabilities, and create measures to correct it from re-occurring. This is done through education, rotation, repetition, counseling, etc. Figure 3.5., provides a list of psychopathological, psychosomatically and behavioral conditions caused by mobbing within the workplace.

Another side-effect of stress is to overindulge by increasing good-feelings such as smoking, drinking, eating, and even taking drugs by stimulating the re-

STRESS caused by MOBBING

Psychopathologic	Psychosomatic	Behavioral
Anxiety reaction	Arterial hypertension	Auto and hetro-aggressive reactions
Apathy	Attacks of asthma	Eating disorders
Avoidance reactions	Cardiac palpations	Increased alcohol and drug intake
Concentration problems	Coronary heart disease	Increased smoking
Depressive mood	Dermatitis	Sexual dysfunctions
Fear reactions	Hair loss	Social isolation
Flashbacks	Headache	Defensive attitudes
Hyper-arousal	Joint and muscle pains	One-way communication
Insecurity	Loss of balance	Mistrust
Insomnia	Migraine	
Intrusive thought	Muscular tension	
Irritability	Skeletal pain	
Lack of initiative	Stomach pains	
Melancholy	Stomach ulcers	
Mood changes	IBS (Irritable bowl syndrome)	
Recurrent nightmares	Tachycardia	

Fig. 3.5. Adapted from the World Health Organization's report protecting Workers' Health Series 4. The symptoms of chronic (long-term) stress caused by mobbing, perceived or real, can be grouped into three segments: Psychopathologic, Psychosomatic, and Behavioral. These affects can be long-lasting and devastating for the individual, team, productivity, and need immediate attention.

lease of dopamine. Dopamine is a natural chemical or neuron. It acts as a neu-rotransmitter and stimulates brain receptors which affect brain processes that control emotional response and the ability to experience pleasure and pain. Unfortunately, when one is under too much stress, lacking control and feeling helpless, a natural response for many will be to take a drink, or two or three, or to eat, or to seek other pleasurable activities such as sex or drugs. Naturally, when there is an up, there is always a down. Consequently, this roller coaster produces a spiral-effect that can set the individual on a path to more chronic conditions such as defensive attitudes, Adjustment Disorders (AD), depression or burnout syndrome.

Defense Mechanisms

When one is threatened or stressed, whether it is perceived or real, the natural instinct is to circle the wagons and defend one's position. All individuals com-municate (verbal or non-verbal) these signals through either psychopathologic, psychosomatic and/or behavior means. These signals can include various stress, anxiety, defense and/or other illnesses. Perceptibly, one's state of mind and cur-rent PMP combined with past experiences will directly effect consequent ac-tions and behavior for a given situation. This behavior can be open and produc-tive, aggressive (fight), regressive (flight), closed or isolationist in nature. To lead and motivate people requires that you have some grasp of this subject matter as it will help you to:

> **1)** understand and interpret these signals,
>
> **2)** to constructively deal with any signals, and
>
> **3)** to recognize and overcome any negative messages/reactions.

As the saying goes, "for every action there is a reaction" this is very true in leadership. How you as a leader react will cause a sequence of events. Your role as a leader is to pro-actively identify and take corrective measures.

According to **Sigmund Freud**, defense mechanisms are created consciously, semi-consciously (pre-conscious) and unconsciously to protect the ego from awareness of difficult facts and ideas or painful feelings (Freud, 1923). Today his techniques are still used widely in psychoanalysis and even leadership. Freud believed that these are normal universal features that signify an unconscious fight between the ***ego of id*** (child-like psyche which is impulsive, wants what it wants, and disregards all consequences thereto), ***the superego*** (the morally right thing to do), and which are balanced by the ***ego*** (portrayed by ones actions after taking into consideration the impulses of the ego of id and the morality of the superego) (Fig. 3.6.).

Freud also introduced the conflict of guilt and how a sense of guilt is established. He believed that this guilt also prevents the individual from conquering their own pathology. His theory, which I might add, is widely accepted and suggests that this conflict happens unconsciously when the superego joins forces with ego of id and blames the ego for the decision.

Defense mechanisms (Fig. 3.7.) are therefore the ego's natural way to defend itself against perceived or actual threat. Freud believed that there were

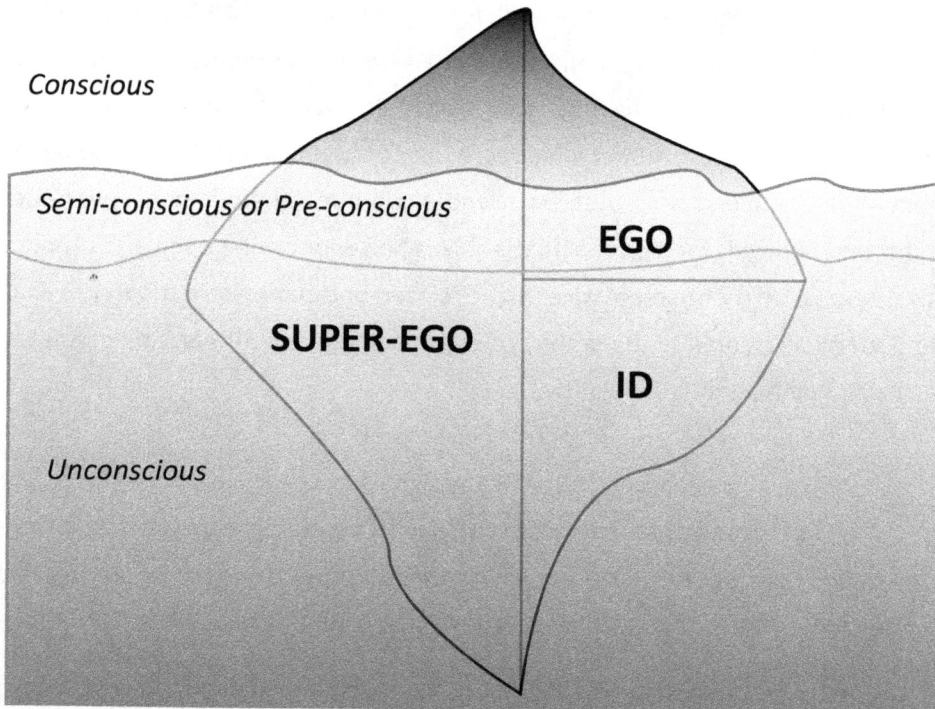

Fig. 3.6. A metaphor of an iceberg is commonly used to illustrate Freud's psyche relationship structure which affects one's personality.

four defense mechanism levels (hierarchy): Level 1, the psychotic defenses allows one to cope with reality by effectively rearranging it; level 2, known as the immature defenses, is associated with minimizing distress and anxiety related to uncomfortable realities or situations brought on by threatening people; level 3, the neurotic defenses, are quick-fixes that usually help the individual to cope with problems in the short-term, unfortunately they can cause problems in the long-term by affecting lifestyle patterns ; and level 4 is the mature or virtue level that consists of the most common defenses found in most normal, healthy adults. These defenses help to integrate conflicting emotions by creating a type of consensus.

The ego is therefore affected by any conflict or any inconsistency. Environmental demands and pressures, blame or guilt and other stresses or threats (physical or psychological), whether or not they are perceived or real, can thereby cause these conflicts or inconsistencies. This conflict can inhibit or distort the normal behavioral responses (isolationism, conflict, one-way communication, etc.) and/or actions (aggression, physical abuse, addiction such as alcohol, drugs, sex, etc.), expected from an individual.

Anna Freud introduced the concept of signal anxiety, which took Sigmund Freud's theory further by presenting anxiety as a biological adaptation (Anna Freud, 1937). This biological adaptation prepares the body for tension, the perceived or actual threat. By providing the individual with more control over his/her environment, Cross-Training helps to prevent development of these issues through counseling, education and rotation; however, if these anxieties are too engrained or complex, external psychologists, therapists or psychoanalysts should be used.

George Vaillant, Robert Plutchick, and others continued on Freud's groundbreaking research into defense mechanisms, moreover, the United States Defense Department created the initial handbook or precursor to the DSM "Diagnostic and Statistical Manual or Mental Disorders" adopted by the America Psychiatric Association and commonly known as DSM-I, DSM-II, DSM-III, DSM IV, and DSM-V (2008) which have long been the standing manuals for professional psychologist and psychiatrists alike.

Psychotic — Level 1

Denial: Refusal to acknowledge certain external realities because they are too threatening.

Delusional Projection: Gross delusions about external reality, normally projected onto someone else.

Distortion: Restructure external reality to meet internal needs.

Immature — Level 2

Acting out: Expressed emotion and/or behavior resulting from an unconscious impulse or wish.

Fantasy: Resolving conflicts by withdrawing into fantasy.

Hypochondria sis: Transforming negative feelings for others into negative feelings of pain, illness and anxiety onto oneself.

Idealization: Subconscious perception of endowing an individual/situation with more qualities than he/she/it actually has.

Passive aggression: Expressing indirect or passive aggression towards others.

Projection: Shifting one's undesirable feelings, thoughts or impulses onto someone else.

Neurotic — Level 3

Displacement: Shifting aggressive impulses to a more amenable or less threatening target.

Dissociation: To postpone or separate oneself from a feeling associated to a situation or thought by drastically modifying one's identity or character to avoid emotional distress.

Isolation: Distance oneself from events and ideas without showing emotion.

Intellectualization: A form of isolationism in that one exaggerates intellectual clarifications in order to avoid emotions or anxiety-provoking situations.

Reaction Formation: Converting unconscious impulses or perceived whishes into the opposite of the actual belief/want or need in order prevent the true belief from causing any anxiety.

Repression: Preventing harmful or painful thoughts from entering the consciousness by suppressing or pushing-back these thoughts into the unconscious through a decrease of awareness or increase naivety in regard to ones own condition or situation. Details could diminish however emotion remain conscious.

Mature /Virtue — Level 4

Altruism: Satisfaction and pleasure derived from proactive service to other.

Anticipation: Rational planning for future distress or anxiety.

Humor: Expressing ideas and feeling in a humorous way to give others pleasure; however, this can also be a negative trait in disguise.

Identification: Forming oneself after another person's character or behavior.

Introjection: Replicating in one's own persona the attributes, behaviors of the environment (surrounding world).

Sublimation: Converting negative perceptions, emotions or instincts into positive behavior.

Suppression: Suppressing conscious thoughts and emotions into the sub-conscious (preconscious) by delaying or prioritizing related needs and emotions so as to best handle current realities, thereafter, accessing and accepting those distressing or uncomfortable emotions.

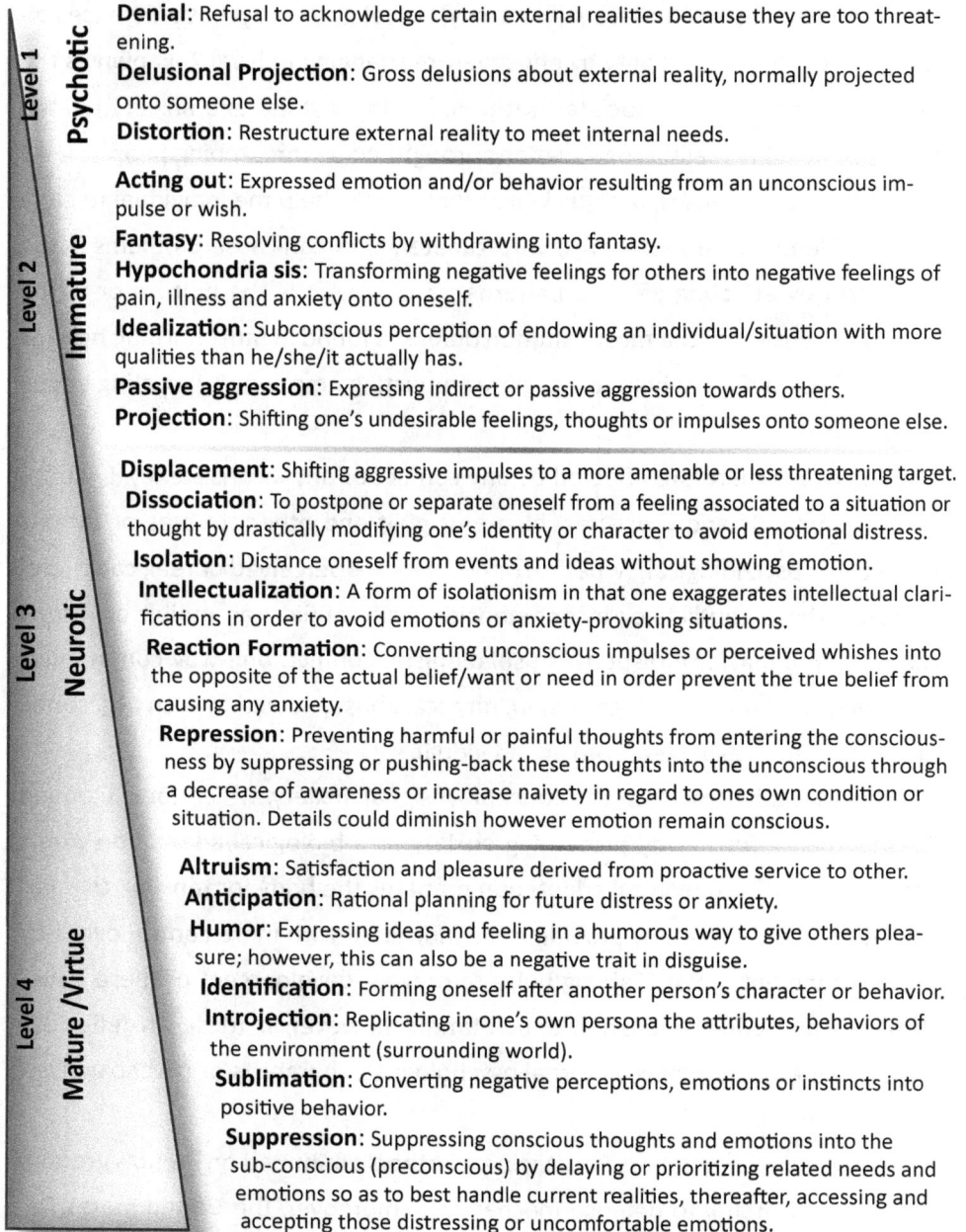

Fig. 3.7. Adapted from Anna and Sigmund Freud's mechanisms of defense. Level 1, the psychotic defenses, *allows one to* **cope with reality by effectively rearranging it***; level 2, known as the* immature defenses, *is associated with* **minimizing distress and anxiety** *related to uncomfortable realities or situations brought on by threatening people; level 3, the* neurotic defenses, *are* **quick-fixes** *and usually help the individual to cope with problems in the short-term, unfortunately they can cause problems in the long-term by affecting lifestyle patterns; and level 4 is the* mature or virtue level *that consists of the* **most common defenses** *found in most normal, healthy adults.*

This chapter is not about making you psychologist or therapist but serves instead to enlighten you, thereby enhancing your ability to recognize patterns, changes in one's behavior, action and reactions, and other defensive behaviors which can inhibit personnel growth, teamwork and efficacy. The manager's role is about people and understanding or interpreting the signals that they give off. These signals include defensive messages transmitted through poor work, low participation, excessive behavior, workaholics, and others.

Anxiety Signals

Anxiety Disorders are brought about through excessive and unrealistic worrying over an extended period of time, 6 months or so. The most common forms of anxiety are *Obsessive-Compulsive, Panic, Post-Traumatic Stress, Social-Anxiety,* and *Specific Phobias.* These worries could include one's family, health, money and even lack of control in a specific situation. Symptoms can include instability, abdominal irregularities, insomnia, muscular aches, and uncontrollable shaking or trembling. Anxieties, fear and phobias are all discussed in detail in the Diagnostic and Statistical Manual of Mental Disorders, the edition (DSM-IV-TR, 2000).

Fig. 3.8. By taking the time to look closely at an employee's behavior with genuine concern and empathy it is far easier to communicate changes and solutions to process and/or prioritization techniques. Anxiety, stress, burnout syndrome are direct causes of complacent managers/leaders and poor leadership skills. By comprehending and recognizing the most common forms of anxiety and/or stress the manger/leader can creatively find solutions to reduce the causes of these symptoms.

Obsessive-Compulsive Disorders are obsessive recurring thoughts of exaggerated anxiety or fear. Howard Hughes was well-known for his exaggerated

fear of bacteria and of being contaminated. This can also include worries about being violent or having improper behavior. Symptoms usually include obsessive rituals or routines such as washing hands, etc.

Panic Disorders or panic attacks are where people feel that they cannot breathe or that they are having a heart-attack. Symptoms can include chest pain, sweating, fear of losing control, fear of dying, etc.

Post-Traumatic Stress Disorder (PTSD) follows exposure to a traumatic event. This can include war/battle situations, sexual abuse, natural disasters, and severe accidents, witnessing death or death of a loved one. Symptoms are grouped into three categories:

1) reliving the trauma in nightmares or flashbacks;
2) avoidance behaviors, avoiding persons or places associated with the trauma or isolating oneself;
3) physiological stimulus or arousal, inability to sleep, sleep deprivation, irritability, and poor concentration.

Social Anxiety Disorder (Social Phobia) is the fear of being embarrassed, ridiculed or being judged by others. Symptoms can include isolationist tendencies, nervousness such as sweating, heart palpitations and light -headedness. Separation anxiety is included within this group.

Specific Phobias are strong fears related to specific situations such as height, noise, speed, flying, hospital visits, etc., and/or objects such as mice, rats, cockroaches, spiders, snakes, etc.

A Subject of Balance (Sleep, Eat, Work & Play)

"IT" is about balance. A known fact that too much or too little of anything can produce a cause and effect scenario. Work, life-style and the demands placed upon them will reap what has been sown. There is always a reaction to the actions. Each individual has their own recommended daily allowances of work, sleep (recovery time) and play (stimulation through various means). Excesses or deficiency will, over time, cause health (physical and/or psychological) illnesses or disorders. A manager's/leader's role is to keep their personnel or human machines, excuse the euphemism, well oiled and trimmed (balanced) so that they can achieve maximize potential effort over extended periods of time and throughout their working careers. This needs to be done through PMP and by balancing corporate policy, culture and life-style to the demands.

Sleep deprivation has been proven to cause a number of health-related problems. A recent study by the University of Chicago Medical center in 1996 linked sleep deprivation to Diabetes Type 2 (Van Cauter et al, 1996 & 2008) by using hormonal rhythms as markers during the circadian clock (melatonin hormone release peeking at night, higher cortisol levels in the morning, etc.). Furthermore, the studies suggest that shift-workers are at higher risk as the disruption of the circadian rhythms may cause a kind of biological revolt leading to obesity, cancer, mental illnesses, reproductive difficulties and gastrointestinal disorders (Fig. 3.9). This disruption causes night-shift workers to sleep less than day workers and to have less quality sleep too as they try to sleep when their bodies want to be awake (Van Cauter et al, 2008). *"Quickly rotating schedules, shift workers suffer from circadian misalignment, since circadian rhythms do not adapt. Very slow rotating shift workers should adapt more easily, and permanent night workers should form a group that maintains a nocturnal orientation* (Olivier Van Reeth, 1998)." Various studies have found that night-shift workers have a 40% to 50% increase risk of heart disease compared with day workers (Shari Roan: LA Times, 2008).

Shift rotations are also under dispute. In Europe a fast-rotating schedules, as in Rexam, where they rotate clockwise (06:00-14:00, 14:00-22:00, and 22:00-06:00) with three days on three days off. Most employees prefer this method although this method includes a small number of consecutive nights of work and resulting in less accumulation of sleep deficit the circadian system of the workers cannot adapt to the imposed work schedule. In the USA most companies prefer slow-rotating schedules (around three to four weeks) which allow the circadian system to adapt to the workers schedule; however, it can

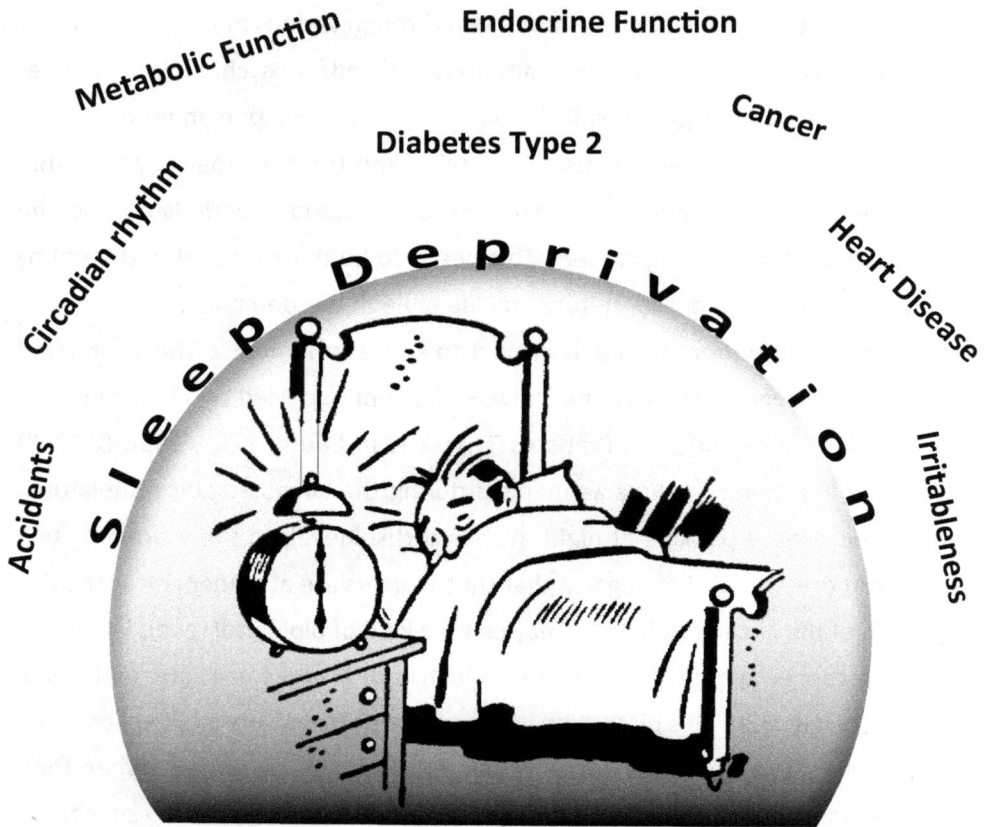

Fig. 3.9. Adapted from text related to Eva Cauter, A. Williamson et al and shows how sleep deprivation can affect health and naturally productivity. As a result of sleep deprivation an employee can expect to make more mistakes due to low alertness and the intoxicant effects of sleepiness, get sick more frequently, be far more irritable (less patience), be vulnerable to cancer and diabetes type 2. Manager's enact policies and leader's should look for creative ways to implement them and to minimize the causes and effects of sleep deprivation by incorporating educational programs into the workplace and activities after hours.

also create a gradual build-up of sleep loss. Weekly rotations represent probably the worst scenario as it does not allow for enough time to synchronize the circadian system (Olivier van Reeth, 1998).

Additional studies by Dr. Even Van Cauter also show that people that sleep less have erratic blood sugars. In one of her studies a group of young men were restricted to four hours of sleep for six consecutive nights resulting in their blood sugar levels (insulin sensitivity) were so abnormal they almost mirrored those of diabetics. Moreover, insulin and other hormone disruptions cause weight prob-

---

Sleep Deprivation versus Alcohol Consumption

OBJECTIVES:

To compare the relative effects on performance of sleep deprivation and alcohol.

METHODS:

Performance effects were studied in the same subjects over a period of 28 hours of sleep deprivation and after measured doses of alcohol up to about 0.1% blood alcohol concentration (BAC). There were 39 subjects, 30 employees from the transport industry and nine from the army.

RESULTS:

After 17-19 hours without sleep, corresponding to 2230 and 0100, performance on some tests was equivalent or worse than that at a BAC of 0.05%. Response speeds were up to 50% slower for some tests and accuracy measures were significantly poorer than at this level of alcohol. After longer periods without sleep, performance reached levels equivalent to the maximum alcohol dose given to subjects (BAC of 0.1%).

CONCLUSIONS:

These findings reinforce the evidence that the fatigue of sleep deprivation is an important factor likely to compromise performance of speed and accuracy of the kind needed for safety on the road and in other industrial settings.

Fig. 3.10. Effects of sleep deprivation and alcohol use. © OEM & Dr. A. Williamsom

lems too. The body produces less Leptin, a hormone that suppresses apetite and more Ghrelin, a hormone that promotes hunger. The result being that the subjects eat more fatty foods, sugar and starch. Naturally, the biological clock does not know if it is coming or going and therefore not in balance either.

According to a study published in the British Medical Journal (Williamson & Fèyer, 2000) evidence shows an equivalent performance and accuracy between persons with sleep deprivation and those with a blood alcohol count of 0.1% (above the legal level in many countries). Figure 3.10. shows the method, results and conclusion.

Studies have shown that **physical training** improved circadian rhythms and sleep quality including improved performance on the job for nurse shift-workers by decreasing fatigue and musculoskeletal symptoms (Ilmarinen, Knauth, Rutenfranz & Nanninen, 1998). Furthermore, additional studies have also shown that nocturnal exercise improved phase shifts in circadian rhythms in relation to their daytime sleep schedule (Eastman, Hoese, Youngstedt & Liu, 1995).

For employees to maximize output, a balance between PMP, work, rest (sleep), exercise, and play is prescribed. Management policy and leadership participation should strive to achieve this balance by providing their staff with the conditions, the resources, and creative means necessary to accomplish this. Train your leaders to know each employee's PMP and to recognize their stress signals. Just like playing the piano, exerting just the right amount of pressure and in a specific order will produce a wonderful sound with perfect synergy. So too, must a manager conduct and a leader play his resources. Mind not to place too much tension on the keys as this stress could cause them to break or weaken. Occasionally, some fine tuning will be necessary and in some cases repositioning of a string too. Humans are the most adaptable species on the planet and if managed correctly the sky is the limit.

Most physical accidents in the workplace are caused by poor processes and most psychological illnesses and even some physical are caused by stress (Fig. 3.11). Both of these, less than optimal, factors can be marginalized or even eradicated altogether.

Regrettably, many managers and leaders become, overtime through complacency, oblivious to their employee's, and even their own, signs of stress or red-flags before it is too late. The author has heard, "Don't fix it or review when it's not broken" literally thousands of times, however, the signs and signals were there, the only problem was that the manager/leader could not recognize them. Proactive prevention is again prescribed. If these signs or signals are addressed, at the earliest convenience, you will be in a good position to solve it before it grows and/or spread to other team members. If left unattended it will develop

Fig. 3.11. Illustrates a process problem causing stress on the individual. The External Demand Environment is out of balance with individual Self-Expectancy. Leaders should be looking at ways to improve on the process in order to balance these demands.

into larger issues causing problems that could affect efficacy, teamwork, and cost the company far more in employee turnovers, and most importantly, causing illness to an individual employee.

Workaholics are also at risk. Usually, management reacts when an individual cannot live up to the expected demands as set by the company and reacts accordingly; however, management rarely corrects someone who works too much. Why is this? Is this not a signal too? Could it be denial or distortion indicating a life-style problem (relationship, family problems, inadequacy of some sort, etc.)? Is it not management's ethical responsibility to look for these patterns too? The author believes so. He has seen many managers overwhelmed as a result of their own PMP tensions. In most instances, their self-expectancy demands, external demands and social demands (private & work) were in tension and out of balance.

Sometimes this scenario becomes a self-afflicting problem of denial and distortion by the individual where he/she voluntarily creates work or extra assignments, which can also be stimulating through participation in a new product, concept, or policy thereby fulfilling a need of satisfaction and stimulation at the cost of recovery and sleep. Naturally, the consequence is usually exhaustion and over extended time periods burnout.

Burnout Syndrome

Too much, too long! The World Health Organization calls burn-out "A State of Vital Exhaustion" caused by high stress over a prolonged period, usually exceeding 6 months. In this chapter and earlier chapters, the author discussed a number of relevant denominators (existing or lacking) which can lead to Burn-Out Syndrome. Denominators that can lead to burn-out:

1. Management that lacks any (one) of the "7 golden rules of management" (Fig. 1.1)
2. Leaders who lack any (one) of the "7 leadership traits" (Fig. 1.2)
3. PMP imbalance (Fig's. 2.9 & 3.11)
4. Long-term stress and anxiety (Fig's. 3.1 – 3.5)

A manager is responsible for creating the guidelines and policies for the leaders to implement, however, without a proper hands-on approach, managers and leaders will not be able to recognize job specific, individual and team limitations and the demands associated thereto. Burn-out syndrome can be prevented with proactive leadership and individual coaching (Fig. 2.14) by emphasizing balance in an individual's PMP.

It is important to remember that managers and leaders need to balance

Fig. 3.12. Persons of responsibility, managers and leaders with little awareness of their own PMPs are at risk for long-term stressor and burn-out.

Fig. 3.13. Persons of responsibility, managers and leaders with little awareness of their employee's PMPs are causing the determinants of long-term stress and burn-out.

their own PMPs too. Their positions are filled with deadlines and other excessive job stresses (Warr, 1984). When 'persons of responsibility' forget their own PMP's and end up with imbalances between their own expectations and the external demand environment they too are candidate for long-term stress and burn-out. Teachers, social workers, personnel managers, management, childcare givers and even volunteers are good examples of these.

Burn-out is caused by a lack of good management and leadership and is preventable through Cross-Training, rotation, flexibility and PMP balance.

chapter *4* *Behavioral Analysis and Management*

In Cross-Training, Behavioral Analysis and Management (BAM) is used to observe and develop individual and group behavior into teamwork. This process begins with identifying signals emitted by the individual, comprehending these signals in relation to the individual's PMP and managing a plan to correct any imbalances by adjusting individual job descriptions, routines, and processes within the individual's landscape.

The individual is the common denominator in all work. Just like a cogwheel in a machine house, it too, must be in balance and sync with other individuals or corresponding parts. BAM in Cross-Training is about the synergy of individual behavior and organizational culture (chapter 12) into the workflow process.

It is well documented that teams complete their goals more consistently, quicker and with less quality control issues than groups. A group consists of individuals working towards set objectives in a somewhat chaotic and sometimes inefficient way. A team works together; they understand the demands of their teammates and have the flexibility to adapt to changing needs and a culture governing deportment. Teamwork is synergy which is the right mix that maximizes potential output with the least amount of friction.

Teams are then individuals in synergy. Therefore, it becomes obvious that the leader/manager naturally has the responsibility to monitor individual PMPs, behaviors and signals in order to achieve optimal synergic efficaciousness. This is accomplished by observing the individual's and the team's behavior, creating a PMP action plan, based upon individual assessment in Appendix D, adjusting the demands on individual's by changing routines, processes, and understanding in order to maximize long-term participation.

Although there is no single accepted theory in regard to behaviorism, the author prefers a more cognitive approach. There are four major objectives in

BAM and they are to (Fig. 4.0):

1) **Understand** (PMP interrelated dependencies, job demands, stresses, anxieties, personality types A&B, team needs, etc.),

2) **Prevent** (too much stress, complacency, façades),

3) **Promote** (change or sustain behavior and attitude), and

4) **Trust** (teamwork, compromise, monitor conflicts, rotate & educate).

1) Understand is your analysis of the association and dependencies of PMP in relation to the individual, the demands of the position, the environment and individual PMP assessment, Appendix D. If you do not know the operating environment and the conditions to which your employees are working you

Fig. 4.0. BAM or Behavioral Analysis & Management in MBCT has its focus on the individual and team synergy at work. This is undertaken by understanding the demands of the positions, managing stress levels, preventing complacency and façade building, promote and motivate through good communication, and manage teamwork though trust, consistency and monitoring.

cannot fully interpret their behavioral patterns, stresses, and anxiety signals. If you do not know the individual or the organizational culture (chapter 12), you cannot understand personality types and behavior as they are individually conditioned, adapted, and modified through situations involving the individual and his/her environment. Obviously, an individual's PMP status will affect susceptibility to cultural conditioning and adaptability. For this reason, leaders should be familiar with ALL positional demands if they are to command behavioral understanding. It is not just a clinical text book explanation of how or what causes the behavior in an individual, but it involves values and demands placed upon the individual at any given time, situation or over longer periods. If the Lieutenants' can't walk in the shoes of their soldiers then they will never understand, cannot lead, and will not be able to make correct decisions. The same goes with leaders/supervisors/shift managers and employees. Not everything is black and white, as a matter of fact, there is a lot more gray in managing behavior.

PMP Interrelated Dependencies Comprehension of PMP and the interrelated dependencies for each are crucial (Fig. 4.1). The interrelatedness can be motivating or de-motivating for the individual. If not in balance (too much or too little) these irregularities will cause internal conflict or tension leading to attitude change within the individual. The leader/manager should assist the individual in achieving better balance in their PMPs by making an action plan together to address these PMP irregularities, and/or by adjusting workflow, process or conditions. Naturally, the leader/manager can only prepare the way by creating new processes, workflows and strategies, but it is up to the individual to take the step.

Naturally, PMP conflict causes stress and if left unabated this stress will spread to the other interrelated PMP dependencies causing further stresses and subsequently producing symptoms. The PMP interrelated dependencies are:

Educational Environment is one of the primary motivators as it provides the individual with an ability to meet the external demand environment and is

Interrelated Dependencies of PMP

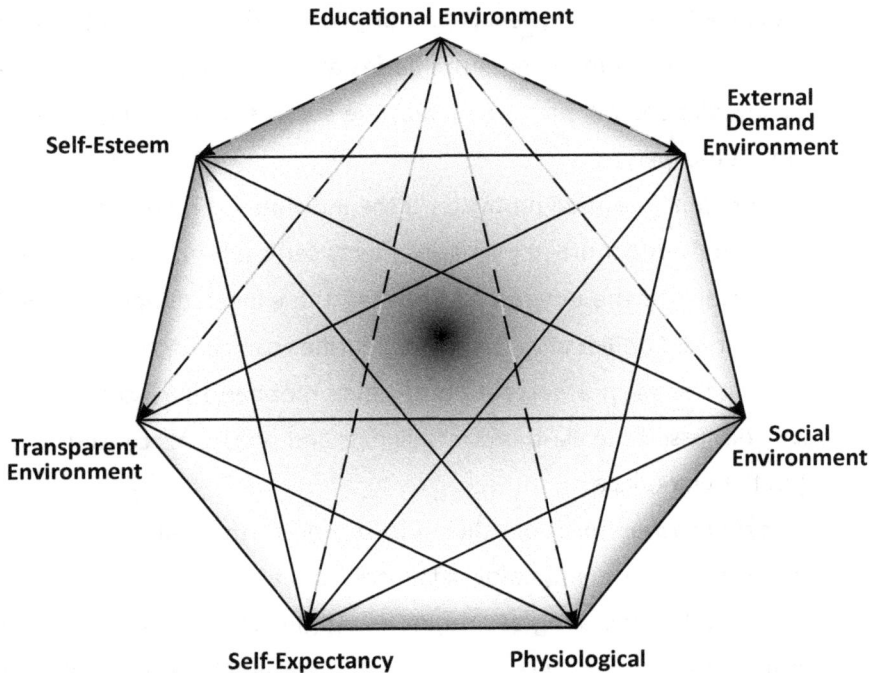

Fig. 4.1. PMP-sociogram illustrates how individual motivators interconnect with the other in PMP. Each motivator is interrelated and dependent upon the other. Here the educational environment has been dashed to better show this. Note that if the individuals educational environment is out of balance (too little or too much) it will affect one or more of the remaining six motivators. If unbalanced for an extended period of time behavioral signs will first appear. These signs or signals will multiple with time subsequently causing psychosomatic and psychopathologic symptoms.

conducive to transparency, participation and belongingness. Too little education affects one's self-esteem, transparent environment, inability to meet self-expectancies and external demands and can affect one's willingness to socially interact. If unresolved this will cause psychological stress and affect trust. Too much education can also cause a conflict if the external demands do not meet the educational and self-expectancy demands.

External Demand Environment is a motivator if these demands are achievable. Achievable demands create a situation where the individual is in control of his/her external demand environment. Naturally, this can also be a de-motivator if the individual is not in control of external demands and/or they are too many. Similarly, if the demands are not adequate enough to meet individual self-expectancy levels and physiological environment, they can also create frustration, workplace injuries and/or complacency and stress. Irregularities here will primarily affect the social environment, physiological, and self-expectancy.

Social Environment is a good motivator if the individual genuinely feels part of a team, family or culture. It primarily affects self-esteem, transparency and self-expectancy if the differential between the expected input and output is unbalanced. Conflict with these irregularities can cause the individual to feel disliked or even a perception of being mobbed (harassed). We have already discussed the various stress signals and symptoms caused by mobbing in the workplace.

Physiological Environment is another primary motivator that is related to all other motivators. The physiological environment needs to provide an ergonomically stable operating environment without which it is almost certain to create stresses that cause long-term illnesses and injuries. A primary focus for leaders is to ensure that individuals are provided a safe (physical and psychological) working environment with adequate rotation from positions inflicting musculoskeletal and psychological injuries caused by repetitive and/or monotone tasks. Irregularities here will create conflict between the external demand environment, self-expectancy, and the physiological motivators. This conflict will also affect the social and transparent environments and even the individual's self-esteem.

Self-Expectancy is related to the individual's own expected achievement/s related to a task/goal for a given situation against that of the external demand and the educational environments. Conflict arises when the individual's normative (perceptive) or subjective vision, goals for each task/goal/situation cannot be satisfied. This can also include an expected satisfaction/reward for achieving individual behavior. Poor planning knowledge of the objective is usually the culprit resulting in increased stress and defense mechanisms. A feeling of lack of control will lead to reduction in the transparent and social environments leading to isolationist activities as one struggles to hide this achievement failure. Communication and individual goal setting together with the leader is important to prevent his spreading to the individual's self-esteem.

Transparent Environment is about openness and trust and naturally if there is any hidden conflict between any of the motivators, this will usually affect the social environment and even self-esteem. This conflict leads to a reduction in the transparent and social environments leading to isolationist activities as one struggles to hide the truth. This guilt can produce an overly eager workaholic or complacency as the individual tries to compensate and covert. Naturally, if gone unabated this will develop into defense mechanisms producing further stress.

Self-Esteem is a tremendous motivator and a real de-motivator too. Sometimes individuals with a high self-esteem can be perceived to be arrogant and cold, when in fact, they are just confident and knowledgeable and willing to take a calculated risk. However, there are those that are arrogant and naturally the leader/manager needs to communicate this behavior as carefully and consistently and possible. Arrogance will inhibit teamwork, decrease transparency, affect trust and the social environment. Whereas, a positive "go-get" attitude will inspire team participation, improve self-expectancy and transparency. Any one of the six remaining PMPs can affect self-esteem as an individual's belief and self-appraisal of his/her own worth, and the perception of what others think of them. Leader's/Manager's focus their attention on the Educational, External Demand, Social, Physiological, Self-Expectancy, and the Transparency environments as this is what they have an ability to affect.

Once you have grasped the environmental and positional demands, and the employee's PMP, it will be far easier for you to interpret behavior, attitude and signals emitted from an individual and your team (Fig. 4.2). There are four levels to an individual's valuation and they are:

Level 1. Valuation or personal values are abstract choices guided by the way individual choices are compared with associated values. They are personal and can be determined by one's environment.

Level 2. Attitude is a combination of hypothetical values which influence positive, negative, or neutral judgments. Attitudes are expected to change as a function of experience (Tesser, 1993)

Level 3. Behavior is affected by one's attitude and what the individual perceives others will see and what others want to see.

Level 4. Environment can cause, observe and question the behavior of the individual.

The environment is the lowest level and it can affect an individual's perceptions and observations, which in hand affect attitude; however, it is the individual who is in actual control of his/her own valuation and any attitude change. Keep

Fig 4.2. Illustrates the four levels related to one's valuation, attitude, behavior, and environment. Understanding this process can help the leader to assist the individual in combating attitude change. The individual is the only one that can affect or change his/her own valuation.

in mind that your own PMP can distort how you interpret and perceive your employee's PMP, so some self-awareness and a critical look at your own PMP is always a good idea.

There are two basic personality types that can aid you in your initial evaluation (Fig. 4.3.). Identifying these personality types can help the leader in understanding the impact that individual stresses, teamwork, conflict and other behaviors will affect each employee. ***Type A personalities*** are more susceptible to stress symptoms as they have a heightened level of stress. They usually try to deal with their stress positively by talking about it and actively seeking help. ***Type B personalities***, although more laid back, could also be under greater

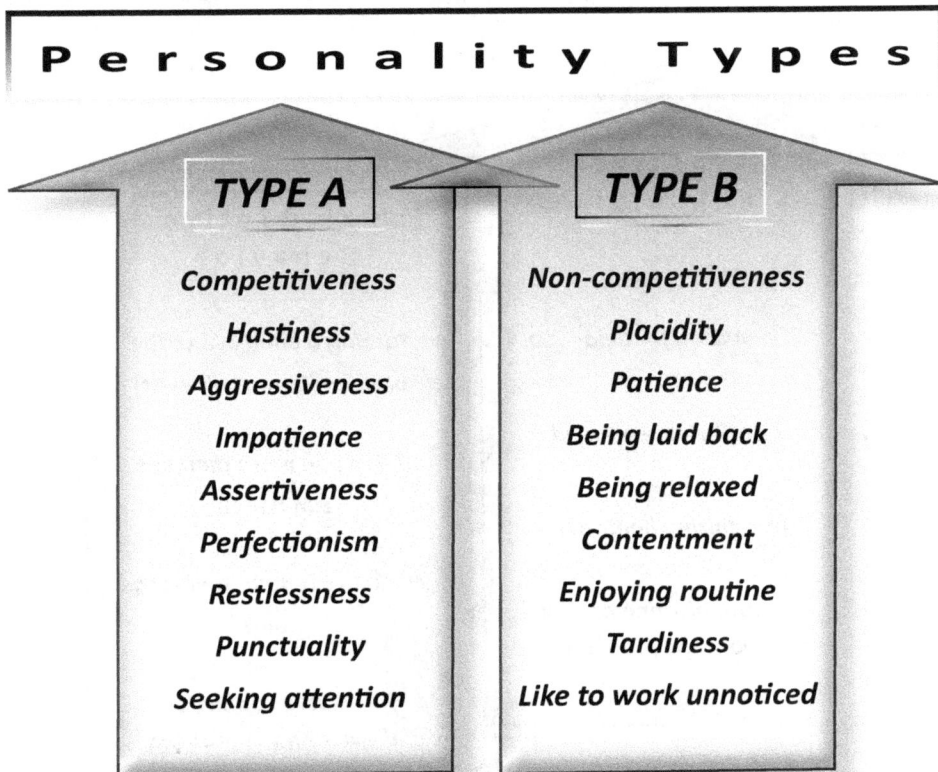

Personality Types

TYPE A	TYPE B
Competitiveness	*Non-competitiveness*
Hastiness	*Placidity*
Aggressiveness	*Patience*
Impatience	*Being laid back*
Assertiveness	*Being relaxed*
Perfectionism	*Contentment*
Restlessness	*Enjoying routine*
Punctuality	*Tardiness*
Seeking attention	*Like to work unnoticed*

Fig. 4.3. Illustrates a few Type A and Type B personality traits. Identifying personality types can help the leader in understanding individual stresses, teamwork, conflict and other behaviors. It can serve to highlight a heightened level of stress (Type A) which might require additional monitoring. It is important that you understand these factors in relation to each specific person as personalities are individual and many work-areas multi-cultural today. You will therefore have to know your employees and yourself.

stress as they could be masking their personalities with de-motivated maladaptive behavior symptoms instead (Fig. 4.4). Maladaptive behavior is a natural defense mechanism namely "denial" and adaptive could be too.

Other signs and symptoms that could affect teamwork include: poor decision making, absenteeism, increased conflict, to blame others, lack of trust, a heightened state of irritability, low participation levels, overly protective or hindering others, poor communication and, avoidance strategies, lack of openness, amongst others.

Power Relations, Boundaries, and Fearless Speech. As the saying goes, for every action there is a reaction, and words like persuasion, perception, reality, rhetoric, vision, images, and the power of communication is at its very

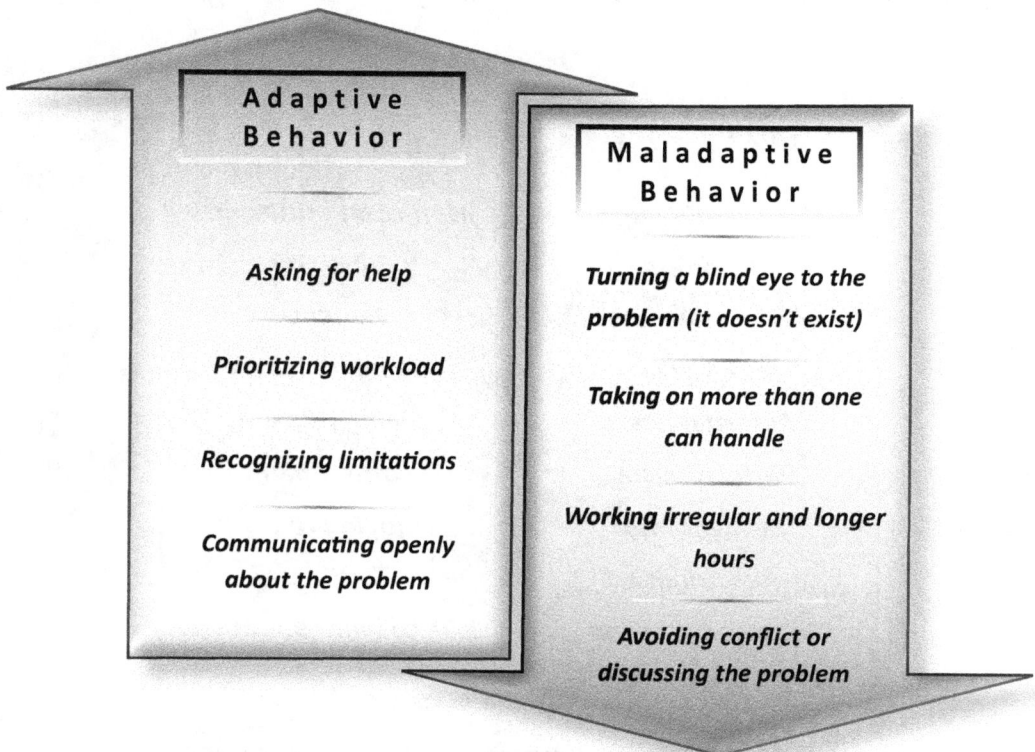

Adaptive Behavior

Asking for help

Prioritizing workload

Recognizing limitations

Communicating openly about the problem

Maladaptive Behavior

Turning a blind eye to the problem (it doesn't exist)

Taking on more than one can handle

Working irregular and longer hours

Avoiding conflict or discussing the problem

Fig. 4.4. Individuals cope with stress in a number of ways, as we learnt in the pervious chapter, and that there are many stress signals that one can look for. As shown by the illustration above, individual behavior can also be grouped into two main categories: adaptive and maladaptive. Individuals showing any of the maladaptive signs are most likely looking for some kind of help. Maladaptive behavior is a natural defense mechanism namely "denial."

best in communities, organizations, and group settings, see also chapters 10 & 12. In all group settings you will find a degree of relational power construction within and between individual and/or group boundaries. Change factors, poor communication, lack of goals, or understanding within one's working and social environment are all natural instigating factors leading to this behavioral pattern. Furthermore, the willingness to conduct 'fearless speech' (Foucault, 2001) within and crossing boundaries. Understanding power relations is therefore important if you are to lead effectively. Power construction can exist between individuals within the same group, between groups, and between individuals and anyone with responsibility and/or authority and is a natural situational reaction whether proactive or defensive in nature. It is obvious, that if the situational rules, guidelines, or goals are ambiguous, the extent of one's participation will vary as a natural consequence. Under these conditions, fearless speech (Foucault, 2001) would therefore play a large role and could even affect power relations within the groups. In order to show my point I address a number of aspects related to power and defense mechanisms. Morgan (1997: 171) lists fourteen sources of power:

1) Formal authority,
2) Control of scare resources,
3) Use of decision processes,
4) Control of knowledge and information,
5) Control of boundaries,
6) Ability to cope with uncertainty,
7) Control of technology,
8) Interpersonal alliances, networks, and control of "informal organization,"
9) Control of counter-organizations,
10) Symbolism and the management of meaning,
11) Gender and the management of gender relations,
12) Structural factors that define the stage of action, and
13) The power one already has.

According to French and Raven, (1960: 607-623) there are *five forms of power*: *coercive* (the ability to force or coerce someone to do something against his/her will), *reward* (the ability to fulfill others needs with financial, satisfaction, and other rewards for services) *legitimate* (the power coming with title or role such as policemen, senators, kings, managers and may come from a higher power or even obtained through coercion), *referent* (derived from someone's admiration such as celebrity fame, social leaders, favorite coach, charisma or wanting to be like someone—those with this power can use it in a type of co-ercion by threatening to exclude you from being part of a group, team or even being close), and *expert power* (ownership of knowledge that someone else wants — this can also include the distribution or controlling of information needed by others).

The Power School (Mintzberg et al., 1998) suggests that power is a negotia-tion between within a group and/or external stakeholders, and that the power instigator is prioritizing his/her own interests before the group. Conversely, this can also imply the support for natural law and the survival of the fittest; or, which is preferable to problem solving, that all sides of an issue are fully debat-ed as it can help to break though facades and obstacles which might be neces-sary for change. Furthermore, this can be useful in understanding support and strategic alliance within a group. Unfortunately, this form of power can take a lot of energy and can be wasteful and ineffective in certain circumstances.

Power Distance (Price, 2004: 245; and Hofstede, 1980) is marked by the status distance between people with high and low degrees of power. Their stud-ies showed that:

1) people were afraid of expressing disagreement with their managers,
2) management style was perceived as paternalistic, autocratic, participative, etc., and
3) employees preferred a particular management style.

The Core Group Theory (Kleiner, 2003) suggests that the power existing within a power group can cause members outside of the group to act or react on guesswork and as a consequence amplify this guesswork in order to please the power group. According to Kleiner these groups are not all bad and or dysfunctional and that the core group can be a source of energy, drive and direction.

The Force Filed Analysis or Diagrams introduced by Kurt Lewin, an American social psychologist, in 1930 (now quoted by literally hundreds of works) suggested that an issue is held in balance by the interaction of two opposing sets of forces' the driving forces and the restraining forces. The driving forces were the advocate for change whereas the restraining forces wanted to keep the status quo. He believed that as things are in a constant state of change there could not be a static pattern and that situations are dynamic and should be in balance or equilibrium with the opposing force or direction. Naturally for the opposing force to succeed (a change issue within a group or organization) the driving forces must dominate (exceed) the restraining forces. Lewin's method follows a basic process starting with:

1) the current and desired situation,
2) desired action,
3) what happened is nothing happens,
4) identify the forces for and against the desired situation or change,
5) evaluate data,
6) assign a priority value to the desired forces,
7) discuss, adjust and implement.

Understanding power relations between team members and the use of fearless speech in relation to individual obligations and participation is therefore very helpful to the leader. Chapters 10, 11 and 12 go into more depth surrounding participation, identity, culture, vision and comfort zones.

2) Prevent the complacency virus and any façade building behaviors from taking hold as they lower PMPs and cause stress and many ills within an organization. It is quite impossible to manage or lead individuals and teams on a weekly basis without a hands-on-approach. Effective leadership requires consistent monitoring and continual adjustment of the demands, rotations, and the individual PMPs. Once you have understood the what, how, when, and who, it is a lot easier for you to set realistic and achievable demands and goals for each person and each position. Sure it's hard work, takes a lot of time, and effort, but it's your job! BAM should be used as your tool to monitor the cardiac rhythm of employee responsibilities. Like a guitar string, keep the stress in balance (Fig.4.5). Too little stress and it becomes lethargic (complacency sets in), too much stress and it breaks (defense mechanisms, anxiety & burnout) so you need a good balance.

The *Complacency Gap Analysis* (Fig. 4.6 & Chapter 13) shows how the gap between a normal productive employee and a complacent employee widens dramatically over time if PMP, job rotational, and job renewal activities are not introduced during the mature phase of an employee's work life-cycle. This widening causes a decrease in IDP

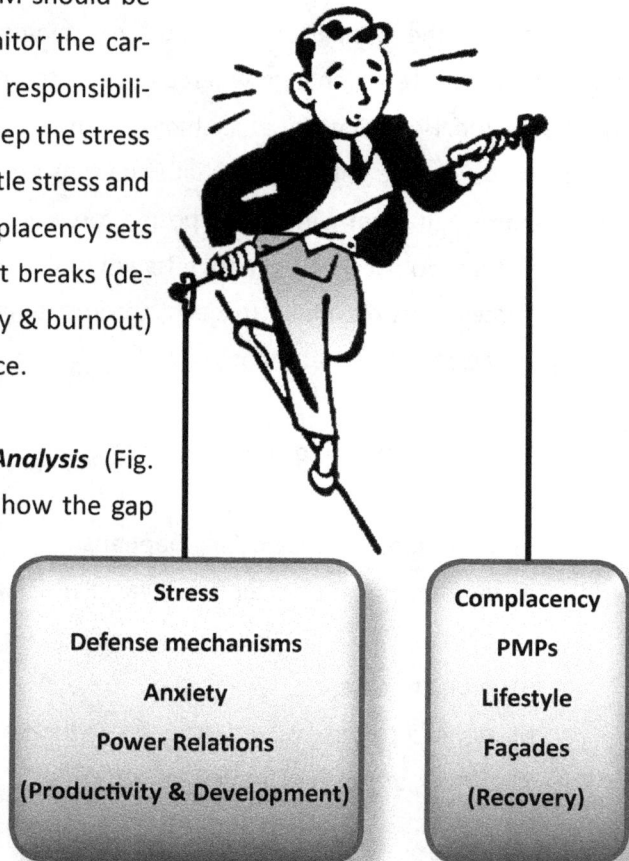

Stress	Complacency
Defense mechanisms	PMPs
Anxiety	Lifestyle
Power Relations	Façades
(Productivity & Development)	(Recovery)

Fig. 4.5. An illustration showing the difficulty in balancing the amount of stress (demands) in relation to company goals with positional and individual abilities. Without a continual hands-on-approach, PMP understanding, rotation, and sufficient control/check points in place it can become a very daunting, if not impossible, responsibility.

Complacency Gap Analysis

Work-Cycle Maturity

C-T Curve

Tunnel-Vision

Complacency Curve
(C-Curve)

Complacency Gap
(C-Gap)
(C-Gap Ratio)

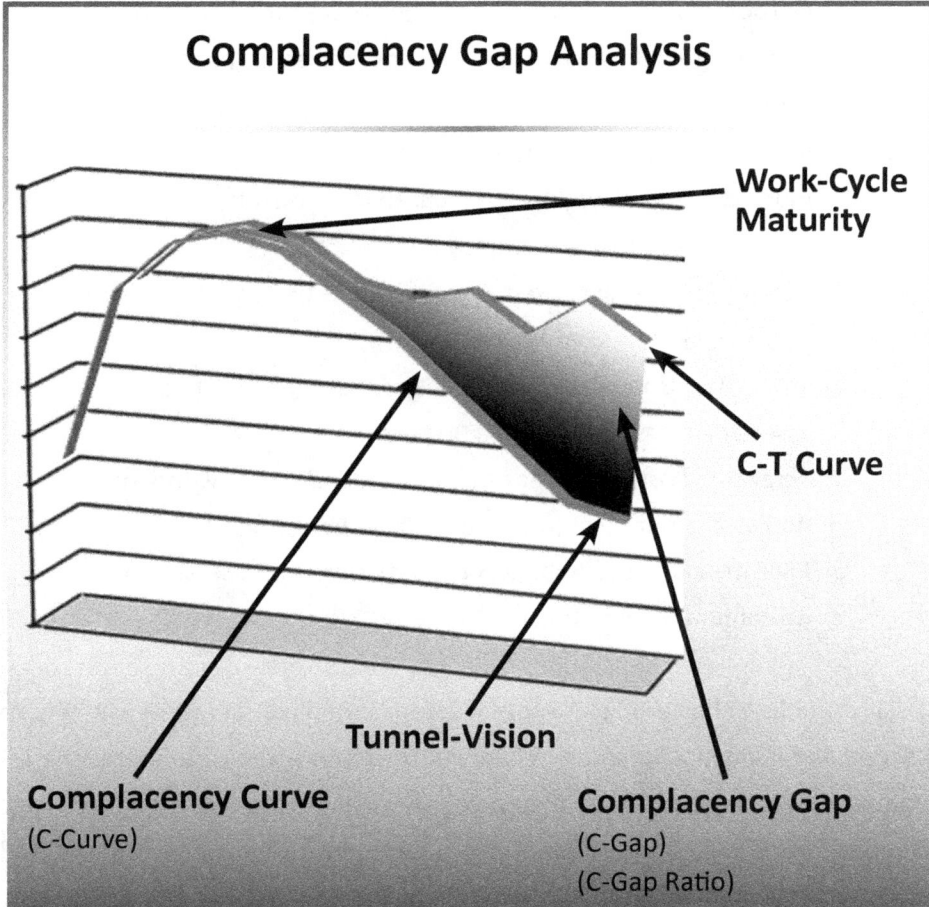

Fig. 4.6. Shows an example of the author's Complacency Gap and Ratio Analysis. These are based on the differential between the established baseline for each individual minus the annual measurement. Measures include Defensive Posturing, Motivation, Stress, and PMP assessments. Behavioral analysis in relation to individual measures and overall output and input is an important step in managing employees as it can assist the leader/manager in rotational and task assignments thereby preventing the complacency virus from infecting individual team members and overall motivation.

(Innovative Development Process, chapter two) if present and/or productivity if absent. C-Gap Analysis is compiled from measures established within the working environment together with employee/team members based upon a number of variables. These variables are represented by the Complacency Gap Ratio $((O^b/I^b)/(O^y/I^y)) / ((M^b \times PMP^b) / (D^b \times S^b))$, and the Complacency Gap: $((O^b/I^b)/(O^y/I^y)) - ((M^b \times PMP^b) / (D^b \times S^b))$. These are calculated using the following:

1) *Output* – O1 (produced quantity measured for sales, production or service) per person / total baseline sales, production or service for 1st quarter / total number of employees,

2) *Input* (total number of hours worked per person per quarter (3 months) – sick days / by total baseline worked hours for total employees/ number of employees,

3) *Motivation* measure, *see Appendix A*, a twenty question assessment test (maximum 400 points),

4) *Stress Assessment* measure, *see Appendix B*, a twenty question assessment test (maximum 400 points),

5) *Defensive Posturing* measure, *see Appendix C*, a twenty question assessment test (maximum 400 points), and

6) *PMP* measure, see Appendix D, a fifty question assessment test (maximum 5 points).

It is evident that proper management of an individual's PMP will help to prevent the complacency virus. Additional preventive reinforcement is the assignment of new and varying responsibilities as in Cross-Training. These new responsibilities can be progressive, seasonal, and rotational and/or delegated to meet a changing environment or situation as in need-based management. It is important to keep in mind that too little work can also cause stress. Stress is an excellent catalyst and incubator for the complacency virus. Some signs of low motivation and complacency are:

1) Very few employees are excited about things at work (things outside of work are far more exciting),

2) The only things they seem to be motivated about are their paychecks, vacations, pensions, and bonuses,

3) The company motto is: if you don't have to do it, then don't; and, try to do as little as possible (classic Theory X, see fig. 2.6.),

4) People seem to be moving in slow-motion, until it's time to go home anyway,

5) When we talk about doing a better job or improving on a process, there are a lot of blank looks,

6) There seems to be a lack of responsibility takers and the attitude is that it is someone else's problem, not mine,

7) People are doing just enough to prevent from being fired and/or reprimanded, and

8) Change is the number one enemy.

Naturally, complacency or PMP imbalances will also lead to façades. *Façades* (Fig. 2.17) are a result of poor PMP management and stress. In order to prevent façades you should ask why would anyone create a façade? Here are a number of reasons:

1) To hide an inefficiency,
2) To conceal an inability,
3) To covert stress and defense mechanisms,
4) To protect low motivation (PMP imbalance),
5) To protect against a lack of trust or openness, and
6) To isolate oneself from poor management and/or leadership.

Façades are rather easy to identify however they take a lot of effort to crack. Quick fixes are inadequate as individuals revert back to their old behavior patterns relatively soon thereafter. A fundamental change in environment, positional demands, and PMP review are prescribed. In most cases those employees suffering from the complacency virus are also afflicted with façades. Openness is a key attribute in PMP and without this it is impossible to prevent façades.

In some cases these façades are caused by poor leadership or management that lacks consistency and motivating praise for a job well done. If employees are working hard and don't receive acknowledgement for good work, the employee will naturally lose motivation and drive.

Managing behavior takes a lot of work; however, the time spent usually produces results that far exceed the effort expended. Prevention of the complacency virus and façades are achieved through understanding position requirements, employee signals and behavioral patterns, individual PMP and adjustment through position renewal, delegation, and job rotation.

3) *Promote* is used to change or sustain and behavior or attitude. Through positive encouragement and consistent leadership a leader/manager can promote behavioral change with emotion, a well known component of persuasion, social influence and change (Brecklar & Wiggins, 1991). Emotion is a part of the cognitive process, the logical way in which we think, for a given situation or issue. Emotional appeals are commonly used in marketing commercials, advertising, political messages, and others using the acronym AIDMA. The objective of AIDMA is to create or persuade the viewer to act on a motivation or in this case an emotion by creating Awareness, Interest, Desire, Motivation and Action (Fig. 4.7.).

1. *Awareness* is where you make the individual aware of a desired or unwanted attitude or behavior.
2. *Interest* is associating that attitude or behavior with a specific result, cause and effect, or scenario so that the individual can logically see it from another perspective.
3. *Desire* is the perceived realization that he/she has the ability to achieve sustainability or change.
4. *Motivate* this desire by showing him/her that they can either sustain or change the behavior through positive feedback using some of the individuals PMPs, past performance and/or

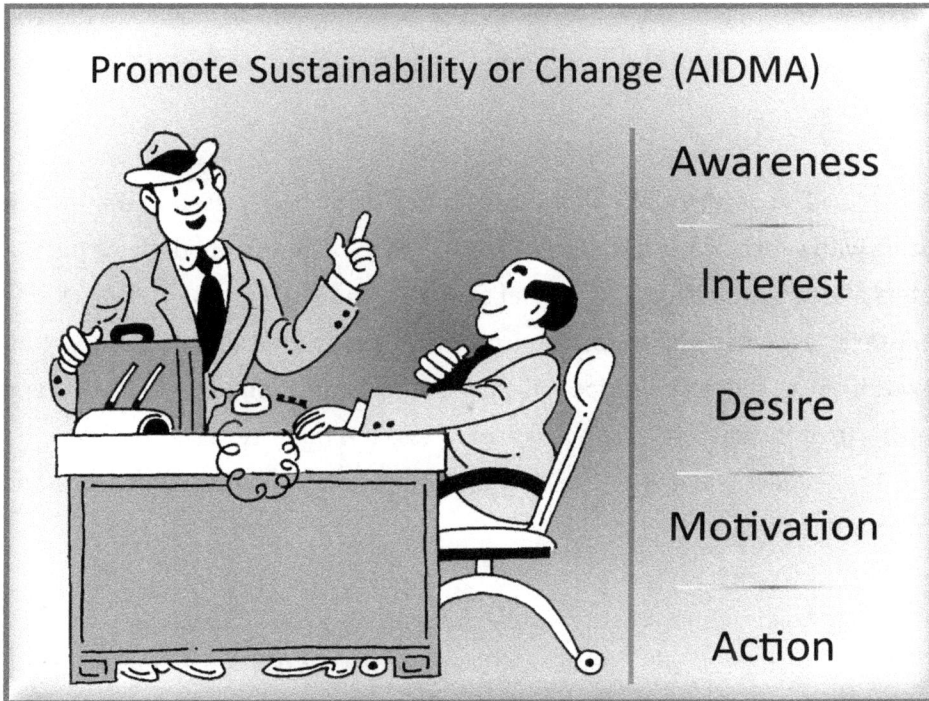

Fig. 4.7. Motivate change with emotion and cognitive persuasion using AIDMA (Awareness, Interest, Desire, Motivation and Action) as a precursor.

future possibilities and goals by helping them to make an action plan.

5. *Action* is to put the plan into action and to provide the individual with feedback as to sustainability or progress on a regular
basis.

Naturally, good leadership and communication skills are required to effectively create a sustainable environment. Easy quick fixes are not the solution
and should be avoided at all costs. They only disrupt by causes inconsistencies.
The role of BAM is to create a tool for the leader/manager/consultant to use
in the quest for sustainable results which are long-term. A quick fix seminar is

just that. They might work for two-days or even two-weeks; however, the end result will in 99.9% of the time be the same as individuals revert back to old behaviors.

4) *Trust* is a VERY BIG word. It is abused and loosely used and in recent years with substance as it is not addressing the root cause or underlying parameters affecting it. It is easy to say "let's all have openness and start to trust one another," yes, right? Being able to trust or tell the truth is about knowing your PMP. It starts with the individual feeling comfortable enough to be honest and open. Trust is therefore awareness, openness, and honesty.

The leader/manager needs to establish trust with his/her employees and this is done through:

1) Leads with the seven leadership traits (Fig. 1.1, Chapter 1),
2) Managers with the seven management rules (Fig. 1.2, Chapter 1), and
3) Improves PMP balance (workplace understanding, PMP action plan, etc. (Chapters 2, 5, 6, 7, 8, 9, 10, 11, & 12)

If any of these are absent then you will never be able to achieve complete trust. Obviously, out goal is to achieve as much as possible. Leaders and use some of the following tips:

1) Communicate your intentions prior to any action,
2) Keep your non-verbal signals in sync with your verbal message. If one contradicts the other you will naturally cause confusion. Keep in mind that verbal communication consists of a message (the information that you want to convey) which is transmitted in a specific tone (affirming how positive or negative the message is), and body language (confirms the tone and message),

3) Communicate in a clear and concise method in a consistent manner,
4) Accept without prejudice responsibility for your actions,
5) Treat everyone with the same respect (do not play favorites and never discriminate)

Section 2 *Cross-Training: System Analysis & Identification*

In section one; we addressed matters related to the individual, leader and manager. Section two focuses on "how" Cross-training looks at the systems which affect production (services or manufacturing) and the synergy of tasks or objectives facing the individual.

EVERY working position on this little planet is a process. This process is part of the landscape and workflow environment and has an optimal system. Management by Cross-Training is not only about using education to enhance rotation and flexibility but its goal is a process of synergy and efficacy where scientific theory teams-up with individual participation and responsibility. The following chapters address a number of functions that contribute to this synergy.

Chapter five *Cross-Training Systems Identification* addresses issues related to identifying your landscape, workflow and workload.

Chapter six *Understanding Basic Ergonomics* discusses various aspects that can affect an individual's participation in relation to a process by considering demands and environmental conditions facing the working environment.

Chapter seven *Process* looks at the theory behind process, process review, and obligations of various stakeholders thereto.

Chapter eight *Standard Operating Procedures* (SOPs) rounds-off this section by discussing the needs for SOPs and who to create them.

chapter 5 *Cross-Training: Systems Identification*

A Landscape analysis assists managers and leaders by providing them with an overall view of their operating environment. Sometimes, "it is hard to see the forest for the trees" and an analysis that can portray both the little and big picture in relation to the department and organization is always helpful in the decision-making process, holding course with the mission statement and synergy with Cross-Training and a rotational program. Naturally, a Landscape analysis will touch on macro process environment; however, detailed processes are left for the Process Analysis and Review in chapter seven.

In Cross-Training, systems identification refers to the recognition of systems integration and synergy of Landscape and process. A spider's web can represent the Landscape, and the spider the process. The web has no purpose or use if there is no spider. Similarly, if the web is in poor shape it cannot fulfill its function or purpose and the spider will weaken and ultimately die. It is therefore in the interest of the spider to build a functional web which can support its statement of purpose. For example, the spider needs to construct a web in the right location, with adequate strength to support the spider's rapid movements. This is the Landscape or system. The capture of the prey is the actual process. One therefore needs the other.

Landscape analysis is just this. It serves to present an almost 3D multidimensional view of the Landscape system through process. This includes individuals, teams, departments, and the organization or region as a whole. There are three major levels to levels to a Landscape analysis. They are (Fig. 5.1):

Macro-Landscape (Horizontal, Internal, Vertical, External)
Micro-Landscape (People-, Integration-, Document-, Decision-intensive)
Process (actual work process, see chapter seven)

Landscape Analysis

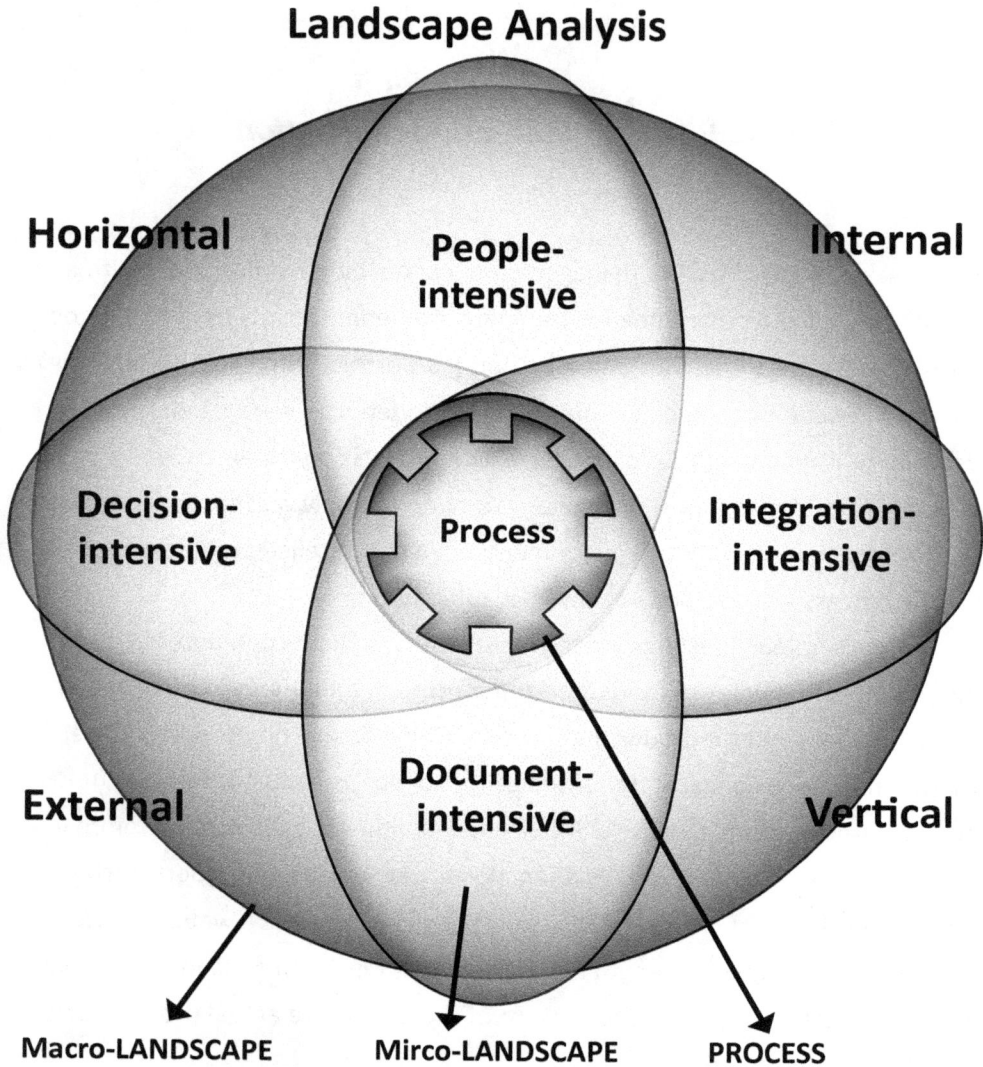

Fig. 5.1. Shows the three integrated levels of a landscape analysis. The lowest, or in this case the foundation level, is called the Macro-LANDSCAPE and encompasses the Horizontal, Internal, Vertical, and External environments. The next level-up is called the Micro-LANDSCAPE and includes four groups of work-intensive demands known as People-, Integration-, Document-, and Decision-intensive. The highest level is the actual Process.

The **Macro-Landscape** is the foundation level where the synergy between internal and external demands are compared to the horizontal and vertical operational structure. In other words, a multi-dimensional look at the statement of purpose in relation to how and what is actually produced. The four areas

Macro-LANDSCAPE

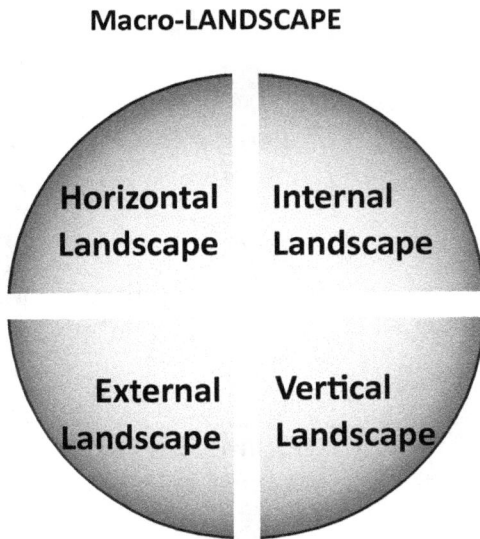

Fig. 5.2. The Macro-LANDSCAPE and encompasses the Horizontal, Internal, Vertical and External environments. It is the lowest or most general levels of a landscape review.

of the Macro-Landscape are the Horizontal, Internal, Vertical, and External environments. It is very helpful to use PERT charts, workflow diagrams, and/or mind-mapping to visually show all connections.

The *Horizontal Landscape* focuses on the lateral workflow of services/production from conception to delivery within a defined area. Naturally, this can include the entire organization or just a department.

The *Vertical Landscape* is a continuum from the Horizontal-Landscape and discusses the hierarchal presence (supervisory, leadership, and management participation) and the demands (expected and actual) for each area related to the flow.

The *External Landscape* focuses on inter-departmental dependencies and synergy, expectations and demands, external supply reliance, and stakeholders. Market conditions, environment, political and other issues can also be introduced here.

The *Internal Landscape* maps inter-department workload demands and expectations, human-intensive versus system-intensive positions, union relations and requirements, rotation, education and competency development needs and resources (money, machine and people) as they related to the statement of purpose.

Mirco-LANDSCAPE

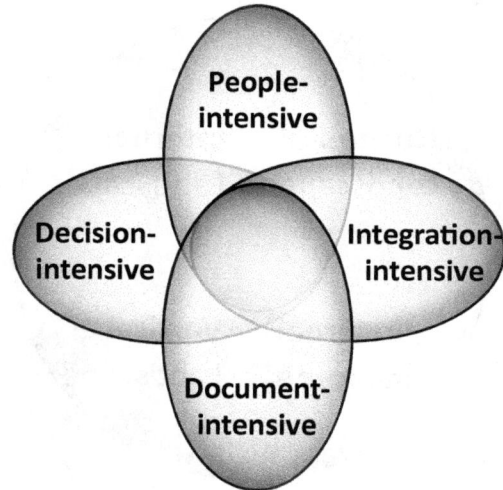

Fig. 5.3. Isolated view of the intermediate level called the Micro-LANDSCAPE. This includes four groups of work-intensive demands known as People-, Integration-, Document-, and Decision-intensive and is the link between the systems function and process.

The **Micro-Landscape** takes the workflow mapped and breaks it down even further. This level includes four groups of work-intensive expectations/demands for each particular position or area of responsibility. These are known as People-, Integration-, Document-, and Decision-intensive.

People-intensive positions are when people are integrated into or required to perform as human-mediators, routers or conduits and are required to accomplish a specific task. This can include things like customer service, medical personnel, purchase requests with a high degree of human interaction, intuition and judgment.

Integration-intensive are positions with little or no human involvement where work-demands and transactions are systematic on a straight-through basis. Good examples of these types of environments are high volume processing with system-integration or system-to-system operation with limited human interaction (industries with high-volume manufacturing, automated high-volume transactions, and others).

Document-intensive are positions that require people to manually enter information into a system or to review a transaction or to make decisions based upon the changing inputs. Actions can be dictated by scanned documents, letters, electronically transferred documents and can include responsibilities such as account openings, quality assurance and quality control monitoring, claims processing, laboratory processing and educational environments.

Decision-intensive are complex manual and automatic decisional systems positions. These usually include mission-critical decision-making responsibilities that require access to information as soon as possible. Some examples of positions include extreme high-volume manufacturing, high value positions in banking, commodity and stock trading, claims and other responsibilities operating by a rules engine.

Synergy between the macro- and micro-Landscape is therefore instrumental to minimize any conflict that may cause delays and/or affect productivity. A good Cross-Training program addresses the Landscape and individual processes, whilst, at the same time, identifying ergonomic issues and eradicating any duplication. Process will be discussed in more detail in chapter seven.

Without frequent Landscape reviews (every three to five years) it is very easy for managers, leaders and individuals to lose sight of the company's statement of purpose. All participants need to be familiar with their macro- and micro-Landscapes because:

1. it keeps them focused,
2. it helps managers, leaders and the individual to understand workload and limitations,
3. provides understanding of the overall processes and their own process,
4. identifies bottle-necking, and
5. emphasizes individual participation in the chain of events.

Workflow

Basically, workflow is a systematic pattern of activity or a sequence of operations for individuals, machines, teams, and the organization. A Landscape review will address the "what, why and when" in an organization. The workflow addresses the "who and how," and the process review the "how" which represents well-defined inputs, outputs, and purposes. The purpose of a workflow design is to address the process of the intended goal or objective through service provisions, physical transformation, or information processing. The workflow and productivity are therefore a series of links represented by a chain. If one link breaks, naturally, productivity will suffer as a result. Poorly designed workflow systems are major problems for many companies today.

Interpreting and questioning workflow/s is a proactive approach activity and should be used by the leader to:

1. stimulate employee participation,
2. establish focus groups (task forces) to:
   a. evaluate existing systems,
   b. recommend changes or tweaks,
   c. design new workflows,
   d. identifying duplications,
   e. establishing measures for output versus input,
   f. review workloads affecting all resources (human & machine), and
   g. establishing workflow, task and process objectives and goals.
3. improve communication channels in the workflow, and
4. enhance proactive and reactive processes within the workflow.

A flow chart is an excellent way to visually identify the demands, movement, and workflow within a Landscape. The smallest entity therein being the pro-

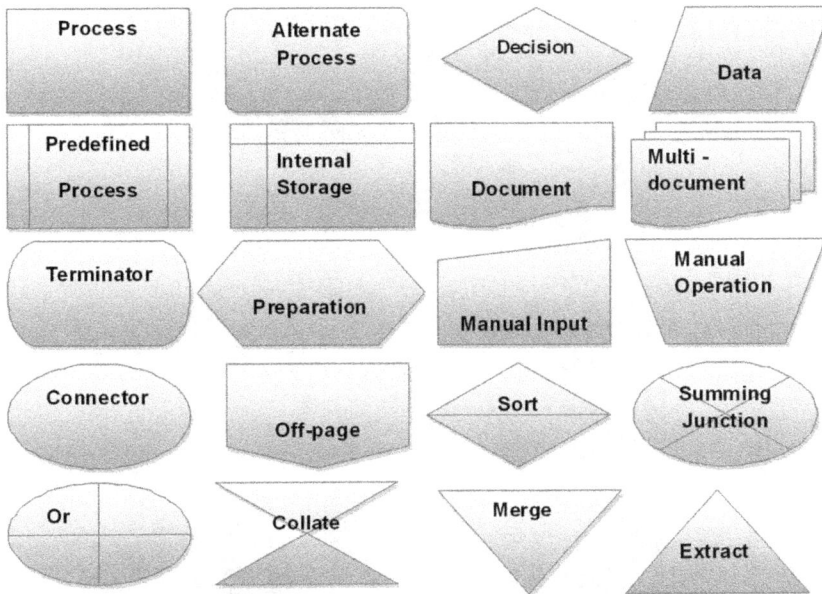

Fig. 5.4. Flow chart symbols used in planning or designing workflow charts. Each symbol represents a process or a part of a process related to point in the workflow such as start, stop, input, output, information, decision and others.

cess, usually described or supported by an SOP (Standard operating Procedure) document. A visual workflow chart consists of a number of symbols representing process, task, decision or movement of the product or service from conception to completion. These symbols (Fig. 5.4.) are standard and well-known in engineering, quality assurance, and business planning.

The workflow chart (Fig. 5.5.) is created in the same manner as a decision tree (see chapter seven) but in a broader perspective and covering the Landscape within a specific working environment. Naturally, this same schematic can be used to show positional responsibilities, resource workloads (individual physical, mental stresses), rotations (need and frequency), and educational needs.

Budget restraints and deadlines will dictate adapting the critical path method (CPM) which is a mathematically based algorithm used to schedule activities. Mostly in project planning, software development and construction it too

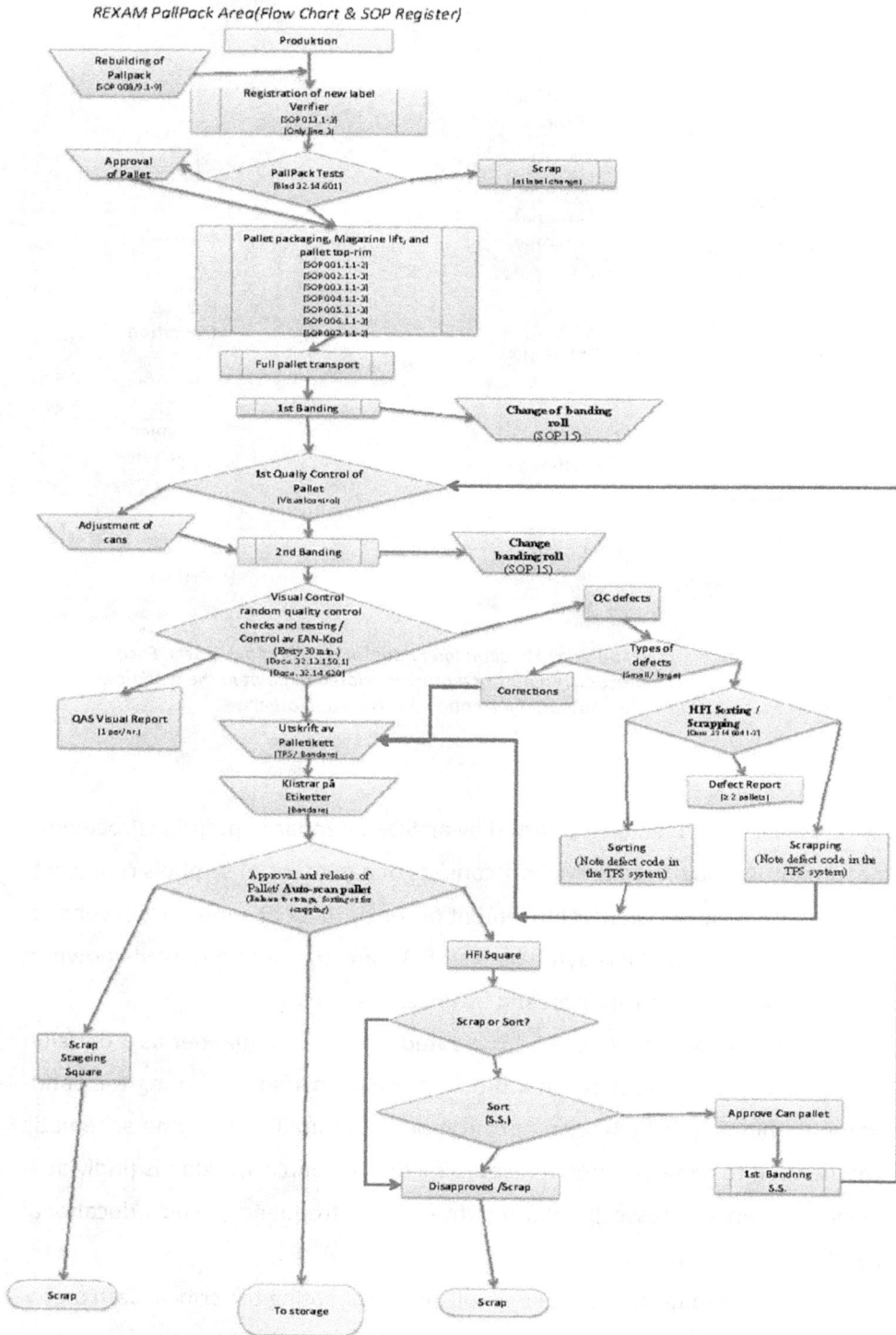

Fig. 5.5. Shows a workflow chart for the pallet packaging area at Rexam Beverage Can Fosie, Sweden. This chart shows the product and workflow within the Pallet Packaging landscape. Naturally, the same chart can be used to identify workloads, physical and mental stresses and other related needs.

can be applied to plan workflow. However, managers should keep in mind that unrealistic budgeting (goals-budget-input-output) will cause PMP conflicts in the external demand, physiological, and self-expectancy environments. In high tension and tight bugetary scenarios managers to increase synergies and short-term goals. Conflict between these PMPs will cause stress and personnel should be rotated more often to allow for recovery. Critical Path Analysis was developed by the US Navy in the 1950s and can be used for any project with interdependent activities. Basically, the CPM model consists of:

1) a list of activities needed to complete the project,

2) a time plan (activity duration) for each activity from start to end,

3) a dependency flow chart between the various activities, and

4) alternative routing for activities within the flow including the critical path.

Program Evaluation and Review Technique (PERT) and Activity-Based Resource Assignments are other spin-off's from the original CPM model (Wolf, 2007). Microsoft Project 2008 has many of these planning tools imbedded into its program and can serve to be very helpful when establishing focus groups.

Workload

Workload models or calculations are simply tasks analyzed and defined in sequence and in relation to how they are performed by individuals and team members. Each task is defined and the demands (capability required to perform the task, capacity and time constraints, capacity to deal with emergencies, lag capacity, psychological demands, physical demands) noted (Fig.5.6.). Obviously, the most consistent method for long-term operation is preferable; however, as discussed earlier, this activity window can be increased for short periods as long as the individual and/or team receives adequate recovery time. Focus groups can be established to evaluate these demands and to recommend adequate

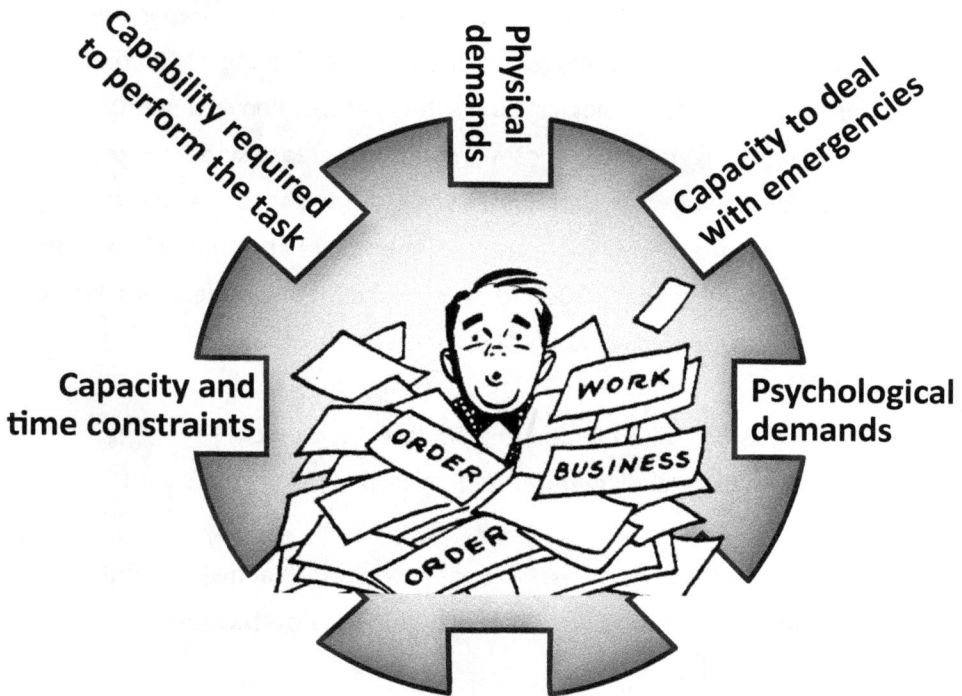

Fig. 5.6. Workload is the demand the position exerts on the individual or team. Workload can be measured in a number of ways; however, it is the task analysis which is critical. Tasks are defined and analyzed by their demands. These are: the capability required to perform the task, the capacity and time constraints, the capacity to deal with emergencies, the psychological demands, and the physical demands.

solutions to the manager.

Capability required to perform the task can include education, equipment, repetitiveness of the task, environmental conditions.

Capacity and time constraints affect specific task demands as input/output demands are in conflict with an individual's ability and self-expectancy. This would imiply that capacity and/or time demands are therefore unrealistic.

Capacity to deal with emergencies by building in some lag capacity to task demands that allow for problem solving, emergencies and development, rotation and training.

Psychological demands caused by poor leadership, unrealistic demands and other environmental conditions.

Physical demands can include one's posture while working, too much sitting or standing, heavy lifting or lifting incorrectly, repetitive tasks, and other dangerous assignments.

Psychological or mental workload is summarized by Bin Xie and Gavriel Salvendycan at the School of Industrial Engineering, Purdue University as:

"1) Put simply, mental workload is the amount of mental work or effort necessary for a person or group to complete a task over a given period of time.

2) Mental workload cannot be detected directly, but through the measurement of some other variables that are thought to correlate highly with it, such as subjective rating, performance and some physiological data.

3) Mental workload has both static and dynamic attributes, which reflect, respectively, the mental workload within a time interval and at a single moment.

4) Each individual has limited processing capacity or processing resources. Mental workload involves the depletion on internal resources to accomplish the work. High workload depletes these resources faster than low workload. The requirements for resources can be unbalanced when performing a task. Some sources may remain under-loaded while other sources are overloaded.

5) Mental workload can be affected by many factors. It is not merely a property of the task, but also of the individual, and their interaction. Meshkati (1988) classified the factors that influence mental workload into causal factors (which consist of task and environmental variable, operator characteristics, and moderating variable), and effect factors (which contain the difficulty, response and performance variables, and mental-workload measures). So each dimension of mental workload can be affected by some factors and their sub-factors. Normally, a hierarchical structure could be used to describe the factors and sub-factors that influence mental workload." (Xie and Salvendycan, 2000).

chapter 6 *Understanding Basic Ergonomics*

Cross-Training is about amalgamating the individual to his/her psychological and physical working environments. Section one dealt with leadership, management, motivation, health, and behavioral analysis. Section two deals with, systems identification, process, and standard operating procedures. Naturally, ergonomics is a critical component in functional organization synergy.

Ergonomics is derived from **ergon** [work] and **nomos** [natural laws] and stems from Ancient Greece. The enlightenment of Hellenic civilization (500-300 B.C.) saw great strides in philosophy and advances in various external demands facing individuals, the design of their tools, jobs and workplaces. Today the International Ergonomics Association (www.iea.cc), which spans over 150 countries, has many of its requirements integrated into the ISO 9001:2000 (quality management systems) and ISO 14001:2004 (environmental management systems) standards. The International Ergonomics Association defines ergonomics as:

> *"Ergonomics (or human factors) is the scientific discipline concerned with the understanding of interactions among humans and other elements of a system, and the profession that applies theory, principles, data, and methods to design in order to optimize human well-being and overall system performance. Ergonomics contribute to the design and evaluation of tasks, jobs, products, environments and systems in order to make them compatible with the needs, abilities and limitation of people."*

Ergonomics in Cross-Training focuses on the individual, his/her psychological environment and the physical environment (Fig 6.0). Organizations lacking any

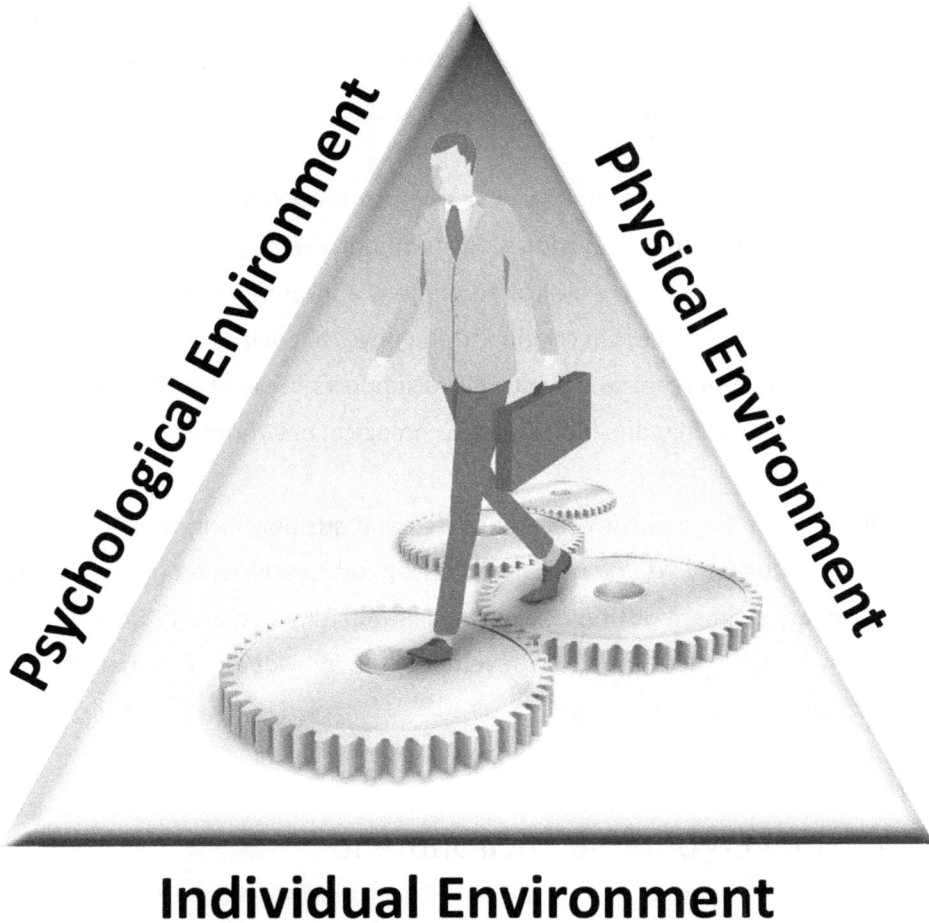

Fig. 6.0. Cross-Training triangulates three environment factors into CT-ergonomics: the individual, the physical and the psychological. Like a three-legged stool, if one leg breaks the stool will fall to the ground if not supported by artificial means.

one of the three components will endurably show signals of low motivation, poor efficiency, increased absenteeism and stress-related illnesses as well as higher employee turnover statistics.

CT-Ergonomics (Cross-Training Ergonomics) provides the individual/team with a secure environment, which is conducive to a balanced PMP. This balance will enable IDP (Innovative Development Process, Chptr. 2) emergence. In the author's experience, IDP with any of its seven derivatives cannot be achieved without first achieving balance in individual PMP. PMP is therefore a prerequisite for this. Obviously, CT-Ergonomics is just one tooth in the cog of the process and focuses on three key areas:

1) the objective of the job in relation to the external demands placed upon the individual environment,
2) the resources or physical equipment appropriateness, workflow and process in relation to the physical environment, and
3) how the organizational structure supports these objectives in policy and leadership in the psychological environment.

C-T Ergonomics focuses on what motivates and sustains long-term participation and productivity. As you would expect, a good rotational program will help to rejuvenate stagnant positions, alleviates or minimizes potential work-related injuries, whilst, at the same time, developing the individual and benefiting the organization.

Individual Ergonomic Environment

Genes are a contributing factor and should not be overlooked. Naturally the individual's genetic makeup can or will affect his/her ability to perform a given task. It is obvious that some positions are better suited to a person's weight, length, sex and age. Obviously, this does not say that only certain genetically oriented persons can only accomplish specific tasks. Sex, age, weight or religion or discrimination has absolutely nothing to do with it. It is about the individual's ability to sustain a workable process over longer periods without causing physical or psychological injury (Fig. 6.1).

    Environment encompasses the individual's knowledge (education, on-the-job-training, and experience) are critical to productivity and well-being. Knowledge is a key fundament to motivation, participation and communication and is without question important in accomplishing positional demands. Knowledge

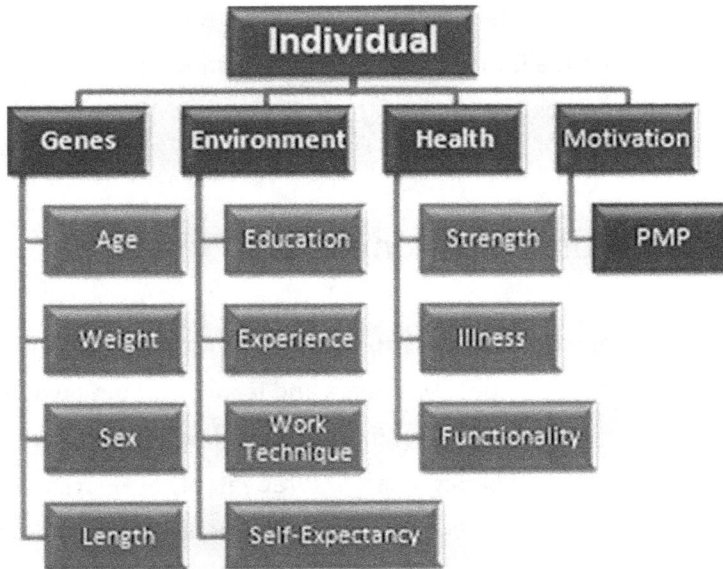

Fig. 6.1. The individual environment consists of items that affect the individual's ability to perform such as genes, environment, health and motivation. Conflict in any of these will affect the individual's ability to participate.

also gives the individual control over his/her environment and improves his/her ability to find or solve problems.

Lack of knowledge will inescapably cause mistakes, affect one's working-technique as well as increase stress, and defensive mechanisms. This will lead to coveting, the formation of façades, and inhibit team-work.

Health is an important ingredient for good. Fitness and functionality are fundamental to sustainability in the workplace. Programs to support a proactive and healthy life-style will benefit both the company and the individual. Clearly, this can reduce work-related accidents and even reduce susceptibility to chronic stress.

Motivation (a balanced PMP) is another key ingredient. Need I say more? It is obvious that motivated individual's are more energetic, proactive, effective and more fun to be around, not to mention that, they have fun at work; whereas, unmotivated employees are a drag on progressive behavior, feel burdened by work, are less productive than motivated employees and, sooner or later, infect other team members with their virus too. Naturally, the cause/s of low motivation should be identified and ratified as soon as possible. In some cases this adjustment needs only to be small by adjusting a process which might cause conflict between one or more of the individual's PMPs.

Physical Ergonomic Environment

Physical environment should be there to support and not to hinder the individuals as they go about their duties. Managers and leaders should be aware of all external factors as they directly affect individual well-being and productivity. If aid, location, workload, and vibration are not repeatedly evaluated, addressed and improved upon, the external demand environment will cause conflict and long-term muscular-skeletal injuries as well as chronic stress (Fig. 6.2). The conflict between the physical environment and the external demand environment (production quotas, competition, globalization, stakeholders) is a determinant factor affecting performance. If you are a taxi driver and your car doesn't support your external demands, you naturally cannot fulfill your potential.

Aid or working tools are tools, equipment (mechanical and electronic) and support materials that assist in the process of implementation. Application of said tools and ease of use also define categories that need to be considered. A good example of this could be a computer and the programs/applications used; furthermore, chairs with the correct support (height, tilt and lumbar corrections), adjustable tables and screens to support long-term sessions, gloves, eye-wear, etc.

Location includes factors related to the working environment including the amount of space one has to operate in. Other aspects include climatic conditions, noise, light, and air quality as well as adequate service facilities such as rest areas, cafeteria, toilets, and access to hygiene services (showers, medical personnel) if needed.

Workload is both mental and physical in nature, it can be either underload or overload, and it is known that it affects individual performance in complex

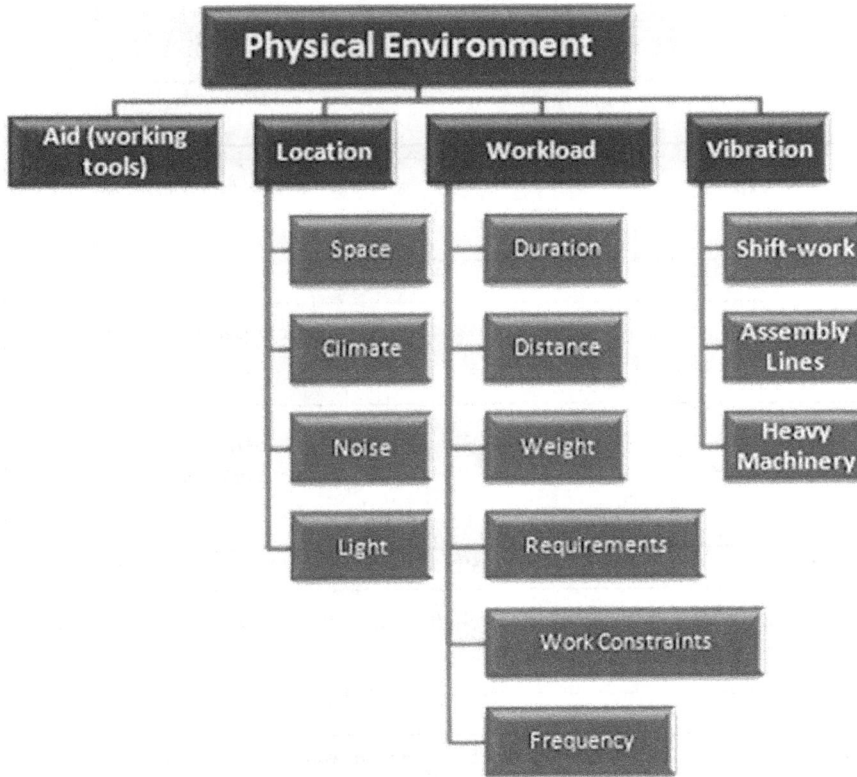

Fig. 6.2. The physical environment of C-T Ergonomics covers aid, location, workload and vibration which are external factors that affect the individual's ability to perform and/or participate in his/her duties.

systems (Xiem et al., 2000). A balance in mental load and stimulation is therefore vital to sustain workload efficiency. C-T Ergonomics looks at alternative systems designs to balance workload.

NASA has used a Task Load Index (Hart & Staveland, 1988) to measure workload on five 7-point scales. There are 21 gradations for each of the five items and they are subdivided into increments from very low to very high and perfect to very high (Fig. 6.3)

Physical workload includes a number of important factors such as distance, weight, requirements, work constraints, and frequency. Mental workload includes not fully controlled situations in relation to dynamic autonomous situations, processes, machines and human operators.

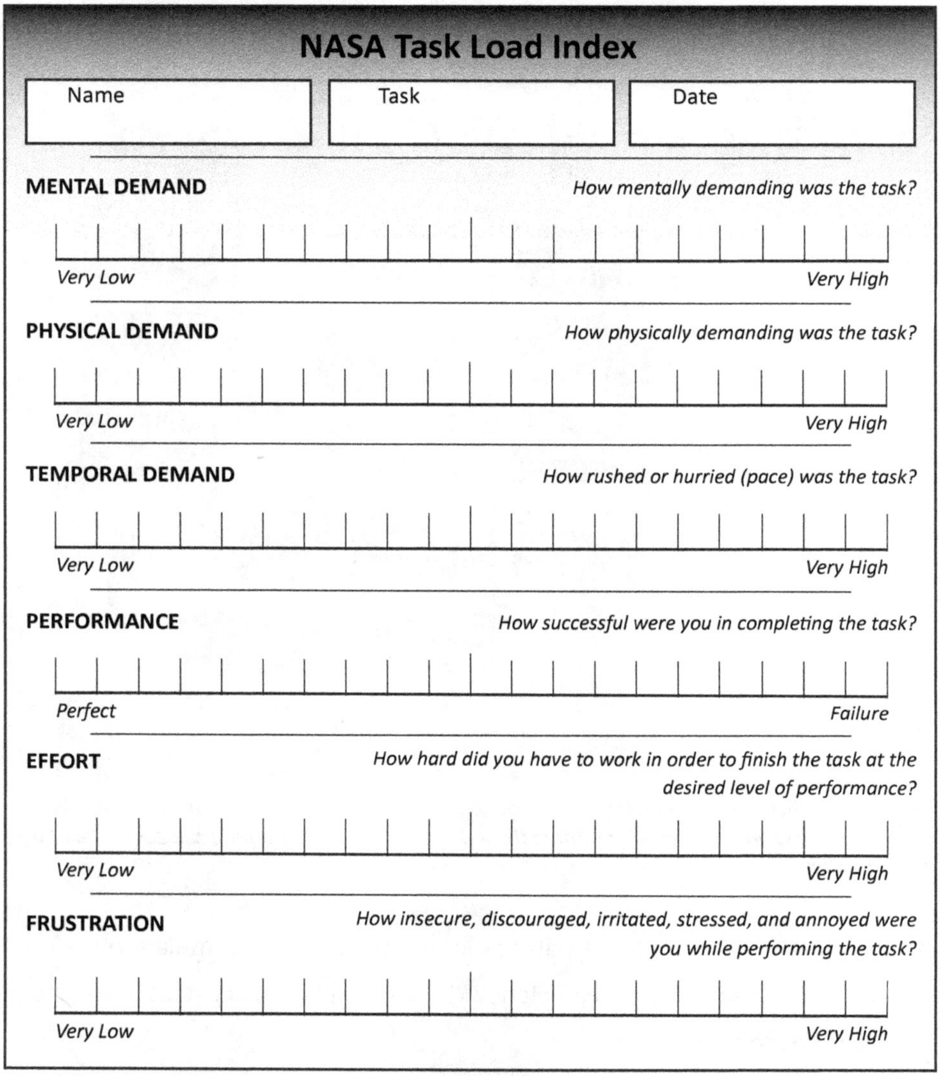

NASA Task Load Index

Name	Task	Date

MENTAL DEMAND   *How mentally demanding was the task?*

Very Low   Very High

PHYSICAL DEMAND   *How physically demanding was the task?*

Very Low   Very High

TEMPORAL DEMAND   *How rushed or hurried (pace) was the task?*

Very Low   Very High

PERFORMANCE   *How successful were you in completing the task?*

Perfect   Failure

EFFORT   *How hard did you have to work in order to finish the task at the desired level of performance?*

Very Low   Very High

FRUSTRATION   *How insecure, discouraged, irritated, stressed, and annoyed were you while performing the task?*

Very Low   Very High

Fig. 6.3. Adapted from Hart & Staveland's NASA Task Load Index (TLX) which is used to measure workload.

"Cooperation between human operators and autonomous machines in dynamic (not fully controlled) situations implies a need for dynamic allocation of activities between the agents, in order to adapt the human-machine system to unexpected circumstances. Dynamic allocation is a way, for example, to avoid human workload peaks. Depending on whether tasks or functions are allocated, the demands made on human-machine cooperation design are different. Task and sub-task allocation assume that both human operator and machine (or its designer) share the same decomposition of the overall task into sub-tasks. Function delegation is less demanding, provided that the human operator explicitly delegates functions to the machine, and within the context of a task representation transmitted by the human" (Hoc et al., 2002).

There are numerous workload assessments; however, the Subjective Workload Assessment Technique (SWAT) developed by the US Air force at their medical research laboratory at Wright Patterson Air force base to assess pilot workload capacity in the cockpit is one of the most widely used. It is a subjective multi-dimensional instrument and assessing three main areas: *stress*, *time*, and *mental loads*.

> **1)** *Stress load* is the amount of stress imposed on an individual while performing his/her task. It measures frustration, anxiety, fatigue, confusion and even risk.
>
> **2)** *Time load* is related to the task's mental demands imposed on the individual while performing said task/s.
>
> **3)** *Mental load* is multi-dimensional and focuses on the imposed time constraints for accomplishing a specific task, while at the same time, the limitations of performance for multiple tasks to be performed concomitantly.

Vibration includes peripheral aspects related to the physical environment such as shift-work, assembly lines, heavy machinery that can affect alertness, focus and concentration.

Naturally, shift work, which can produce sleep deprivation, will also affect workload one's knowledge, skills and ability in relation to performance of assigned tasks, and more importantly one's safety. This too, is evident in performance on assembly lines and when operating heavy machinery for extended time periods.

Psychological Ergonomic Environment

The Psychological Environment is related to organizational structure, job descriptions, level of control over your working environment, coworkers and leadership (Fig. 6.4). The title "Psychological Environment" is somewhat vague; however, it is a combination of physiological and psychological factors and demands related to, and governing, the individual within his/her working environment.

Leadership is a critical component of an ergonomic climate as many problematic situations become far worse when there is a lack of leadership or a conflict between leadership and policy. This environment should be rife with open horizontal communication reinforcing policy and proactive behavior. A leader with a good hands-on-approach will have the opportunity to lead by example, forging process-critical development and igniting stimulating feedback. This in turn fosters informational flow and participation.

Coworkers is the climate of social responsibility within the workplace. The individual's/group's ability and willingness to belong, participate, and take responsibility. Teamwork involves helping one another to best achieve established goals and to minimize the encroachment of pretense, isolationism and facades. Naturally the social culture needs to be a part of the organizational culture and policy and "do as I do and not as I say."

Control over one's working environment should include all personnel and should be supported by policy. Social normalization will work to an extent; nevertheless, we must remember that all personnel are individuals. These individuals make up the teams, so teamwork starts with individual behavior, knowledge, attitude, and control (actual or perceived). Control over one's working environment includes the fundamental aspects, knowledge related to the landscape and workflow processes (laterally and vertically within the individual and team's environment) and the skills and ability to perform them.

Therefore, it is without question, the external demand environment (workload and demands) must be in balance with the individual's self-expectation

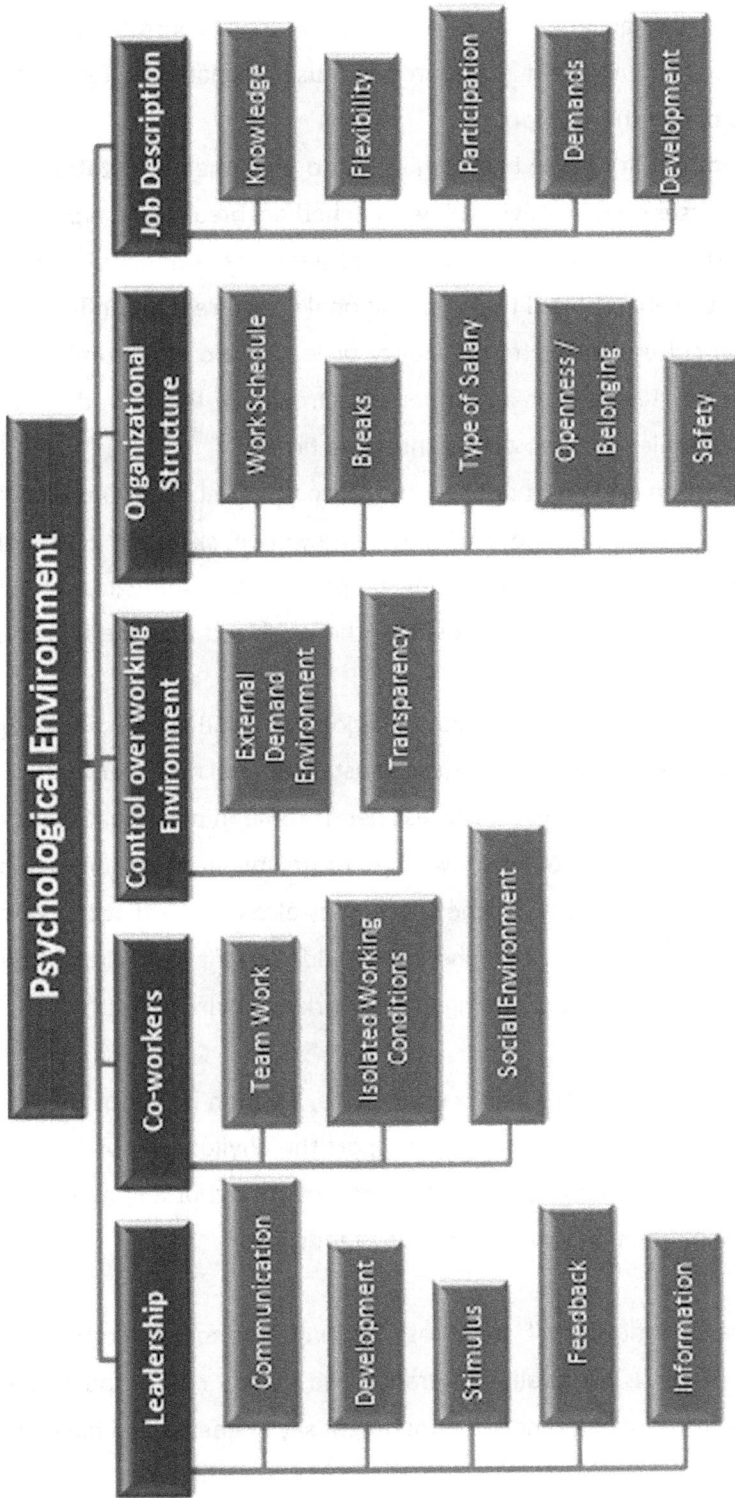

Fig. 6.4. The psychological environment has to do with fundamental management and leadership practices and how they affect the individual's environment.

otherwise this imbalance will cause conflict and loss of control. Furthremore, this lack of control will affect transparency causing isolationist tendencies as well as a loss of communication.

Organizational Structure has nothing to do with the organizational chart but instead focuses on the individual's work schedule, breaks, and type of salary as well as on the organizational culture, which deals with openness, belonging-ness, and safety. Perceptibly, if the organizational structure is in conflict with the organizational culture through poor policy or leadership, ergonomics will fail sooner than later. I have seen a number of examples of this in both industrial producing companies and knowledge intensive firms.

Job Description is without doubt a critical component in ergonomics. If the demands of the position do not match the knowledge, skills and ability of the implementer, the consequences can only be problematic. Ambiguity and inter-pretation of the demands of the position, the workload and the individual is naturally vital.

Matching the individual to the job or the job to the individual can be argued until the cows come home; nevertheless, most personnel managers with whom I have had contact believe that a process needs to be in place that guides and manages the individual through knowledge, flexibility, participation, demands, innovation and development. Furthermore, they also believe that the vast ma-jority of positions (at work or on the sportsfield) benefit from Cross-Training, rotation and a greater understanding of the working environment.

Mr. Ulf Larsson, HR Manager at Rexam in Fosie, Sweden is one of those great visionaries. His methods and practices support the phyilosophy of Cross-Train-ing by empowering personnel to take charge of their working environments through participation and workplace understanding.

You might have noticed that the Cross-Training Ergonomic model overlaps slightly. This design is for quality assurance and quality control purposes and provides support between functions. You might say a "checks and balances."

chapter 7 *Process*

In Cross-training, PROCESS is a fundamental building-block which spreads throughout the organization like a web or an electrical circuit. The process determines, and is always responsible, for the outcome. If the process is not critically and repeatedly reviewed though analysis and measures, it cannot be sustained or improved upon. In my experience, new models advocating a LEAN process, an innovative process, Six Sigma and others are dependant upon a process of critical review.

Process is therefore the corner stone of quality control and quality assurance and the management of all processes is vital. Empirical evidence has shown that poor output is the result of either a single or a number of process failures where management have either turned a blind eye, in order to save money or time, or have not established adequate controls or measures. This includes innovative as well as human-machine and mechanical processes.

Naturally, the purpose of a process is to reproduce a specific effort (electrical, mechanical, decisional and physical) consistently with an objective to achieve a desired outcome, which is either constant or innovative.

Process Analysis Management

Process analysis management in Cross-Training consists of focus group/s (from within the process and interrelated processes within the macro- and micro landscape that are familiar with said workflow, workload and synergy) with the responsibility to critically question, review and suggest changes or improvements to the process activities. This is done by looking at: 1) Intention, 2) Significance, 3) Extent, 4) Outputs, 5) Measures, and 6) Resources.

1) **Intention** addresses the purpose of the function, product, process or service, which can be either proactive or reactive in nature. What quality requirements or issues the customer (end-customer, intermediate customer, or workflow customer that can be someone or even an entity within the workflow) has or might have with the product, service, task, input or output. The intention is to isolate requirements for correction, innovation or prevention.

2) **Significance** is the importance of ranking of how the change will either prevent (pro-actively) or reduce (reactively) the issue in relation to the customer (end-customer, intermediate customer, or workflow customer that can be someone or even an entity within the workflow) has or might have with the product, service, task, input or output and why it should be done now.

3) **Extent** and scope of the team's focus includes what information and how the information is to be collected to identify the proactive or reactive issues. The extent of the team's jurisdiction which should include the parameters pertaining to the actual process or part of it, workload, or synergy and at which point of the process or flow should they begin and end. Furthermore, the need to establish deadlines, time limitations, reporting milestones, and other constraints thereto should be done in relation to the scope and customer (end-customer, intermediate customer, or workflow customer, that can be someone or even an entity within the workflow).

4) **Outputs** or the expected deliverables necessary in relation to the objective. This can include a time frame for a particular objective including finish dates or dates for submittal and presentation of finding. What will be considered successful or failure. These parameters need to be clearly established.

5) Measures and statistical controls are vital if the analysis is going to carry any weight. Naturally not all employees will be able to establish statistical controls themselves, and the team might need to rely

on additional resources to establish these; however, they should be able to identify and establish points and criteria for practical measures. Participation in establishing these measures are psychologically very important as these measures are also used in workload and other performance related issues. How measures will be tracked and the objectives for the measures should be agreed upon and noted. If improvement is needed then targets and a realistic date and time (date) should be established and the issue tagged and tracked.

6) Resources and responsibilities need to be assigned. Accountability needs to be established. First, the team will have to report to a manager or sponsor within the organization. Second, a process owner, who has the ongoing responsibility to monitor the process and to strive for gains, will have to be assigned. All key stakeholders need to be identified the focus group/team needs to be established. See the appendix for tips on how to select and establish teams. Fix a budget and obtain approval for nominal expenditures and set limitations for each. Assign someone as a team leader. Create the guidelines on how the meeting minutes are to be kept and meetings organized and how a decision making process will be reached by measures, statistical controls, voting, consensus, a combination or all of the above. Ambiguity will only cause chaos.

Process

The Cross-Training process involves seven parameters starting with objective, input, knowledge, decision, workload, measure, control, and output (Fig. 7.1). The OIK-DW-MCO process method helps to identify task/objective specifics by conforming data specific information into meaning and knowledge within the working environment. By interpreting the individual process components employees can more easily identify or participate with synergic ideas and improvements in both the micro- and macro-environments.

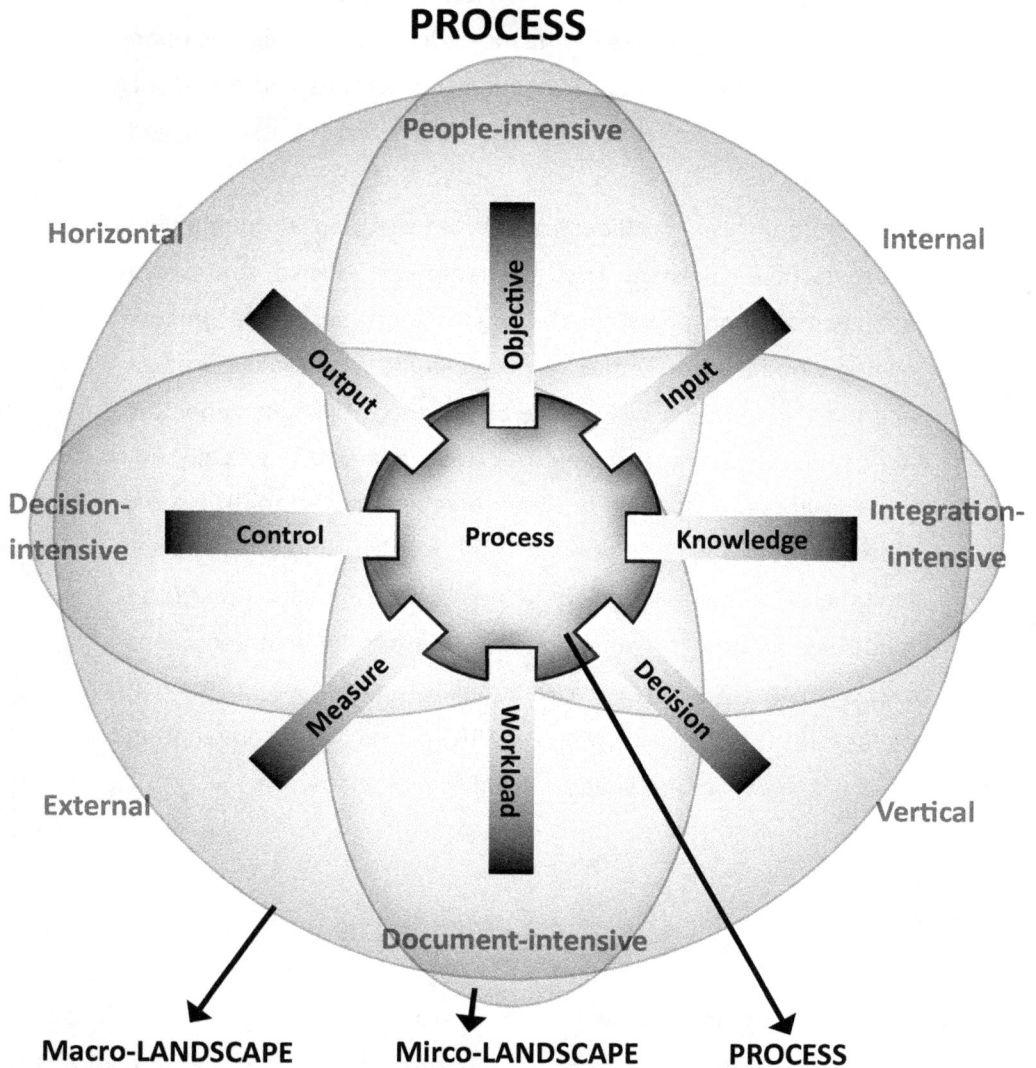

Fig. 7.1. Illustrates how the Cross-Training PROCESS and its eight components are the building block of the landscape. The process therefore integrates and affects all levels of the landscape. Furthermore, OIK-DW-MCO method used in Cross-Training improves identity and a greater understanding of purpose which in turn enhances the employee's ability to innovate, create or participate.

Objective Whether machine or man, every process has an objective or goal. This goal needs to be clearly defined, otherwise conflict with the remaining components of the process is obvious. Whether or not the specific process is knowledge-intensive, skills, ability, physical or just plain mechanical, the sequence remains. By defining this sequence, one provides a perspective view and target. This view catalyzes practical and even philosophical thought processes, but, more importantly, it forges assists in establishing measures, controls and output.

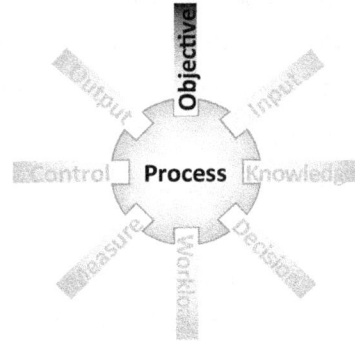

Input Actual inputs can include data, information, ideas, resources (electrical, mechanical, physical, psychological, environmental) needed to move the process forward, without which the process would not progress. Input could therefore be considered an actual effort or even delayed effort such as storage of information or goods.

Knowledge Human, natural, and machine knowledge is the applied data, information, skills, ability and the nature of the environment incorporated in the operational laws of the said process. A changing landscape will affect knowledge and process should develop ad infinitum with technology, science, and individual capabilities. However, knowledge limitations and the management thereof in relation to process objectives, and the micro- and macro-landscape is always a governing parameter. Chapter nine discusses knowledge, skills and abilities and the applications within Cross-Training in more detail.

Decision reflects the fundamental and applied use of knowledge in relation to the needs within the process. The objectives might, for example, require adjustment because the workload and measures indicate so; or, the controls could indicate a quality problem which in turn could also affect the needs of the objectives. Decision is therefore fluid; nevertheless, it is guided by the established parameters and can be automatically programmed or learned. Classic decisional matrix methods such as the Recognition Primed Decision approach (Klein, 1998), Naturalistic Decision Making (NDM) (Klien, 1993 & Todd et al., 2001), Zero-Based Decision Making also known as the Slippery Slope (Eugene Volokh, 2003), Tacit or Implicit Assumptions (Schein, 2004), Image Decisions (Alvesson, 2004) and many other cognitive models.

Workload reflects the demands the process places upon itself and anyone or thing (electrical, mechanical or environmental). These demands if excessive will cause subsequent conflicts with the other processes within the process. For example, too much input can overload the decisional process thereby causing poor decisions in relation to quality controls and objectives. In humans, excessive workload can affect mental, physical, temporal demands and performance, effort and cause stress or frustration. On the other hand, too little workload can result in under-capacity and loss of concentration, which can lead to similar symptoms exhibited from excessive workload.

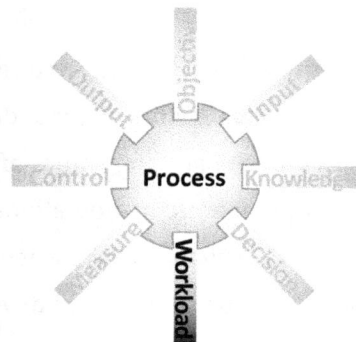

Measure All processes have measures. In Cross-Training measures are established from focus groups using the objective, input, workload, and output vari-

ables for the process. The focus group evalu-
ates the process and decides upon measures to
be used (time, length, volume, weight, amount
and space) which best fit the parameters. Measures are integral to the process as they provide
data and information to the process operator
whereby decisions can be made for adjustment
to the process. Monitoring these measures help
to set new objectives and to understand or cor-

roborate workload versus input and output. Whether philosophical or mechanical measures, these are helpful to the process.

Control The process needs to include quality
control points. These can be coupled to the
output or even as part of the measures; however, it is important to understand the distinction
between these two. The control function of the
process is solely responsible for the quality of
the expected objective's output. Naturally, this
will have implications on input, knowledge, decision and output.

Output The processing of the process functions is the output. The output should naturally
be in synergy with the objective. The input/s,
knowledge, decision/s, workload, measure/s,
and control/s are the means to achieve the expected objective outputs as consistently as possible.

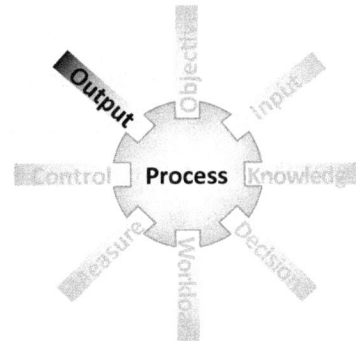

Any errors or misunderstanding is a direct failure of process. Therefore, Cross-
Training focuses on understanding process related to standard operating pro-

cedures for specific tasks within the workflow and macro-landscape. This knowledge helps to provide identity and greater participation within a working environment. See **Appendix F** – Process Assignment Guide for practical application.

There are many process forms and many processes within process too; nevertheless, the OIK-DW-MCO process method will be found in the majority of them. Other methods include process engineering and business process modeling or business process management used in change management.

An interesting model to consider is the Meta-process modeling used in systems engineering, construction of models, dealing with predefined problems and even in software construction. Naturally, unlike OIK-DW-MCO, the Meta-process is often supported through software and provides an instantiation and assembly technique (Rolland, 1999).

The CPRET process is a representation or an integration of company mission and the environment and is used in systems engineering and the chemical industry. CPRET stands for: Constraints, Process, Resources, Environment (mission & products), Elements (inputs) and Transformation (operations).

Processes naturally have to integrate into a system within the macro-environment. The understanding of this interaction and participation within the system is fundamental in linking the micro- and macro-environments. Considering things in requisites of process help you to develop a common understanding of the job constraints, operating procedures, workload, and more importantly, to re-evaluate the synergy and efficaciousness leading to IDP (Innovative Development Process, chapter 2).

chapter 8 *Standard Operating Procedures*

Standard Operating Procedure or commonly called SOP is a fundamental building block in Cross-Training. Not only does it serve to document procedures and guidelines in daily duties, but it also serves as a reference library or not so common procedures which can either be forgotten over time or lost due to transfer or rotation. An SOP is also a living document which is continually reviewed and updated to suit the changing environment. Furthermore it is a management and leadership tool used to implement participation and process understanding. In Cross-Training, SOPs go far beyond the basic description of methods, materials, and safety requirements. C-T SOPs cover quality procedures, job responsibilities for that procedure, process, conduct, corporate culture, and policy as they relate to unambiguous procedures. Keep in mind that SOPs are about communication, quality assurance and quality control too.

SOPs cover all the spheres of working life and no position is free from their scope. If one is not responsible for implementing a SOP, then one is responsible for insuring that they are created, maintained and followed. SOPs can be used in research methods, clinical studies, inventory procedures for stock, laboratory security and reference cultures, disposal of hazardous materials, including needles, chemical and biological materials, surface decontamination, spill procedures, operation and maintenance of equipment, transportation, lifting, sealing, packaging, production, and thousands of more examples.

SOPs are also used as tools for compliance procedures in regard to regulations and certifications such as:

OSHA (occupational Safety and Health Administration) Safety,
FDA (Food & Drug Administration) Good Laboratory Practices or
the production of edibles.

> **ICH** (International Conference on Harmonization) Clinical Research,
>
> **ITAA** (Information Association of America) Computer Based Information Systems,
>
> **SIS** (Swedish Standards Institute) Thousands of Standards from SS, SS-EN, ISO, IEC, ASTM, and others.

Basically, SOPs compels individuals to think through procedures and processes step by step thereby standardizing methods and updating or improving processes, for example, OIK-DW-MCO (Objectivity, Input, Knowledge, Decision, Workload, Measures, Controls, and Output).

In Cross-Training, we link each SOP to a specific workflow, process diagram or Microsoft Visio document (Fig. 8.1) for easy of use and identification purposes thereby reducing the confusion found in many computerized and manual systems. Naturally, easy access and availability to all SOPs is essential if they are to be incorporated in the daily/weekly and monthly activities and duties.

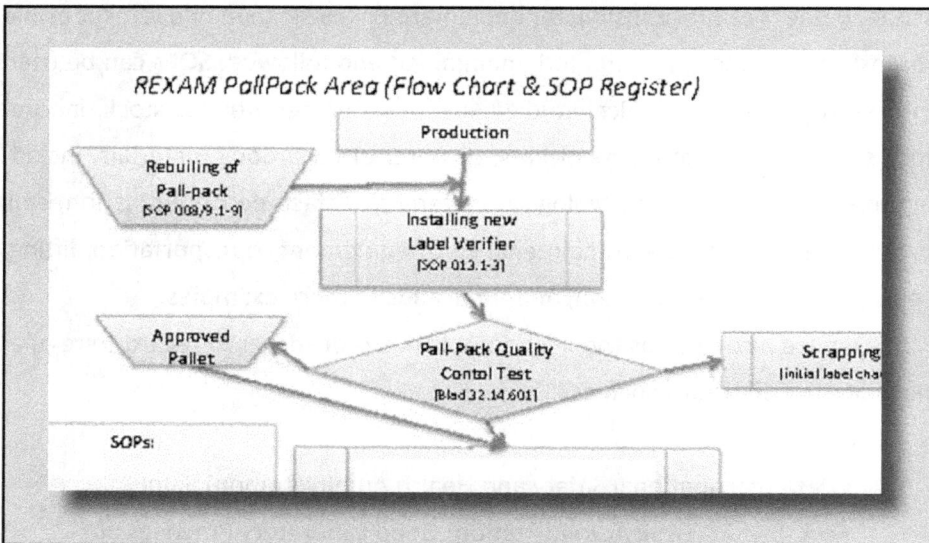

Fig. 8.1. Shows the SOP linked to a specific task within the workflow diagram. This way the SOP becomes easier to locate visually within the workflow and the macro-environment.

Writing an SOP

A typical SOP contains a number of elements: a Header (Fig 8.2) which shows the Title of the SOP, Original Issue Date, Revision/Review Date, number of pages contained in the SOP, who wrote the SOP, and the Approval Signature.

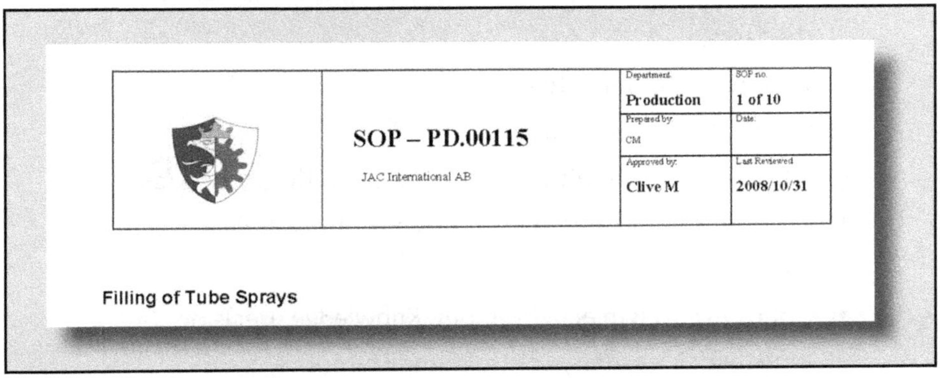

		Department: Production	SOP no. 1 of 10
	SOP – PD.00115	Prepared by: CM	Date:
	JAC International AB	Approved by: Clive M	Last Reviewed 2008/10/31

Filling of Tube Sprays

Fig. 8.2. Shows a typical SOP header. The header links the SOP to the flowchart and the SOP register.

If the SOPs or policies are incomplete, inconsistent or even outdated, then you can expect that problematic and systematic situations will arise. Resolving these will take time and influence performance. SOPs assist to improve efficacy and increase stakeholder and customer satisfaction.

One important factor that most people tend to ignore is that the individual that receives the product or service from you, within your workflow environment, can also be construed as your customer. If they received the product or service on time and in order as per the SOP then they will be able to do their job.

There are a number of basic elements which can help you to write a good SOP. They should include:

- a clear and concise heading,
- a clear purpose and scope,

- exact key definitions of process or scope ,
- all the materials and equipment needed,
- safety concerns related to the task at hand,
- a list of who is responsible for the task, or is process owner,
- step-by step procedure with the "critical steps within the task listed,"
- the measures (input/output and quality controls) related to the tasks,
- what records should to be kept,
- copies of forms to be used,
- references related historical changes in to the process/es
- list of applicable laws, regulations and any compliance com-munications, and finally
- OIK-DW-MCO (Objectivity, Input, Knowledge, Decision, Workload, Measures, Controls, and Output).

To be valuable it helps to insure that your procedures and policies are written in a consistent format allowing for ease of use and comprehension (Fig. 8.3). SOP documents are a medium of communication, and as we are aware, poor communication only leads to errors. Your SOP format and style should be taken seriously as it not only portrays your guidelines and procedures but also affects company culture and identity.

SOPs therefore have a large part to play in the transference of knowledge, individual skills and ones ability to develop.

Chapter nine will discuss the definition and importance of knowledge, skills and ability; however, it should be kept in mind that SOPs form an integral part of an organization's management culture and SOP information serves to empower the individual within his/her working environment.

Furthermore this empowerment, the gained knowledge, skills and/or abil-ity within ones environment, helps to improve transparency and teamwork by increased flexibility, rotate-ability, and formation of focus groups to review and/

or improve on SOPs. This in turn enhances belongingness and supports social culture within the organization.

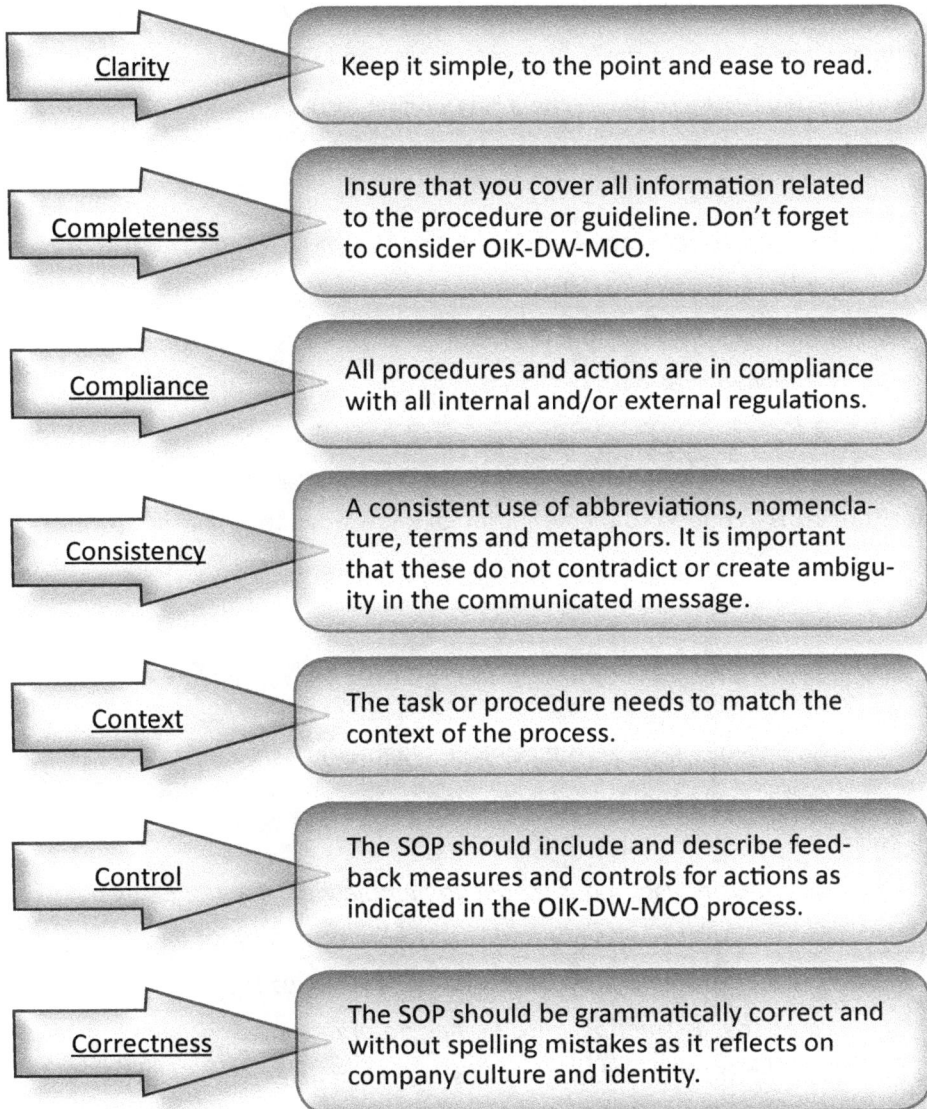

Clarity →	Keep it simple, to the point and ease to read.
Completeness →	Insure that you cover all information related to the procedure or guideline. Don't forget to consider OIK-DW-MCO.
Compliance →	All procedures and actions are in compliance with all internal and/or external regulations.
Consistency →	A consistent use of abbreviations, nomenclature, terms and metaphors. It is important that these do not contradict or create ambiguity in the communicated message.
Context →	The task or procedure needs to match the context of the process.
Control →	The SOP should include and describe feedback measures and controls for actions as indicated in the OIK-DW-MCO process.
Correctness →	The SOP should be grammatically correct and without spelling mistakes as it reflects on company culture and identity.

Fig. 8.3. The illustration shows the importance of precision in SOP formulation. SOP documents communicating guidelines and procedures and their accuracy and completeness affect corporate culture and identity.

chapter 9 *Knowledge*
(Sustain, Generate, Innovate)

What is the meaning of knowledge? Professor Mats Alversson, Head of Organizational management at the School of Business and Economics at Lund University in Sweden has been researching this subject for a couple of decades and in a recent lecture he gave the following four meanings:

1) knowledge as data and information,
2) knowledge as a social good,
3) knowledge as truth, and
4) knowledge as a tool.

To frame a dialogue from Plato in reference to a discussion between Socrates and Theatetus in regard to the definition of knowledge they consider three possibilities:

1) knowledge is perception,
2) knowledge is true judgment, and
3) knowledge is an account of true judgment or true judgment with an account.

"The Socratic method is meant to be objective, or at least unbiased. Socrates asks questions of Theatetus and masquerades as knowing nothing. This is aimed to convince us that what Socrates says is true; because he has no prior motive or knowledge he must be objective. This is a clever deceit on Plato's part because it means he can manipulate the reader or audience into accepting anything Socrates says and he can keep his

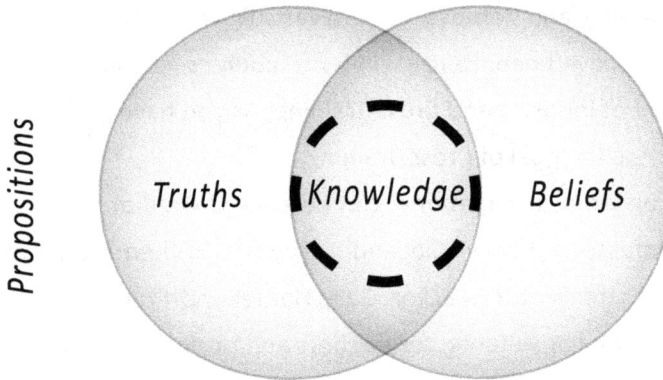

Fig. 9.1. Adapted from Theatetus by Plato (Project Guten-berg, Release #1726, April 1999) to illustrate knowledge as a subset of what is both true and believed.

agenda i.e. the Forms, concealed from view, at least initially. Socrates asks questions to produce certain answers from Theatetus and from this seemingly innocent position he dictates the enquiry. This betrays the inquiry as exclusive , not objective as it might appear, this exclusivity being Plato's already existing conception of knowledge. The type of questions used dictate the possible answers, "Tell me how you are searching and I will tell you what you are searching for." (Wittgenstein, 2000, p18) Asking questions is the most effective way to shape a discourse about something, particularly when you are trying to exclude certain possibilities. The argument that all he is doing is asking questions is a poor one because there are long sections of the inquiry where Socrates speaks for many sentences and Theatetus merely agrees. Furthermore Plato's enquiry presupposes there is truth and is directly concerned with what truth is. This means he also presupposes falsehood as something which truth is not." (http://journal.ilovephilosophy.com)

Knowledge, Skills, Ability, and Competence are very big words and books can be written on each, and have been. Here I will try to address, in shorthand, these issues in the context of industry and Cross-Training. As you have gathered, contextual competence is the goal of Cross-Training.

The modern version of occupational competence started at Harvard Business School by Professor David McClelland in the 1960s then Professors Michael Porter, John Kotter, Peter Drucker, Gary Hamel and Prahalad; however, many other well-known consultants, researchers and professors such as Ikujiro Nonaka, Mats Alvesson, Hugh Willmott, Dan Kärreman, Etienne Wenger, and others have risen to forefront with stimulating, original and thought-provoking ideas on knowledge, identity, power, subjectification (Alvesson, 2004: 213) and the ambiguous nature of knowledge addressing this ever growing and important field of management.

According to Malhorta (1998, p.59) 'knowledge management caters to the critical issues of organizational adaptation, survival and competence in face of increasingly discontinuous environmental change...' He believes that it embodies organizational processes with the synergic goal of combining, information and innovative and creative capacity of employees.

Management by Cross-Training's objective is to understand these critical micro-components and to provide a platform of policy, guidelines, and personal development incentives, and leadership for them to flourish within the macro-environment using situated learning (Willmot & Contu, 2003), concerted control methods, teamwork, and corporate culture (see chapter twelve for more detail). To support this Alan Price (2004: 63-64) reported from various studies that team-working (community and tacit transfer) was better for organizational learning that IT (explicit or formal):

> "The Institute of Employment Studies launched a report stressing the importance of learning in teams straddling cross-functional boundaries. Based on in-depth research among teams in a number of leading British employers, one of the au-

thors of the report – IES Research Fellow Polly Kettley – concludes that this is neglected potential deserving proper recognition.

Modern Businesses tend to stress sophisticated networks and 'groupware' but they tend to leave their project teams or special task forces unsupported by their colleagues. And their objectives are often not understood or misused. According to Polly Kettley: Few of the lessons of even successful teams make in into the 'organizational memory,' and new teams repeat many of the mistakes of the past. Organizational learning has been hijacked by IT, in the guise of 'knowledge management,' and employers are struggling to address the human issues associated with knowledge creation and exchange. The reality is that the majority of knowledge sharing and innovation within organizations occurs through the interaction of people with people – especially within networks, groups or teams of people who cross conventional organizational boundaries. Moreover, for the ambitious employee, time spent on a cross-functional team is now one of the most popular, and potentially, rewarding, forms of career development – though it in not without risks. The study found that what helps team members learn was:

- *Learning is made an explicit and important part team-working for team members and their organization/s) before, during and after this team 'experience.'*
- *Team members' departments have a positive attitude and interact well across their boundaries with other parts of the organization.*
- *There is a diverse membership within the team.*
- *Members can organize their own work within the team.*
- *They can work together in one place.*
- *Team membership is continuous and consistent because this*

> *'maintains the team dynamic' and builds the mutual trust that is essential for team learning.*
> - *They use recognized team processes for learning and are able to discuss problems honestly."*
>
> **Source**: HRMGuide.co.uk (http:www.hrmguide.co.uk), 30 October 2000.

Michael Porter with his models on Identifying value activities (1998; 39-45); Increasing competitive advantage (Porter, 1998; 202-206); The growing impor-tance of a horizontal strategy (Porter, 1998; 320-322); and the Diversification of corporate resources (Porter, 1998; 380) all stress the importance of knowledge, competency and flexibility as a precursor which providing corporations with the capability to meet competition through knowledge understanding.

Prahalad and Hamel (1996) claim that a corporation should be built around a core of shared competencies. Prahalad & Krishnan (2008) present excellent cases and arguments on the importance of understanding business process. They show that understanding this process provides enablers for innovation (2008: 44-79). They also show that innovation is not the only product of this understanding and they go further to illustrate how this understanding leads to increased flexibility and efficiency (2008: 174-203). Moreover, they stress that a dynamic re-configuration of talent needs to occur; in addition, an agenda for managers focus on the essence of innovation from this talent should also take place (2008: 204-266).

The author believes however, that this talent is actually competence and that understanding one's competence for a given task, job description, or even professional field is therefore critical as it directly affects one's: willingness to participate, transparency, efficacy, and teamwork. To illustrate this, more effec-tively, we can consider a discipline which carries the most prestige, a practicing doctor of medicine. The knowledge of their profession is usually undisputed; nevertheless, I have, and I am sure everyone has, come into contact with an M.D. that lacks either skills or ability to apply his knowledge in an effective or most suitable manner. These M.D.s might be more suited to academia or re-

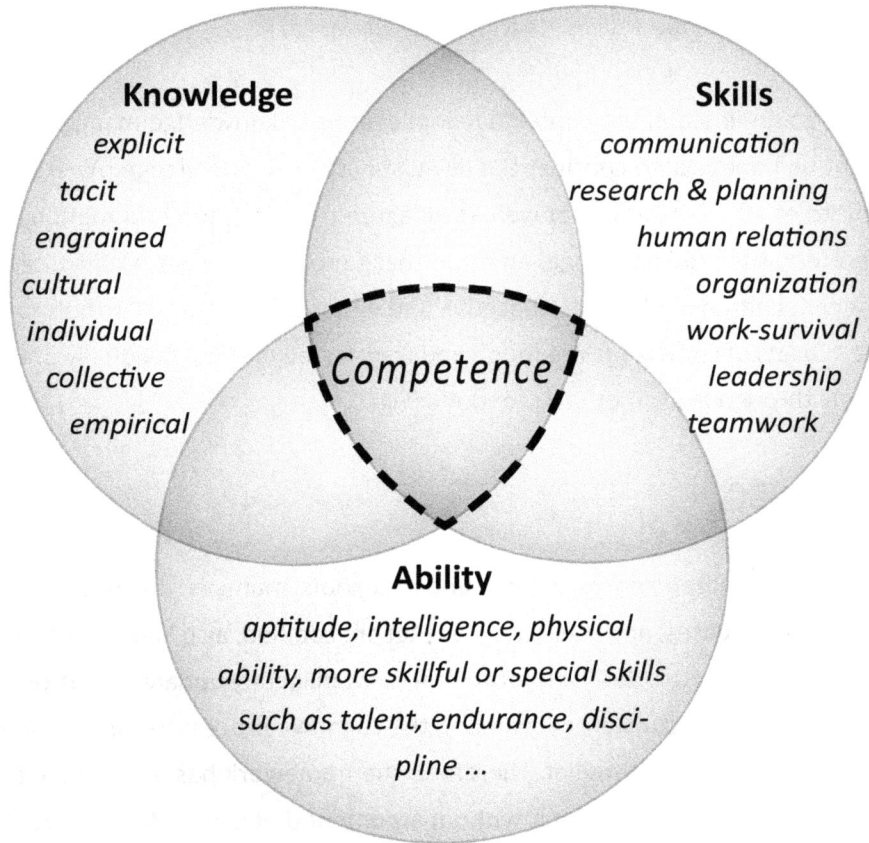

Fig. 9.2. Adapted from Hamel and Prahalad's theory on Core Competence. The illustration shows the associations and the product of ones competence. Here contextual competence is a combination of knowledge, skills and ability for a specific task, process, procedure and/or ones job demands. Herein after known as KSAC.

search rather than medical practice. Ones competence therefore lies at the core for one's knowledge, skills, and ability (Fig. 9.2).

Chapter seven discussed the parts of process and chapter eight highlighted SOPs in a codification or cognitive context of required knowledge within the working environment; however, there is far more to empowering individuals with knowledge, skills, ability and competence (KSAC) as KSAC also affects both identity, organizational culture and motivation. Therefore, KSAC should be considered a process in perpetual motion.

KSA=C *(Knowledge + Skills + Ability = Competence)*

In order to understand the contextual implications of knowledge management it might be beneficial to consider the key distinctions of knowledge (Alversson, Willmott, et al). I am sure that we can all agree that data and information are the prerequisites to knowledge, and that these prerequisites are explicit, tacit, engrained, cultural, individual, collective and empirical in nature. Furthermore, these subsets of knowledge are found and transferred either individually or collectively through explicit or tacit conduits (Fig. 9.3).

Knowledge

Explicit or formalized knowledge is found in schools, manuals, documentation, SOPs, files, databases, and other sources that are codified, also known as codification. Naturally, if this data or information is not diligently updated, controlled, measured and/or in constant movement, the cognitive process becomes unreliable and the object of disbelief. Therefore, the framework has to fit the needs of the situated environment. It is without argument that explicit knowledge is a product of modern day society and is needed to form the building block or theoretical foundation for specific processes, job descriptions and/or professions. Thereafter a combination of tacit knowledge, skills and ability are required for Innovation Development Process (IDP).

Tacit information is found in the heads of an organization's employees (Price, 2004: 65). Also known as implicit knowledge it can include empirical or posteriori knowledge, cultural, and basic intuition which is easy to verbalize. Engrained is rationalism – priori processes – and even intuition – as suggested by Plato's Theory of Forms in the Seventh Letter 342-345: The epistemology of 'Form." Form here is a mind-independent entity whereas 'form' always written with a small 'f' indicates the outward or appearance of something. Metaphysical connections are therefore drawn for perception, reality, and being. Being relates as sense of being, truth or belongingness. The problem with being as a Form is that if it is participatory then non-being must exist and be being too. Plato also discusses (Sophistes 246-248: True essence of a Form) that 'Form' is an effective solution to participation problems. Therefore, tacit knowledge in Cross-Training helps to form cultural identity through form specific and/or personification means resulting in improved individual knowledge, and to a greater extent, vast collective or community knowledge.

Individual knowledge encompasses use of ones competence (KSA: knowledge, skills and judgment) in relation to ones PMP (self-expectancy, self-esteem, and transparent environments) within the situated context.

Collective or Community knowledge is the informal explicit knowledge which exists within an organization combined with the tacit knowledge.

Procedural knowledge is the interplay between individual knowledge and community knowledge (Alversson, 2004: 46) within the situated environment.

Substantive knowledge is the interpretation and amalgamation of community and individual knowledge in context to the situated environment.

Forms, Frames, Being, Power and Identity represent a relationship between the rhetoric of storytelling, genre, KSA, PMP and the organization. This relationship creates a perception of how one sees oneself, and how one imagines others sees one. Understanding this relationship of awareness, perception and interpersonal relationship is best realized by considering the Johari-Window (Boyd and Chinyol, 2006: 65). Naturally, knowledge is a key to identity construction (Alversson, 2004: 215). Within his text, Alvesson creates a correlation for identity construction and three major categories: cultural values (autonomy, flat organizational structure, innovative, ad hoc, etc.), status (reliability, hierarchical position, control, etc.), and moral virtues (integrity, fair trade, equal opportunity, etc.), which all lead to a self-construction of ones identification. These are achieved through broad discourses and situational construction processes.

Obvious correlations between belongingness, power, forms and frames are therefore made. This correlation therefore supports and links the author's process theory of Perpetual Motivation Positioning of the educational environment to the social, transparent, self-esteem, and self-expectancy environments.

Key Distinctions of Knowledge

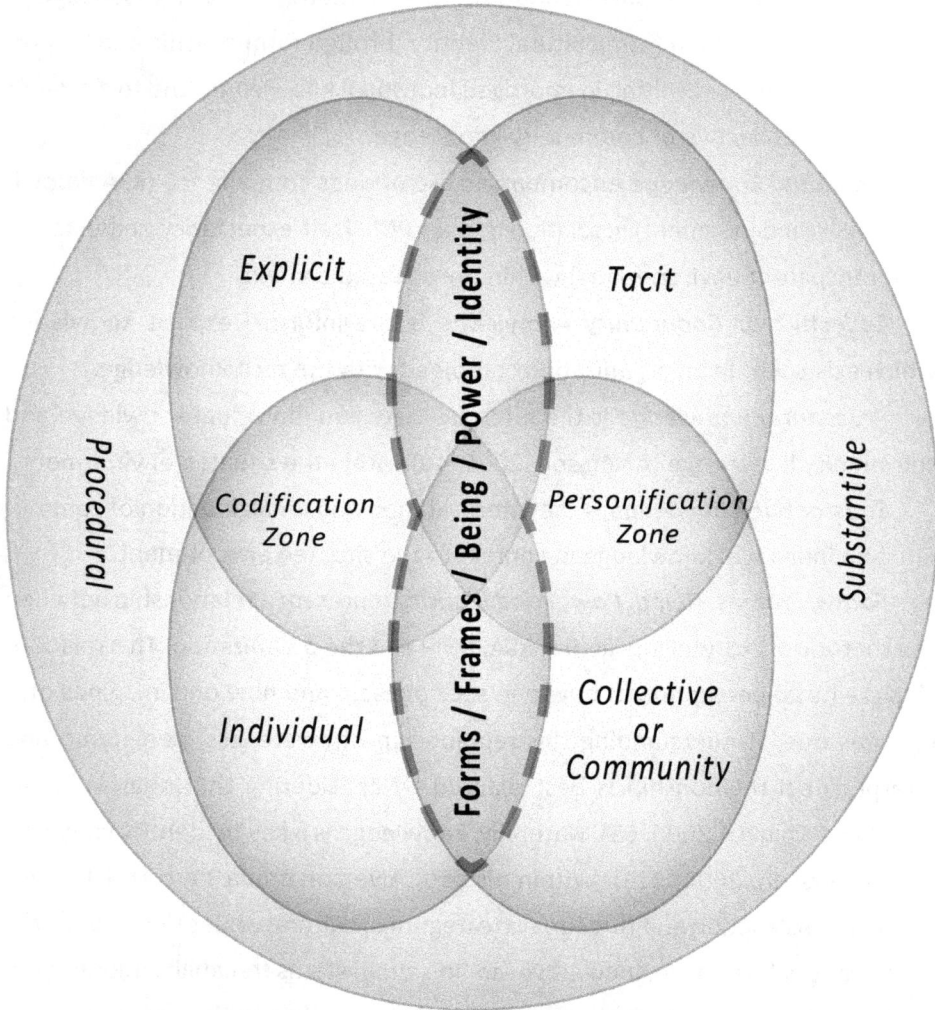

Fig. 9.3. Adapted from Allvesson's key distinctions of knowledge (Alvesson, 2004: 45). Here the author tries to illustrate the flux or motion of knowledge between the explicit and tacit forms in relation to individual and community based knowledge and how the four sets of knowledge interact to create forms, frames, being and power which are derivatives of identity, belongingness, control and motivation.

Nota bene: *Knowledge management is the ability to maximize knowledge capital within the organization through policy, leadership and organizational culture to best suit the situational conditions and objectives.*

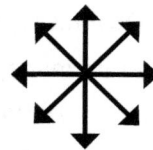

Knowledge Mngt.

Skills can include communication and feedback, research and planning, human relations, organization, work survival, coaching, delegating, appraising performance and goal setting, motivating or inspiring performance through identity, culture and other means. Harvard Business School has a program called "Talent Management" which focuses on improving these management skills and other, commonly called, soft strategies.

Ability is having the aptitude, intelligence and judgment to understand and conceptualize the physical and educational environments in relation to the external demand environment and the self-expectant environments of the macro- and micro-objectives. This can include skillful or special skills.

Competence is the aptitude to interpret and apply the knowledge, skills and ability in the most productive and most appropriate manner, even when ambiguous, which best suits the situation in both the short and long term. Naturally, this application also applies to the ability to adjust, change and set a course as judgment so indicates.

Autonomy through Competence

Whether perceived or actual, autonomy in the workplace weighs heavily as a motivator. The feel of competence control, having the ability, skills and knowledge (tacit or explicit) to interact with the required processes or to design or alter these processes produces autonomy. Empowering the individual, at all levels of the organization, to take control of positional understanding is by far the most important factor facing managers (Fig. 9.4). Let's take two examples at either end of the spectrum, a cleaner and an engineer.

The Cleaner Fundamentals of ergonomics naturally require that we have a clean working environment. This is obvious to all of us, is it not? How creative or effective would you be if you had to work in an unclean environment? The cleaner has his/her daily routines and routes, he/she uses various cleaning supplies and equipment and goes about his/her job year after year. In Cross-Training, the role of the supervisor would be to guide the cleaner through a number of steps in order to achieve this autonomy or empowerment.

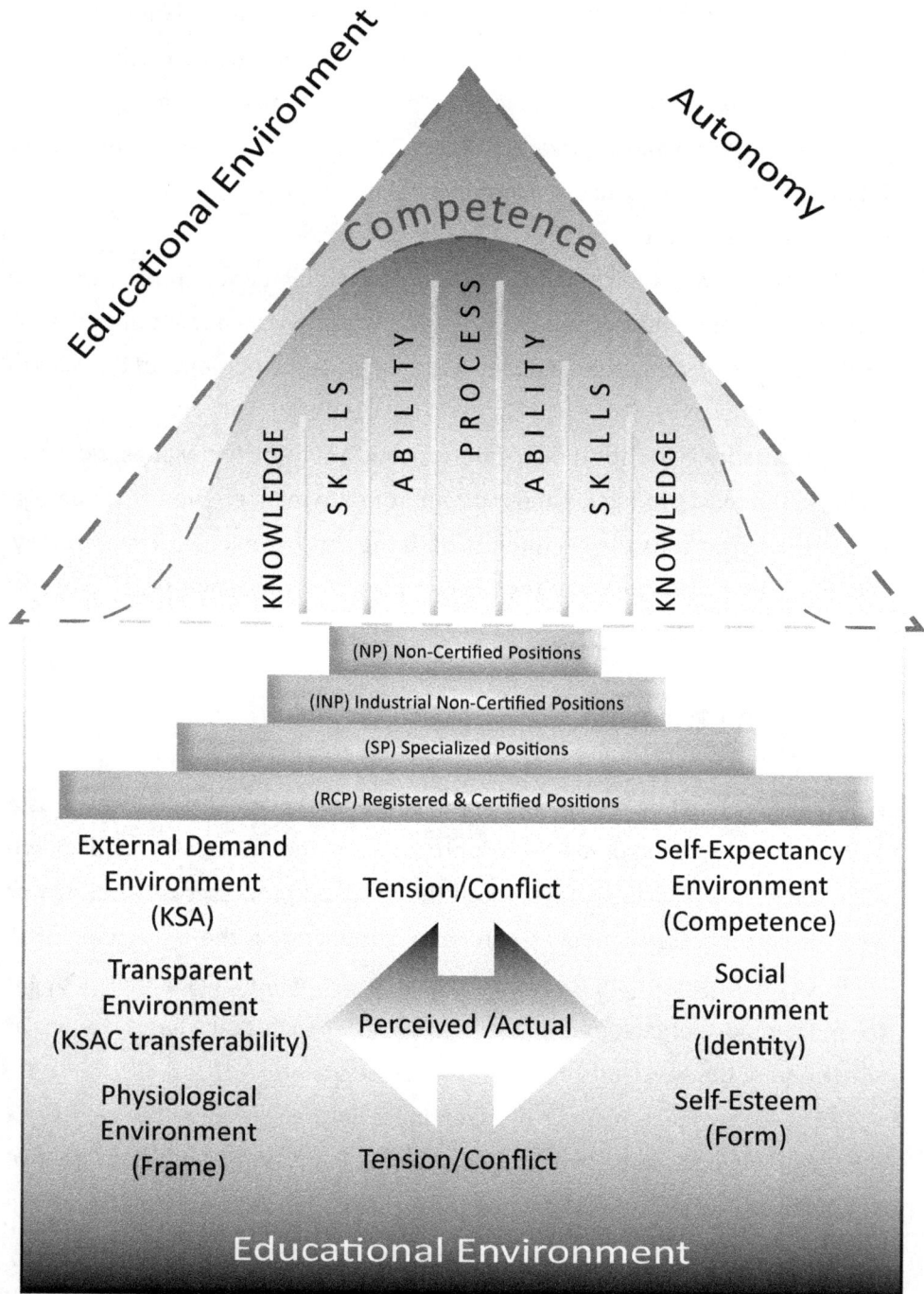

Fig. 9.4. Shows the complexity of knowledge resource management in relation to KSAC, Process, and the perceived and/or actual personal autonomy. Positional competence therefore leads to a sense of autonomy resulting from of control over ones working environment.

Step 1, create an understanding of where the cleaner fits into the organization and why his/her role is important,

Step 2, create a workflow of the working environment to illustrate individual importance,

Step 3, design SOPs related to processes and routines which should include process information (OIK-DW-MCO) on how to clean and how to self-evaluate, measure and control specific tasks. Creation of a focus group in facilities management could be a good way to address understanding and some identified issues as well as serving to enhance, individual PMP.

Step 4, create a test group (of cleaners) to evaluate SOPs, equipment, chemicals used, etc..., and to empower them to make decisions and alterations to their objectives and inputs in relation to the company culture and goals,

Step 5, challenge and train all cleaners to question processes and SOP routines, to learn (through tacit or explicit means), to set quality standards, the process of cleaning and to suggest improvements,

Step 6, provide a budget to realize their efforts and or suggestions, and

Step 7, allow cleaners to present their work to management and used effective storytelling to show that you are pleased with their input and that you would like to get a follow-up report biannually in regard to procedures, further development.

You have put them in control of their environment and this control will provide identity and a perceived and/or actual autonomy thereby improving motivation and greater participation. Naturally, there are always some employees that can't take the initiating role. Here the supervisor leads them through the processes and includes them in evaluation or focus groups. Everyone should be kept active.

The Engineer. The engineer comes to us with a high degree of explicit knowledge and in many cases possesses the skills, ability and competence to fulfill his/her responsibilities too. His/her responsibilities, although more advanced in nature, have many similarities to the cleaners'. They both have goals, need to improve processes, controls and measures. Naturally, these measures and controls are far more advanced and even ambiguous on occasion; nevertheless, deadlines are deadlines, objectives are objectives and everyone has to report to someone. If output lags behind competition and costs more heads will roll here too. The engineer therefore creates SOPs, uses more frequent and accepted controls and measures, and although highly regulated as to process understanding he/she still has the perceived and/or actual autonomy if in control of his/her working environment. The fundamentals are therefore similar; however, interaction with external partners and stakeholders is usually prevalent.

Naturally this perceived or actual autonomy is dependant upon there being no tension or conflict in one's PMP. Figure 9.4 illustrates how tension interplays within the educational environment and in relation to and between: self-expectancy environment and external demand environment, social environment and transparent environment, self-esteem, and physiological environment. Autonomy therefore lies in the balance of these environments.

It is quite important to keep in mind that too much autonomy may cause tension and even complacency. If not managed correctly tension can emerge as a consequence of greater autonomy. In some cases, the more autonomy one achieves the more distant one becomes from core team participation and as a result the formation of boundaries to protect this autonomy also emerges. These boundaries are forms of defense mechanisms and facades and will eventually reduce the organizations ability to transfer knowledge, thereby making it vulnerable to attack from competitors.

Sustain, Generate & Innovate

Sustain, generate and innovate are very easy words to say; nevertheless, they are a lot harder to implement as this entails a community of openness, trust, knowledge capital and knowledge transference. Cross-Training's goal is to accomplish this through tacit knowledge, rotation, and by adopting some well known techniques such as SECI by Nonaka and Takeuchi (1995: 284 pages) and von Krogh, Ichijo and Nonaka (2000).

George von Krogh, Kazou Ichijo and Ikujiro Nonaka suggest that because knowledge is constantly evolving they have identified five enablers to harness this knowledge (2000:5). These five enablers are to:

1) instill a knowledge vision,
2) manage conversations,
3) mobilize knowledge activists,
4) create the right context, and
5) globalize local knowledge.

They stress "The ultimate success of knowledge creation depends on how these and other organizational members related through the different steps of the process" (von Krogh et al, 2000:5).

Nonaka and Takeuchi (1995: 61-67, 70-73, 197-198 & 230-231) suggest that knowledge is a spiraling process of interactions between explicit and tacit knowledge (Fig. 9.5.) which lead to the creation of new knowledge and that "ba" (Fig. 9.6.) facilitates the conversion of this knowledge. They go further to state that there are four categories of knowledge assets (Fig. 9.7).

As Nonaka describes in his model, cross-training also realizes the importance of knowledge assets and the importance of being able to interchangeably covert one form into the other in order to secure, question and generate ideas, new methods and innovate through participation.

Nonaka's SECI Model

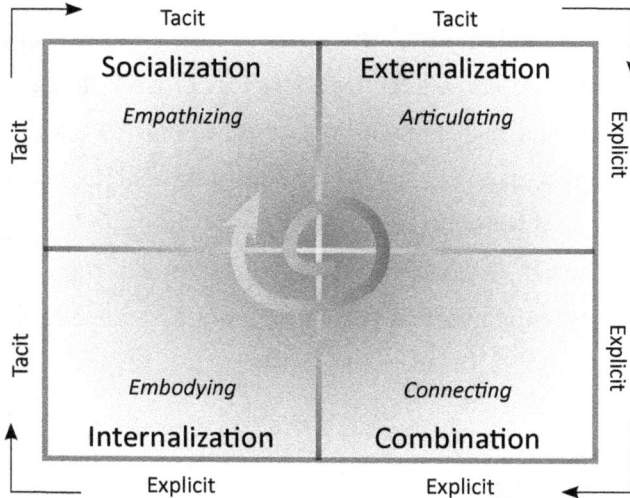

	Tacit	Tacit	
Tacit	**Socialization** *Empathizing*	**Externalization** *Articulating*	Explicit
Tacit	*Embodying* **Internalization**	*Connecting* **Combination**	Explicit
	Explicit	Explicit	

Fig. 9.5. Shows ow Nonaka and Taleuchi conceptualizes the foundation of knowledge and the interaction of explicit with tacit knowledge. **Source**: *Adapted from Nonaka and Takeuchi (1995).*

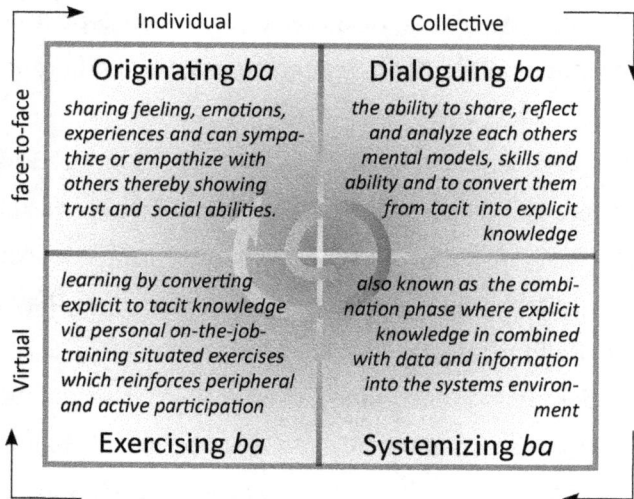

	Individual	Collective
face-to-face	**Originating** *ba* — sharing feeling, emotions, experiences and can sympathize or empathize with others thereby showing trust and social abilities.	**Dialoguing** *ba* — the ability to share, reflect and analyze each others mental models, skills and ability and to convert them from tacit into explicit knowledge
Virtual	learning by converting explicit to tacit knowledge via personal on-the-job-training situated exercises which reinforces peripheral and active participation — **Exercising** *ba*	also known as the combination phase where explicit knowledge in combined with data and information into the systems environment — **Systemizing** *ba*

Fig. 9.6. Ba is CONTEXT which encompasses meaning (originating, dialoguing, systemizing and exercising) and is considered a shared space which acts as the foundation of knowledge. In Cross-training we call this understanding process. **Source**: *Adapted from Nonaka and Takeuchi (1995).*

Four Categories of Knowledge Assets
(Nonaka & Taleuchi)

Experiential Knowledge Assets *Tacit knowledge* - Common skills and intuition or know-how of individuals (being able to read someone) - Openness, trust, care and love - Energy, passion and tension	**Conceptual Knowledge Assets** *Explicit Knowledge* - Articulated through language, symbols and images and can be seen as: - Product concepts - Designs - Forms
Routine Knowledge Assets *Embedded or engrained tacit knowledge* - Knowledge of daily tasks or operations - Organizational SOPs or routines - Organizational Culture	**Systemic Knowledge Assets** *Explicit codified knowledge* - Specifications, manuals and documents - Databases - Patents, licenses and certifications

Fig. 9.7.Shows a variety of knowledge assets that you could expect to find within your organization. **Source**: *Adapted from Nonaka and Takeuchi (1995).*

I hope that this chapter has started to put the preceding chapters into context and the correlations between management, leadership, motivation, health, behavior, the macro- and micro-environments, workflow, and process interconnect and one large puzzle.

Section three, a short section, which includes chapters 10 to 13, covers aspects related to the implementation and change process and how to constructively look at synergy, teamwork, a social culture, flexibility and other practical issues relating to the negotiation of participation, comfort zones and more.

Section 3

Management by Cross-Training

Change Implementation

In order to implement any systematic change in routines or process one needs to understand the nature of change. This section covers change in a number of forms from the individual to corporate. It also addresses organizational culture and strategies associated with change process in relation to *Perpetual Motivation Positioning* (PMP), intent and the environment. For clarity purposes, this chapter draws from two case studies illustrated in the appendix section at the back of the book.

Chapter ten *The Politics of Change* looks at change and the politics of change in relation to the individual. Addressing change in its various forms from comfort zones to resistance, communication, and vision.

Chapter eleven *Strategy & Structural Change Decisions* focuses on strategy and structural change decisions in relation to the synergy of people, objectives and production (SOPOP) and analyzed or framed by workflow, process, participation, rotation and boundaries and other action-based methods.

Chapter twelve *An Organizational Culture* addresses organizational culture, identity and vision framed by the change process and supported through management of the organism (monitoring pulse, temperature and flexibility signals) and union partnership.

chapter *10* *The Politics of Change*

The Individual and the Nature of Change

In order to adequately address the highly complex question about the nature of change, we will have to draw upon a number of issues already discussed within this book and to create some additional facets through correlations thereto. Greater understanding of PMP, Competence, Subjectification, Learning, Identity, Reification, Vision and Negotiation will help to clarify the nature and tension found within the individual when facing change.

One important aspect to reflect on is the saying "it is what it is." A good friend of mine in Oregon, Dr. Don Olson, renowned and now retired neurological surgeon, used this saying often. I asked him about his frequent use of the saying and he replied with a smile on his face, "it is what it is." How profound, I thought. If everyone could have such ease in accepting uncontrolled situations, processes or tasks for what they really are, and if one could focus on applying one's best judgment in regard to the job-at-hand, life would be so much easier. For that reason, I initiated the four dimension rule in Cross-Training. The four dimension rule states that there are four dimensions to every task, process, and thing and they are:

1) the way you see it,
2) the way I see it,
3) the way others see it, and
4) it is what it is.

Naturally, leadership in Cross-Training is about understanding vision, the fluidity of the workflow and process and questioning what, where, why and how specific tasks are to be done through continual process reviews, work improvement groups and establishing new visions with purpose and striving towards achieving "it is what it is." What does *it is what it is* have to do with change and the individual? Well, it's about one's comfort zone and the willingness to leave situationally framed areas where one is in control, even if only for a short time. Changing boundaries and the frame of one's environment directly affects one's identity, knowledge, ability and skills in relation to one's competence (perceived or real) and consequently the variables or demands (internal and external) placed upon the individual.

Unfortunately, explaining this phenomenon is not as simple as one might anticipate. In my opinion, the human mind is in a constant state of Yin and Yang or tension between participation and reification, which is further confronted by one's PMP, identity and vision. Furthermore, individuals are bombarded with changing variables on a day-to-day basis. Whether these variables are framed by a situation which is objective or subjective, perceived, abstract or it is what it is, is irrelevant, as it is this tension of multiple dualities that permits the extent of participation in the change process. In his book Communities of Practice, Etienne Wenger (1998: 63) introduced the duality of meaning and suggested that participation and reification cannot be considered in isolation as they come in a pair. I agree with his hypothesis and argument that this duality is fundamental in the constitution of communities of practice (1998: 65). However, I would suggest that this duality is not just horizontal in nature but represents various layers which affect Yin and Yang negotiation.

Adapted from Wenger's duality of participation and reification (1998:63) figure 10.1 shows the inherent tension present in the negotiation between participation and reification. This negotiation is an ongoing battle between the conscious and semiconscious and directly affects the level and extent of use of one's defense mechanisms, thereby also the individual's willingness to leave his/her comfort zone.

Regrettably, it is not as simple as that. Individual PMP status will directly affect one's stress levels, use of defense mechanisms, creativity, and willingness

The Yin & Yang of Participation and Reification

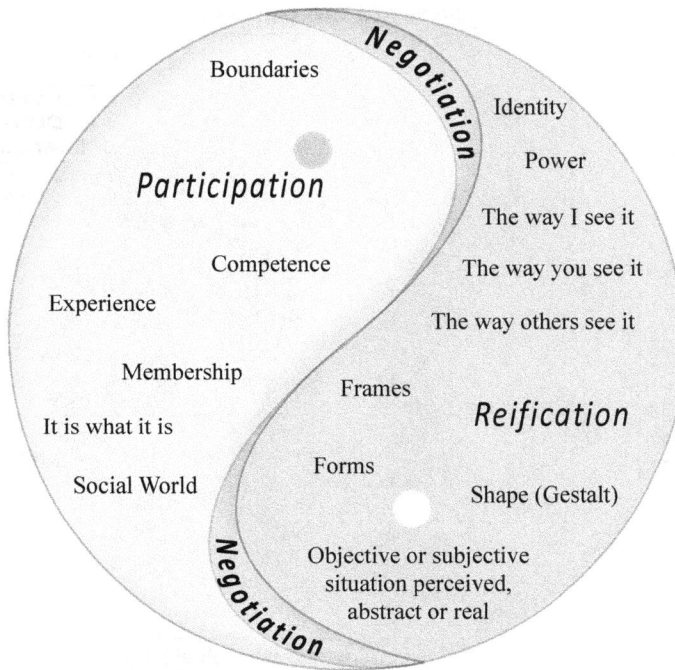

Fig. 10.1. The Yin & Yang of Participation is an ongoing conflict or negotiation between the conscious and semi-conscious in relation to reality as interpreted or perceived by the individual in relation to his/her situational environment. This environment can be framed by forms and identify, membership, competence, boundaries and 'it is what it is'.

to venture outside of one's comfort zone. In figure 10.2, I have placed the PMP sociogram as an overriding dimension which supersedes the Yin and Yang of participation and reification. As you may recollect from the earlier chapters, I discussed the tensions between the seven elements of PMP. These seven factors are interrelated and directly affect the Yin & Yang of participation and reification. Inequities within the interrelatedness cause conflict and tension leading to the adoption of defense mechanisms in forms such as attitude change, resistance and within the individual. PMP Yin/Yang is therefore fundamental prior to change if that change is to be effective and long-lasting.

The Yin & Yang of PMP, Participation and Reification

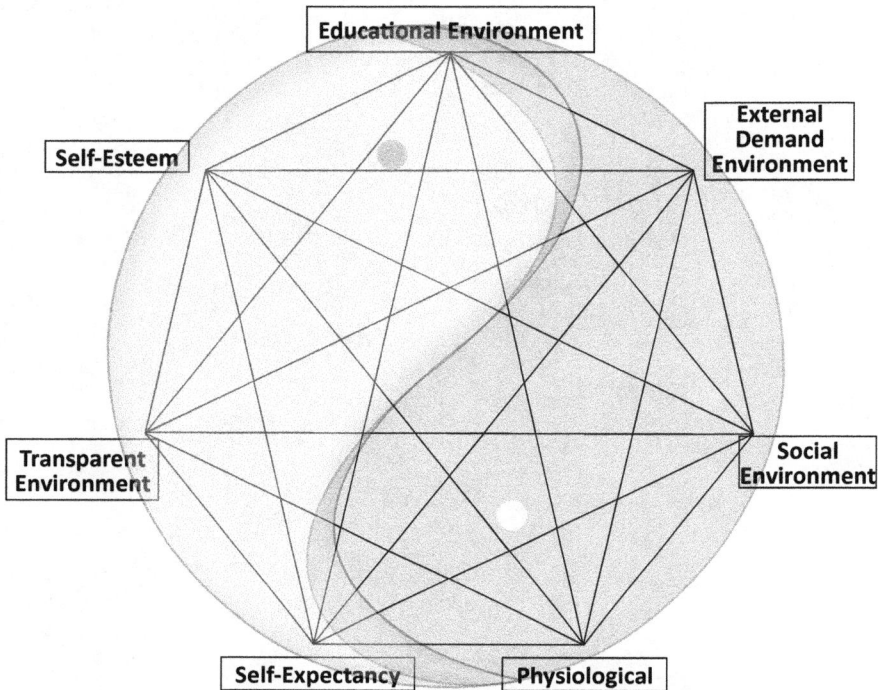

Fig. 10.2. The Yin & Yang of PMP, Participation and Reification is always in motion and ongoing. This conflict or the negotiation between the conscious and semi-conscious is the reality as interpreted or perceived by the individual in relation to his/her situational environment and their PMP and will determine the outcome and sustainability of the change process.

The Yin and Yang of PMP interrelated dependencies are:

Educational Environment is the knowledge, skills and ability (competence) to meet the external demand environment and is conducive to transparency, participation and belongingness. Too little education affects one's self-esteem, transparent environment, inability to meet self-expectancies and

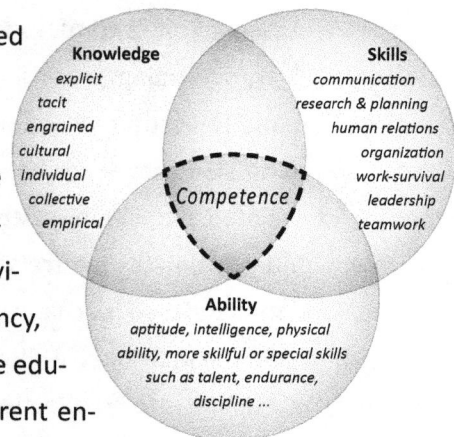

external demands and can affect one's willingness to socially interact. If unresolved this will cause psychological stress and affect trust. Too much education can also cause a conflict if the external demands do not meet the educational and self-expectancy. The Yin is one's competency and the Yang is the reification of one's competency within the perceived or real environment.

External Demand Environment includes all the demands from the environment, process, workflow, associates, boss, family and the situation, the Yin, and the Yang, is the perceived reality of these demands plus the control of these demands within the environment.

Social Environment is the belongingness to the social environment, team, family and the ability to identify the Yin and the Yang how one perceives the willingness of others to accept oneself within said situation.

Physiological Environment is the ergonomically stable situational environment which is a safe (physical and psychological) working environment that also supports adequate stimulation through assignments and rotation from positions inflicting musculoskeletal and psychological injuries from monotonous to repetitive tasks the Yin. The Yang consists of the belief, perceived and/or real that the physiological environment is either under or over stimulating, thereby affecting 'it is what it is'.

Self-Expectancy is the individual's personal goals, the ability to achieve them, and is the Yin. The Yang is the perception of one's ability to achieve said goals. It is important to remember that individuals sometimes over or even under estimate their capability/ies too. As a result, this over- or under-estimation can cause a loss of control (either too much control or too little control).

Transparent Environment is about openness, trust, mutually beneficial situations, and is the Yin. The Yang is the perception of this openness and if 'it is what it is,' is really 'it is what it is' and the interpretation to whether or not defense mechanisms are needed to protect one's domain.

Self-Esteem is about feeling comfortable or competitive about one's self-image and competence (Knowledge, Skills and Ability) within a scenario or situation and is the Yin. The Yang is the perception of this position within a scenario or situation and whether that 'it is what it is' or not.

Individual participation in change is therefore dependant upon the negotiation of reification in relation to an individual's PMP and the situational context. The further the change goal from an individual's comfort zone the greater the tension will be on the individual's PMP. Cross-Training is about widening the operating scope of the comfort zone by introducing continual development programs to enhance understanding of the operating or situational environment facing the individual. However, by pushing this envelope the leader or manager can achieve various IDP (Innovation Development Process) components.

The Comfort Zone

Comfort zone, boundary, and my bubble are all metaphors used to delineate the scope, distance, or area where one feels most comfortable, capable, and/or in control. Leaving one's area or comfort zone requires a lot of mental deliberation and negotiation on an individual basis. An individual's self-awareness of his/her PMP status and self image all play an important part in individual willingness to extend boundaries or comfort zones. Figure 10.3 shows the extent of the internal negotiation that individuals have to go through. Each new demand (perceived or real) will create a new set of PMP conditions.

Knowing oneself, one's PMP, self-image, identity and subjectification are all mental conditioning mechanisms contributing to the creation of mental boundaries, comfort zones and in some cases behavioral patterns. The boundaries create a sense of security, perceived and/or real, by providing physiological and operational control within said comfort zones.

Therefore the four dimension rule also works as a tool in counseling and analyzing one's self-image. It is also very helpful and could assist the individual and leader in understanding their PMP positions by asking these four basic questions:

1) the way you see it, (How do you see your PMP image?)
2) the way I see it, (How do others see your PMP image?)

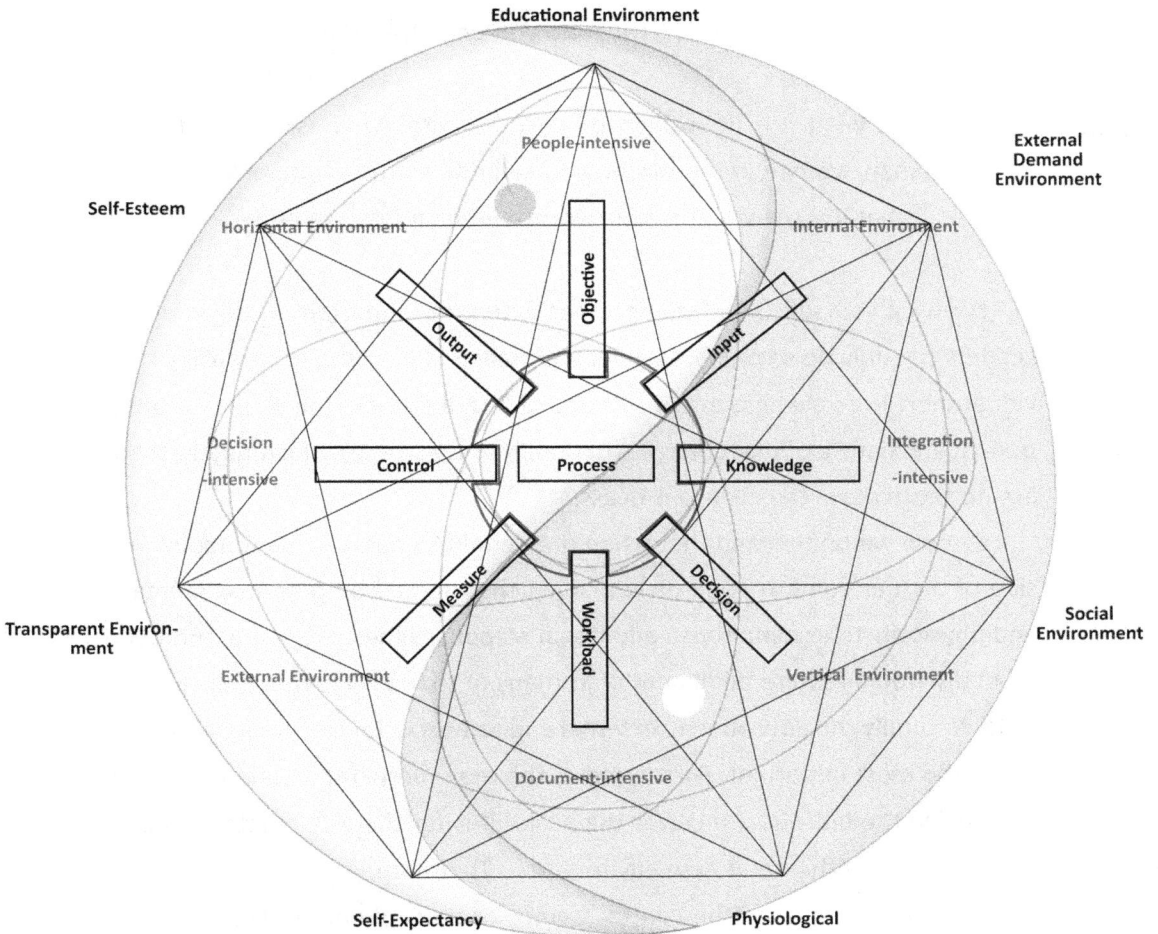

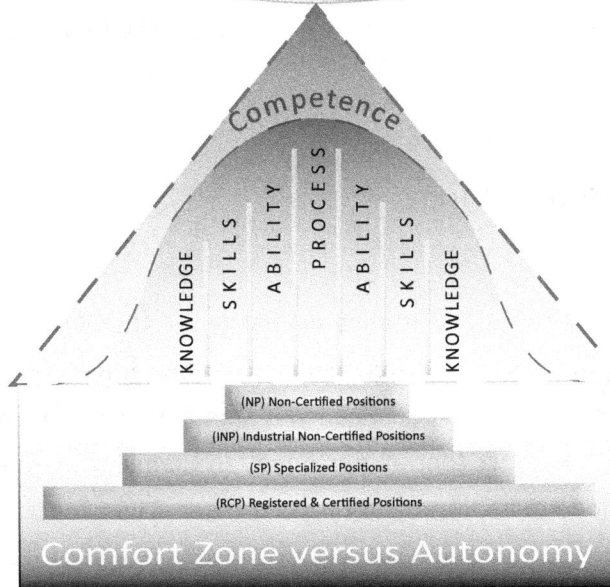

Fig. 10.3. Comfort zones are multidimensional and include the Yin & Yang of PMP, Participation and Reification is always in motion and ongoing. This conflict or the negotiation between the conscious and semi-conscious is related to reality as interpreted or perceived by the individual in relation to his/her situational environment and their PMP and determines how far the individual will extend boundaries when faced with change.

3) the way others see it, (How do you perceive others see you PMP?), and

4) it is what it is (If you looked into the mirror and asked, the man/woman in the mirror, yourself, the status of your PMP, what it is then?). The man/woman in the mirror never lies.

Knowing yourself therefore becomes extremely important in this process. Leaders can only do so much. Sustainable change must come from within. Individual short-lived changes are only fronts or façades where the actual purpose, benefit and nature of that change is not really understood. Unfortunately, there are no shortcuts in the change process.

By now we understand that when one requires an individual to move outside of his/her comfort zone or boundary, they should be prepared mentally and physically to assume those additional responsibilities. Preparing someone mentally would require fulfillment of as many of their PMP parameters as possible. Naturally the educational, external and self-expectancy environments are by far the most important. Furthermore, the more preparation and peripheral knowledge the individual receives the easier it is for them to create an image of themselves within their new environment. Therefore, preparing adequately will assist in transferring the control frames of perception, predictability and trust. Both predictability and trust are important facilitators to ease through the minefield of change.

Resistance to Change

The mechanisms causing resistance to change are therefore more clearly understood when considering the elements of the bigger picture.

While doing my military service I was stationed overseas for a three year tour of duty. I recollect that all personnel and families were required to go through an indoctrination program upon arriving. This program was designed to prepare us to adapt, live and work in a foreign country. It included programs and lectures in the differences in communication style, culture, work, leadership, environmental factors, etc... Years later, I can still remember the story about individual 'bubbles'. This centered on individuals having a bubble covering their entire bodies. The distance between one's skin and the bubble would vary, expand or decrease, depending upon the environment, situation and to whom one was talking. In this particular country, bubbles were very close to the skin and therefore we were taught to understand that this was their custom and not an encroachment into our space. Naturally this encroachment into our bubble could cause us to resist by increasing the size of our own bubbles.

Individual resistance to change has a lot to do with the bubbles. Our individual bubbles or boundaries are multi-dimensional and complex in nature as they adjust to the pressures of the changing environment. These bubbles/boundaries change throughout one's life span and they include:

1) Individual PMP bubble (Education, External Demands, Social, Physiological, Self-Expectancy, Transparent and Self-Esteem)
2) Identity bubble (Subjectification and Self-Image)
3) Yin and Yang bubble (participation and reification)
4) Situational bubble

The ***Individual PMP bubble*** is our controlling mechanism responsible for adjusting both the distance and impermeability of the bubble's/boundary's wall. Any perceived strengths or weaknesses within one's PMP will affect negotiation and resistance.

The ***identity bubble*** engulfs subjectification and self-image in regard to oneself within any particular situation. Subjectification (Foucault, 1976) is connects oneself to a particular model of self-knowledge. This could be your competitive advantage, specific knowledge, a unique skill or ability. The individual sees himself/herself as a distinct kind of subject with a clear-cut self-definition and/or image. Ambiguity of self-awareness is thereby framed by this subjective definition.

The ***Yin and Yang bubble*** is an individual's negotiation measured in resistance and/or the level and willingness to participate or to venture outside of one's own bubble/boundary in an effort to participate.

The ***situational bubble*** is just that. It is the situation in which the individual finds himself/herself. The situational environment will affect an individual's PMP, Identity and Participation and whether or not resistance to change in one's bubble will be tolerated.

Lack of trust and predictability within the environment fosters a number of forms of resistance. Adapted from Flemming and Spicer (2003; 10; 157-179) these resistance forms include:

1. collective resistance, which can progress from the individual to the umbrella of the union;
2. sabotage, in the form of physical destruction of equipment, computer viruses, etc.;
3. careful carelessness; making silly mistakes or forgetting to meet deadlines;
4. hidden transcripts, creating a 'smoke-screen;'
5. subjective resistance, a perceptive feeling of loss of control projected into a resistance of cultural control and loss of individual identity;
6. cynicism, using words and comments to show mistrust or disagreement with an individual view;
7. skepticism, always procrastinating through non-proactive means;
8. humor, used in a cynical way;
9. alternative interpretative repertoires, by interpreting messages and directives logically but incorrectly; and
10. tactics of transgression, the individual will transgress or withdraw in efforts to thwart the cultural colonization of his/her identities.

Resistance is as much about the change process as change itself and the context of how change is communicated is also important. The role of a change agent therefore requires a number of management disciplines. One is mastering the transition of change by minimizing the effects of resistance towards the process of change and is more clearly about the ability to create un-threatening short-term goals and vision in line with individual abilities, and towards established milestones. Company core values and tradition of communication, guidance, coordination, teamwork and belongingness (all PMP parameters) and the style of leadership are therefore critical in order to prevent or minimize resistance and to enable success of any change process.

Learning, Communicating Core Values, and Vision

"All that we are is a result of what we have thought." Buddha (563B.C. – 483B.C.) As you have noticed by now, politics surrounding change are vast and complex.

Naturally, change is also about learning and advancing one's understanding and competence within one's working environment. Cross-Training helps to create a systematic approach to leadership, adaptable learning, flexibility, crossing boundaries and Innovative Development Process. Therefore, knowledge transfer and knowledge transformation or attainment of knowledge, skills, ability, and competence (KASC) is an integral facet within this process. Chapter nine discussed knowledge in some detail; however, it did not address three distinct types of knowledge: data, meaning and practice (Fig. 10.4).
Cross-Training takes all of these aspects into consideration by combining them into practical landscape, workflow, process and leadership applications. According to JC Spender (2008), data, meaning and practice are explained as:

- data collection, distribution, warehousing, optimization
- data mining (analyzing data and extracting various perspectives, knowledge discovery and inductive learning)

Type of Knowledge	Focus	Learning Mode
data	*objective*	*accrual*
meaning	*subjective*	*holistic*
practice	*embodies*	*situated*

Fig: 10.4. Used with permission from JC Spender, guest lecturer at the University of Lund. The illustration shows knowledge type, focus and learning mode for the three types of knowledge. Cross-training combines all three modes.

- data infrastructure

- oversight, accountability, security

* meaning management, corporate communications

* leadership

* identity

* values, held in place

- best practices

- intellectual capital management

- human capital management

The act of getting someone to actually participate in both the learning and teaching process requires some effort. Individuals are not just willing participants to changing their comfort zones without due negotiation. Framing language and vision to communicate learnable and achievable goals are therefore vital steps in the change process. Communicating these images well will vastly improve your success rate. By well, I mean that the image/message needs to be understood and transformable into an identifiable vision for each person receiving said message. According to Fairhurst and Sarr (1996) there are three elements in Framing:

    1) Language

2) Thought

3) Forethought

Unlike traditional rational thinking the communicator frames vision and achievable goals through one or more of the following techniques by using:

1) Metaphor/s which give new meaning to an idea or to a program by comparing it to something else,

2) Stories/Narratives which aid in building identifying images of myths and legends or by telling an anecdote in a memorable or vivid way,

3) Tradition/s core values, rituals and showing this value at different milestones to confirm these organizational values,

4) Slogans and jargon within the organization to achieve or describe a subjective thing or process in a familiar fashion.

5) Contrasting perspectives to show what it is not,

6) Illustrations/diagrams showing process and or workflow, and others.

How Vision and Core values Change the Outcome

Let's start by considering vision. It is commonly known that sports coaches use vision and images to train their athletes. High jump for instance is a good example. You'll see the jumper internalizing and practicing the run-line, steps, and actual jump process of his/her jump prior to attempting it. If unsuccessful he/she adjusts or ratifies his/her vision until he achieves his/her goal. The same goes for sprinters and even rugby players within a team sport. You visualize your participation prior to the game and even during the game. Your game plan, plays and moves are played out in your head prior to implementation. This process creates a comfort zone giving the participant a feeling of control over his environment. I would argue that, as an organization is comprised of individuals and individuals have goals and visions, by adjusting or changing this vision it will produce results.

The internal organizational environment consist of three main factors: "1) the guiding beliefs and principles of the organization, 2) the enduring organization purpose that grows out of these beliefs; and 3) a catalyzing mission that is consistent with the organizational purpose and, at the same time, moves the organization towards the achievement of that purpose (Collins & Porras, 1989)."

In the Rexam Cross-Training project within the warehouse, the employees lacked a corporate vision and were low on motivation. Teamwork was poor and company loyalty non-existent. Instead they had their own vision entailing: "being there for their shift, doing their time and leaving" (Michelsen 2007). The lack of organizational core values and vision could have been due to the fact that the warehouse manager was not physically employed by Rexam but on contract from their distribution company to oversee and coordinate all logistical activities. Moreover, the warehouse manager had his own external vision. An action plan was created for the warehouse manager and progress is being made; however, it is extremely slow and the entire Cross-Training, action-based program is moved at a snails pace. In 2009 the two key floor supervisors will retire at 65 years of age and together with a newly employed middle manager we will try to revitalize the department with some radical structural and organizational changes, leadership and motivation programs and more practically based ideas generated from the employees on the floor.

To drawing from another example of vision at Rexam we can look at the Palletizing area. After landscape and workflow reviews our recommendation was to remove all the SuperSorter responsibilities from the area in question, as these were being grossly overlooked by the vast majority of the 37 staff. We staffed this new department with two individuals, one from the Palletizing area and one from production and created a cross-training program together with them. Their new responsibilities were to create a vision in line with the organization, restructure procedures and processes and to align working schedules to maximize effectiveness. Our changes created a positive working environment which, during this fiscal year, should save Rexam more than 20,000,000 Swedish Kronor, about 2.8 million USD. It can be construed that the success of the realignment of the SuperSorter was a combination of factors including creating a vision, empowering the employees to rethink, and to implement purpose and process, thereby creating followers who believe in the organization's mission.

Lessons learned in this department helped us immensely in redesigning our approach in regard to learning, core values and vision in Rexam's Palletizing area. The Warehouse project started on January 15th, 2007 and the Palletizing area project on January 15th, 2008. In November 2008, the Palletizing area's participation rate was over 75% of the employees within the area and has far exceeded the expected participation rate. Conversely, the warehouse participation rate was a meager 10%.

Identity

Recognizing the duality of personal identity and social identity in relation to the working environment and change is important. This is both complex and in continuous motion. Naturally, this negotiation is always dependant upon context and individual PMP. The duality of identity and participation within a Cross-Training program is quite evident in Rexam scenario above.

Figure 10.5 shows the Yin and Yang interplay between negotiation and identity (participation and power, belongingness and social status, self-image and the way others see it as well as change and learning) is important for the leader to consider as it causes tension on an individual's interpretation of his/her external demand, self-expectancy and self-esteem environments. This interplay creates individual forms and these forms lay foundations to the contextual extent of one's rigidity and malleability.

Cote and Levine (Fig. 10.6) introduced identity formation strategies in the field of social psychology which states that individuals might adapt their behavior to suit their social context. This typology of identity shows some behavioral characteristics that young adults display by grouping them into five categories: refuser, drifter, searcher, guardian and resolver. These identity categories are then defined by their psychological, personality and social symptoms. Parallels between identity, participation and change are therefore quite evident.

The Yin & Yang of Identification and Reification

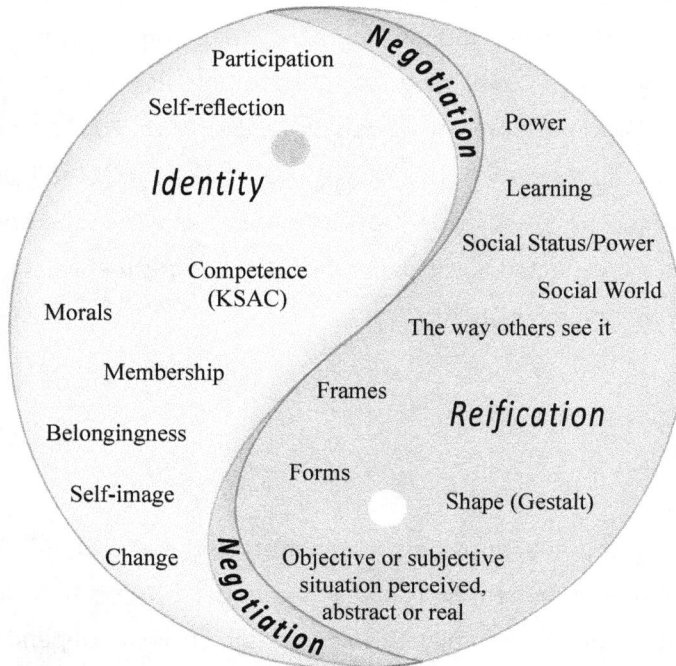

Fig: 10.5. The illustration shows the Yin & Yang negotiation of identity. Forms created by identity result in the rigidity and malleability of participation.

Naturally, the Yin & Yang negotiations and an individual's tension in relation to PMP, participation and identity will affect one's ability to step outside of one's comfort zone. Therefore, leading any change effort is not done by directive but it is done brick-by-brick through meticulous dedication. Change agents are compelled not only to understand the functional aspects of process, workflow and the demands thereto, but also the complexities surrounding sustainable change. Real change is achieved individual by individual and there is no short cut for change that is sustainable.

	Psychological symptoms	Personality symptoms	Social symptoms
Refuser	Develops cognitive blocks that prevent adoption of adult role-schemes	Engages in child-like behavior when resisting.	Shows extensive dependency upon others and no meaningful engagement with the community of adults.
Drifter	Possesses greater psychological resources than the Refuser (i.e., intelligence, charisma)	Is apathetic toward application of psychological resources	Has no meaningful engagement with or commitment to adult communities.
Searcher	Has a sense of dissatisfaction due to high personal and social expectations	Shows disdain for imperfections within the community	Interacts to some degree with role-models, but ultimately these relationships are abandoned
Guardian	Possesses clear personal values and attitudes, but also a deep fear of change	Sense of personal identity is almost exhausted by sense of social identity	Has an extremely rigid sense of social identity and strong identification with adult communities
Resolver	Consciously desires self-growth	Accepts personal skills and competencies and uses them actively	Is responsive to communities that provide opportunity for self-growth

Fig: 10.6. Adapted from Cote and Levine's strategies of identity formation in adolescents. Some of these symptoms can be evident in low educational requirement positions typically found in mass production facilities. The typology of identity shows a number of behavioral patterns one might adapt in order to suit social contexts. Strangely enough, change behavioral characteristics seen in teamwork, participation, belongingness, resistance are all evident here.

chapter 11 Strategy & Structural Change Decisions

Although both chapters ten and eleven deal with change, ten focuses more on the individual aspect of how one negotiates with change within oneself; whereas eleven deals with organizational fundamentals such as purpose, strategy, synergy, teamwork, values and policy which support continual and sustainable change. As I have mentioned before, there is no single model for change but rather interchangeable models that encompass various models or parts of models best suited to the situation. Furthermore, as situations are in motion and not static so too must solutions if they are to be sustainable.

In Cross-Training change comes in two major forms: *first-order change* and *second-order change*.

First-order change is adaptive and incremental with initiatives focusing on developing an individual's workplace knowledge (KSAC) in regard to process, tasks, routines, job description, and workflow within individual, team and department environments. The objective is to create individual participation in questioning and improving on process, tasks, routines and workflow, thereby increasing various frames of identity and individual control. This is partly accomplished through established goals created in one-to-one counseling sessions with supervisors and by forming focus groups. Naturally, updating work descriptions to include analysis of process, tasks, routines and workflow and participation in focus groups is therefore important.

Second-order change in Cross-training is more about structure, strategy and synergy of workflow from process through micro-, macro- and landscape-environments and incorporates transformational changes related to downsizing, re-engineering, restructuring and the nature of the organization.

Management by Cross-Training is about balancing management decisions and leadership styles in a congruent and flexible way by empowering subordinates to understand and develop their working environment through creativity, innovative solutions and change as part of their organizational culture, identification and, moreover, the integration of PMP as a core value. Therefore, I will start this chapter with a quick review of a number of these well-known change models used in Cross-Training coaching sessions to help individuals reinterpret and identify with their working environments. These are the:

- Ashridge Mission Model
- Star Model, Galbraith
- 7-S Model: McKinsey & Co. (Waterman, Peters and Phillips)
- Congruence Model, Nadler and Tushman
- Causal Model of organizational Performance and Change, Burke-Litwin Model
- Balanced Scoreboard, Kaplan and Norton
- Business Process Reengineering Model (BPR)
- Competing Values Framework, Quinn and Rohebaugh
- SOPOP, Michelsen
- Transformational Change Phases, Kotter

Ashridge's Mission (Campbell and Nash, 1992)

A *mission statement* or *statement of purpose* is management's way of communicating core values, a sense of identity, and corporate images both internally and externally. Unfortunately most mission statements are misinterpreted or even unknown to many employees, and as a consequence management's philosophical guidance is lost.

Ashridge Mission Model (Fig. 11.1) incorporates four aspects closely associated to a statement of purpose and serving to inspire and motivate employees and manages to increase levels performance by providing them with a sense of identity, direction, shared values and focus. They are purpose, strategy, values, and policies and behavioral standards:

The Ashridge Mission Model

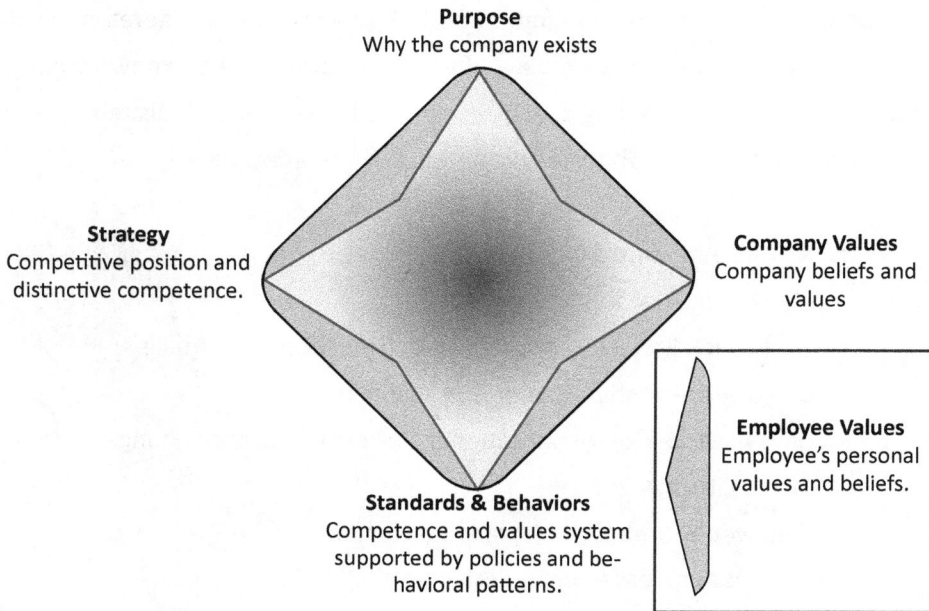

Purpose
Why the company exists

Strategy
Competitive position and
distinctive competence.

Company Values
Company beliefs and
values

Employee Values
Employee's personal
values and beliefs.

Standards & Behaviors
Competence and values system
supported by policies and behavioral patterns.

Fig. 11.1. Adapted from Campbell and Nash's (1992) interpretation of The Ashridge Mission Model. The model serves to negotiate individual alignment to the organization's statement of purpose.

1. Purpose: Benefits to shareholders, stakeholders and company ideals which serve a higher cause.
2. Strategy: The commercial reason "why are we here" behind the company.
3. Values: The beliefs and moral principles engrained in company culture and aligned with personal values which provide meaning to practices and standards in the company.
4. Policies and Behavioral Standards: Guidelines and expectations to assist all employees in deciding to participate from day-to-day.

In Cross-Training we encourage leaders and supervisors to use the statement of purpose during stage one of their individual counseling sessions. Here they discuss the employee's interpretation and perspective in relation to the macro- and micro- environments and if and how they can identify their specific duties and responsibilities to the statement of purpose.

The Star Model

Stage two incorporates adaptation's of the Star Model (Galbraith and Kates, 2002) and discusses perceptions, on both the individual and departmental level in regard to alignment and deployment of five mechanisms within this model and their company (Fig. 11.2). Here we employ another perspective incorporating strategy, structure, process and lateral capability, reward systems and people practices. Strategy is elevated to the pinnacle where alignment thereto is vital

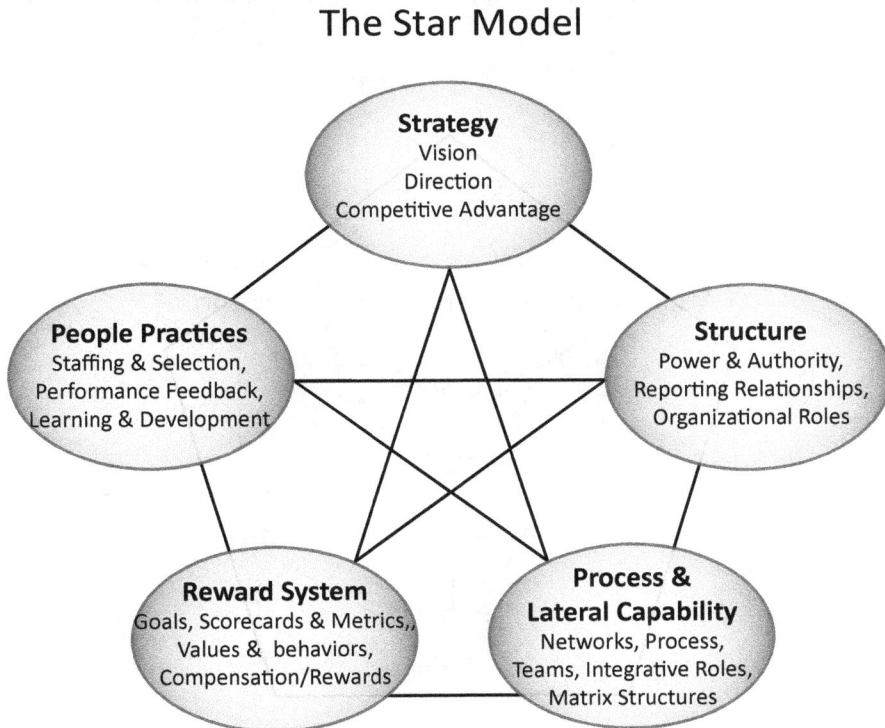

The Star Model

Strategy
Vision
Direction
Competitive Advantage

People Practices
Staffing & Selection,
Performance Feedback,
Learning & Development

Structure
Power & Authority,
Reporting Relationships,
Organizational Roles

Reward System
Goals, Scorecards & Metrics,
Values & behaviors,
Compensation/Rewards

Process &
Lateral Capability
Networks, Process,
Teams, Integrative Roles,
Matrix Structures

Fig. 11.2. The Star Model is adapted from Galbraith and Kates (2002) and serves to reinterpret on alignment with the organization. Misalignment in any of these five mechanisms will naturally be a signal that optimal performance is not being achieved.

as it incorporates vision, direction and competitive advantage. Structure is the chain of command and organizational chart, reporting and the like. Process and Lateral Capability represents activity (formal or informal) coordination through the macro- and micro-environments. Reward systems identify individual actions (output) to organizational objectives and self-expectancy (PMP). People practices include all human resource programs and activities.

The 7-S Framework Model

Like PMP and SOPOP (Synergy of People, Objectives and Production) the 7-S Framework model is based upon the postulation that organizational effectiveness comes from the interaction of multiple factors and that any sustainable change demands the inter connectedness of the various mechanisms or variables. The 7-S model was developed by McKinsey & Company consultants

The 7-S Model

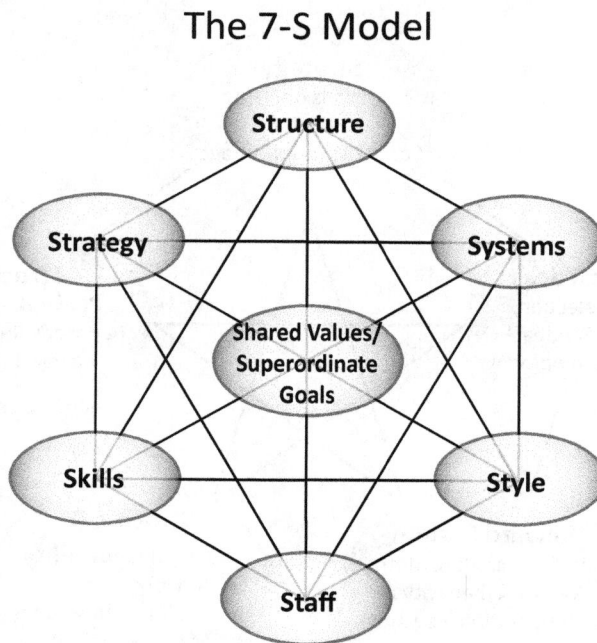

Fig. 11.3. The 7-S Model or Framework is adapted from McKinsey & Company consultants Waterman, Peters and Phillips as is used during coaching and counseling session in Cross-Training to provide additional perspectives (landscape and departmental) when evaluating one's working environment.

Waterman, Peters and Phillips (Fig. 11.3). It encompasses seven variable factors: structure, strategy, systems, style, staff, skills, and super-ordinate goals.

Structure refers to the formal organizational design (hierarchical, flat, centralized, decentralized, etc.) or synergy, and focus. *Systems* involve SOPs, processes, routines on a day-to-day basis, how things are done, within the organization. *Style* is the accepted company culture, behavior and patterns displayed by individual actions (individuals, leaders and managers) in relation to situations and conditions within one's environment. *Staff* includes the process for human resource development, numbers and types of personnel within the organization. *Skills* can be described as the crucial attributes and competencies that differentiate it from its competitors. *Strategy* refers to the direction and action the company takes in response to or in anticipation of changes to its internal or external environment. *Super-ordinate Goals* or *Shared Values* are the organization's vision, image and beliefs.

The Congruence Model

David Nadler and Michael Tushman's Congruence Model is based upon the postulation that organizational effectiveness is determined by consistency or "Congruence" in four components: task, individuals, formal organizational arrangements and the informal organization (Fig. 11.4). In Cross-training we have adapted this model to create a perspective or an image and vision of inter connectedness between task, workflow, and the organization.

Task represents specific tasks or work activities within the workflow and landscape. *Individuals* represent what an individual needs to accomplish in terms of Knowledge, Skills, Abilities and Competence (KSAC). *Formal Organizational Arrangements* considers methods, processes, structure and workflow within the macro- and micro-working environment. *Informal Organization* includes behavior, culture, values, beliefs and other implicit or tacit information gathered from the individual or collective.

The context is naturally the environment, resources and historical perspective. This environment can include historical procedures, multiple or varied tasks,

Congruence Model

Environment,
Resources & History   *Context*

Feedback   *Feedback*

Strategy

Task

Informal
Organization
Arrangements

Individual

Formal
Organization
Arrangements

Transformation
Process

Feedback   *Feedback*

Organization
Group
Individual   *Output*

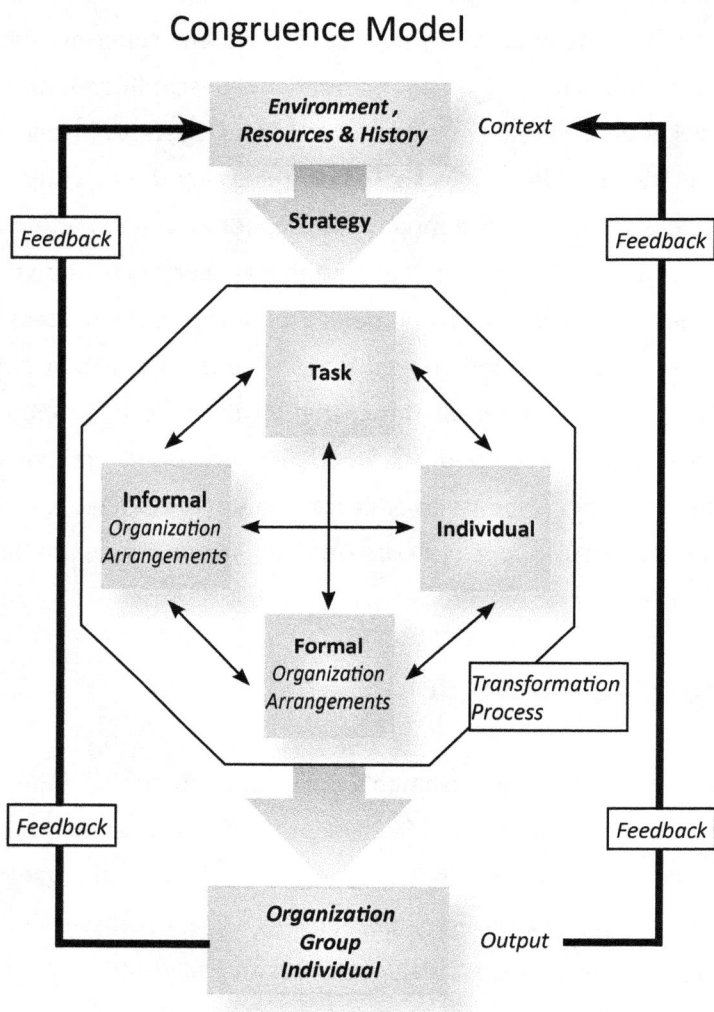

Fig. 11.4. The Congruence Model is adapted from Nadler and Tushman (1998) and used in Cross-training to identify process, task, workflow, input and output in relation to one's working environment.

process (see chapter seven) and historical implementation methods internally and crossing boundaries. This model serves to support the inter connectedness of PMP and task implementation and fits well into the thinking behind Cross-Training and SOPOP, later in this chapter. It also affords the individual another perspective of his/her adapted image in relation to his/her working environment. Cross-training is about understanding one's working environment and questioning historical, current implementation methods with the purpose of generating improvements, participation and identity whilst creating continuity in transformational change.

The Burke-Litwin Model

Warner Burke and George Litwin (1992) introduced the 12-factor model, which illustrates and differentiates between two important elements that are a major source for change. Distinguishing between **transformational** (four major change) and **transactional** (incremental change) and these authors assist lead-

The Burke-Litwin 12-Factor Model

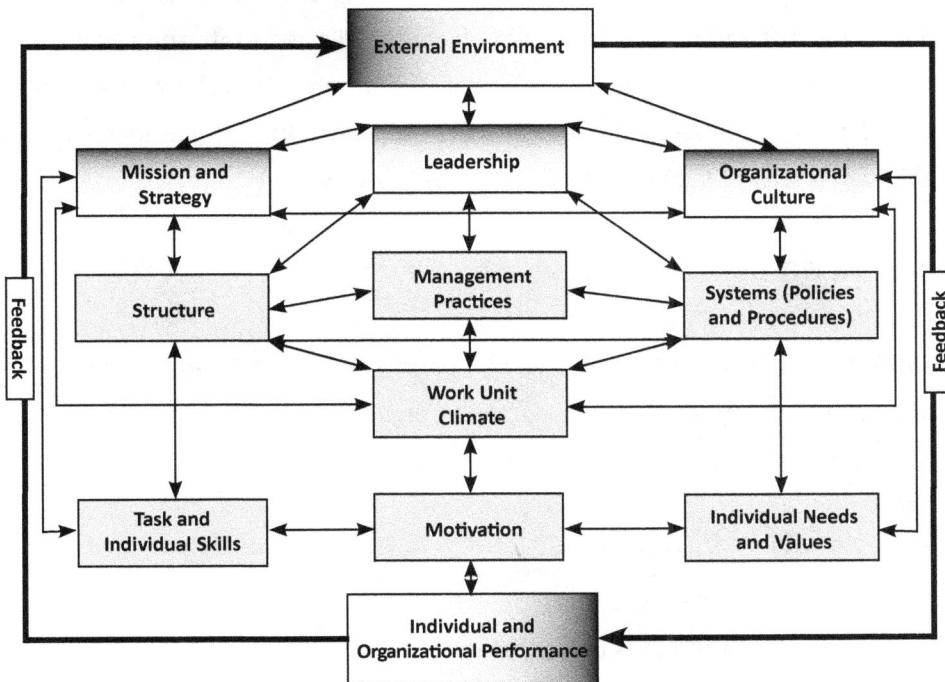

Fig. 11.5. The Burke-Litwin 12-factor Model (1992) is an illustration of the inter connectedness between elements of transformational, transactional change and PMP. Understanding and practicing these concepts will contribute to a greater employee involvement and participatory change.

ers and managers to better predict, understand, analyze and manage change (Fig. 11.5). The inter connectedness between these and the pervious models is always useful for participation negotiation and persuasion purposes.

The framework integrates a number of major change factors that influence and are influenced by the organizational climate or environment (daily, transactional level represented by the shaded boxes) and those influenced by organizational culture (fundamental, transformational level represented by the white boxes).

This model therefore illustrates a good connection between culture and working practice. The *Transformational Change* occurs in response to the External Environment (although not necessarily the catalyst or starting point) but affects the Mission and Strategy, Leadership and Organizational Culture. *Transactional Change* is governed by the inter connectedness of Structure, Management Practices, Systems (Policies and Procedures), Work Unit Climate, and Individual Needs and Values, Task and Individual Skills and Motivation. Naturally, motivation directly affects Individual and Organizational Performance. Moreover, a correlation between management and leadership competence and the ability to interpret individual PMP becomes more evident.

Balanced Scoreboard

The Balanced Scorecard Introduced by Robert Kaplan and David Norton (1996) translates Strategy into Action and enables organizations to implement a strategic vision from four perspectives instead of just a financial one (Fig. 11.6):

1. Financial perspective
2. Customer Perspective
3. Business Process Perspective
4. Learning and Growth Perspective

One could argue that the *Balanced Scorecard* is a runoff from Management by Objectives (Odiorne: 1979) as they both strive to set goals and monitor performance. Kaplan noted, "The experiences revealed that innovating CEOs used the Balanced Scorecard not only to clarify and communicate strategy, to manage strategy. In Effect, the Balanced Scorecard had evolved from an improved *measurement system* to *a core management system*" (1996: ix).

In Management by Cross-Training these perspectives (with their needs, goals and measures) are also covered during individual coaching sessions. By introducing all personnel to these methods it is easier to maintain a deeper understanding of *SOPOP* (Synergy of People, Objective and Production). The Balanced Scorecard therefore helps to support implementation of the various Cross-training programs and combines performance, accountability and customer service (someone that is dependent upon what you produce: individuals, tasks or processes; within the workflow who either precede or follow oneself). Managers and Leaders should therefore break down strategic measures to understandable levels so that employees can interpret and identify with them, making them easier to adopt.

   The Financial Perspective and financial data are always important aspects to consider; nevertheless, they should not be a dominating one. In a strategic frame the financial perspective can create stability but also instability in regard to other policies. The financial banking and automobile industry is a crisis born out of pure individualistic greed and a lack of perspective and is a good example of this. However, it should be noted that good financial prudence in use of resources (time, equipment, people, raw materials, etc...) is extremely important in optimizing any given situation and should always be a perspective within one's image of vision. The ability for the individual employee to work with simplified financial tools such as risk analysis and cost-benefit analysis in relation to their tasks and objectives is vital and should be supported by supervisors and leaders.

   The Customer Perspective is increasing in importance and scope. This scope is not only external to the organizational environment but also internal. In Cross-Training any individual within the workflow chain, participating through support or physical action in delivery of a product or service (in part or finished), is responsible for satisfying the customer. The internal customer is someone receiving what you have produced or participated in. If your customers receive an inferior product or service, their performance criteria, product and service will also be affected. If your end customer receives a product inferior to what he/she ordered then you could either lose that customer to a competitor and/ or the product would have to be replaced, which naturally has a cost. Poor performance in this perspective is therefore a key indicator of future decline.

The Balance Scoreboard: Measure Drive & Performance

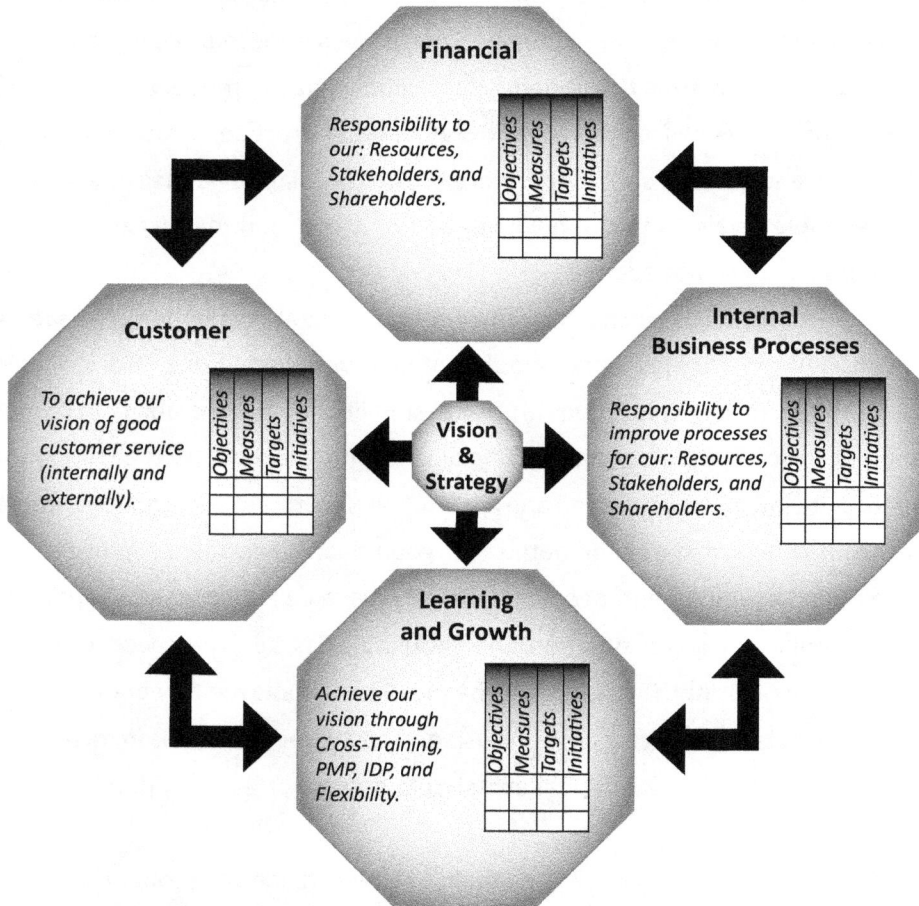

Financial

Responsibility to our: Resources, Stakeholders, and Shareholders.

Objectives | Measures | Targets | Initiatives

Customer

To achieve our vision of good customer service (internally and externally).

Objectives | Measures | Targets | Initiatives

Vision & Strategy

Internal Business Processes

Responsibility to improve processes for our: Resources, Stakeholders, and Shareholders.

Objectives | Measures | Targets | Initiatives

Learning and Growth

Achieve our vision through Cross-Training, PMP, IDP, and Flexibility.

Objectives | Measures | Targets | Initiatives

Fig. 11.6. Adapted from Kaplan and Norton's the Balanced Scoreboard: Measure that Drive Performance (1996), this illustration shows how the Scoreboard can be used in Cross-Training as a tool to measure, drive and communicate vision and strategy.

The Business Process Perspective refers to internal processes that affect workflow. These are tools used by managers and leaders to show how well their business is running. However, in Cross-Training employees set measurements and goals based upon the seven parameters starting with objective, input, knowledge, decision, workload, measure, control and output (Fig. 7.1). The OIK-DW-MCO process method helps to identify task/objective specifics by conforming data specific information into meaning and knowledge within the working environment. By interpreting the individual process components employees can more easily identify or participate with synergic ideas and improvements in both micro- and macro-environments. Naturally, output is in accordance with customer requirements. Leaders and supervisors are responsible for finding the best balance between demands of output and self-expectations of input for each. In the larger perspective mission-oriented processes and support processes are also taken into consideration and measured.

The Learning and Growth Perspective refers to employee training and corporate cultural attitudes in relation to individual and corporate self-improvement. By now you should realize that Cross-Training is about individuals representing a corporation's main resource. It is also about empowering the individual and corporation to develop, innovate and to grow through various tools from *management* to *leadership* and *PMP* to *IDP* and *process* via *knowledge* and *understanding of one's work environment*. This is done through leadership, coaching, PMP balance, vision & corporate culture (core values, images, goals measures, targets and initiatives) and teamwork.

Double-Loop Feedback was added to the 4 perspectives of a balanced scorecard to shield customers from unnecessary defects. Traditional quality control and zero defect measures are not always effective if, in production plants like Rexam (leading beverage can producers in the world), one cannot measure all processes within a process workflow system without proper feedbacks. Feedbacks are necessary as they provide the supervisors, leaders and managers with the data necessary to isolate problematic areas and to reassess and fix subprocesses. Cross-Training is about learning where to place these measurements by fully understanding one's working environment.

Business Process Reengineering Model (BPR)

There has been a lot of talk about BPR in recent years. Hammer and Champy (2003) describe it as "the fundamental reconsideration and the radical redesign of organizational processes, in order to achieve drastic improvement of current performance in cost." They believe that one should organize corporations as whole processes. By this they mean not in the traditional sense of production, accounting, marketing and facilities management but by the complete work-flow process instead. Davenport (1992) suggests that a five step approach to business process reengineering is most helpful, they are:

1. Develop the business vision and process objectives: vision implies specific objective as in the Balanced Scoreboard; finance, customer, process and growth. However, this can also include working patterns.

2. Identify the business process to be redesigned. There are two approaches here: The exhaustive approach which identifies the processes within an organization and then redesigns them based on priority. In Cross-training we redesign them based upon workflow and vision. The other approach is the 'high-impact' approach which redesigns process after the most important in relation to the vision.

3. Understand and measure the existing processes: creating base line measurements to repeat old mistakes and to prepare goals and vision for new innovation and to test the level of the bar. This is a good method when testing workload on the individual. The NASA workload index is a nice tool to use to get feedback from affected individuals.

4. Identify IT levers: check and become aware of al IT resources used for feedback, maintenance, measurement etc..., and

5. Design and build a new prototype for the new process: in Cross-Training we reconsider the landscape and workflow, personnel resources, workload, continuity and consistency in

the redesign together with the individuals affected in focus groups, task forces or team sessions.

It is important to remember that BPR is only part of the solution. Individual participation and an individual's understanding of his/her working environment (PMP, IDP, Process, Workflow, Landscape and Vision) are vital to any BPR success. However, there is always a Yin & Yang somewhere in the picture and most models require a balanced negotiation based upon the situational context.

Competing Values Framework

The Competing Values Framework of Cameron and Quinn (2005) propose a number of dimensions in regard to effectiveness and leadership. Multi-dimensional in use, their framework can produce images and perspectives in regard to organizational strategy, culture, gaps, leadership, individual coaching and even functions and processes. These competing values help to negotiate a good balance of adaptability and flexibility and are very useful in counseling and coaching sessions when trying to communicate an image and vision of organizational change.

Competing Values in Organizational Effectiveness (Fig. 11.7) illustrates two two-dimensional focuses of competing values. The horizontal dimension deals with the *internal* and *external* the focus on well-being and development, and the vertical dimension deals with organizational preference for structure and looks at stability in relation to *flexibility* and *control*. These two dimensions form four quadrants represented by four major management and organizational theories for both frameworks: *The Human Relations Model, The Open Systems Model, The Rational Goal Model, and The Internal Process Model.*

1. ***The Human Relations Model*** emphasizes human resources development, cohesion, personification and morale in approaching effectiveness.

Competing Values Framework: **Organizational Effectiveness**

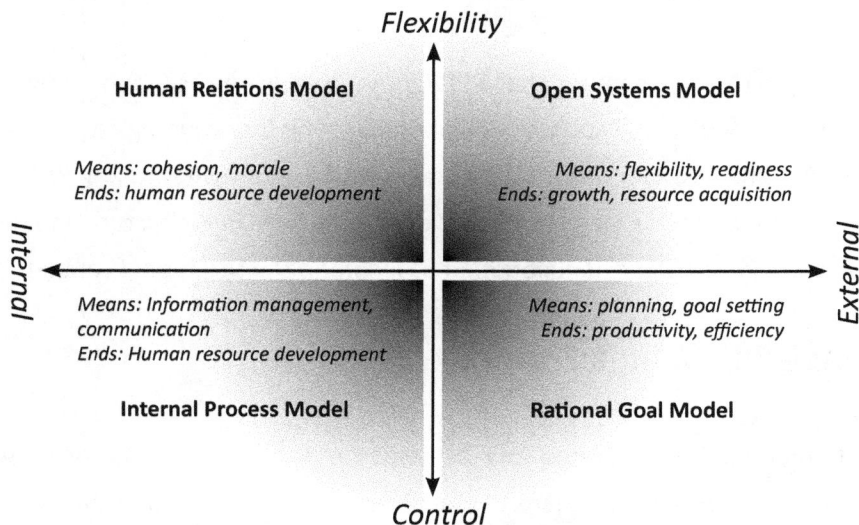

Fig. 11.7. Adapted from Cameron and Quinn's the Competing Values Framework: Organizational Effectiveness (2005) the illustration shows the tension represented in change between flexibility and control and internal and external and the relationship to various organizational theories.

2. ***The Open Systems Model*** stresses growth, readiness, re-source acquisition, external focus and support with empha-sizes on flexibility.

3. ***The Rational Goal Model*** emphasizes control with an exter-nal focus. Productivity and efficiency is key and is achieved through planning and goal setting.

4. ***The Internal Process Model*** stresses an internal focus with control with emphasis on codification, ICT, communication, stability and control.

Competing Values Framework: leadership Roles (Fig. 11.8) illustrates two, two- dimensional focuses of competing values represented in the quadrants by the four management and organizational theories above producing eight categories of leadership behavior style: *mentor, facilitator, innovator, broker, producer, director, monitor* and *coordinator* roles. Naturally, transformational change requires leaders to have an adaptable style best suited to the situational

Competing Values Framework: **Leadership Roles**

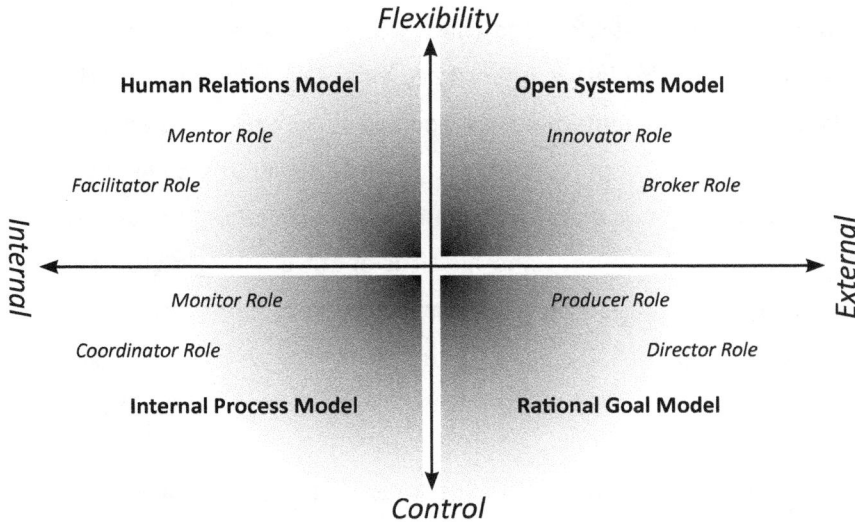

Flexibility

Human Relations Model	**Open Systems Model**
Mentor Role	*Innovator Role*
Facilitator Role	*Broker Role*

Internal ← → *External*

Monitor Role	*Producer Role*
Coordinator Role	*Director Role*
Internal Process Model	**Rational Goal Model**

Control

Fig. 11.8. Adapted from Cameron and Quinn's the Competing Values Framework: Leadership Roles (2005) the illustration shows the adaptability a leader needs in order to maximize change efforts by balancing one's role and leadership style to match the context.

context. This does not suggest inconsistency in policy but rather using leadership approaches to maximize communication, understanding and motivation related to the context.

If you recollect, in the previous chapter, I addressed individual negotiation in respect to reification, participation, identity and meaning. A leader's role is to assist the individual in this negotiation by adopting various models which best fit the context and by simultaneously balancing the competing demands and expectations.

Synergy of People, Objectives and Production (SOPOP)

In Cross-Training our change objective is SOPOP, Synergy of People, Objectives and Production. Production in this context is producing something whether a tangible product or an intangible service. This model encompasses all the applications found within this book, such as: PMP, KSAC, Yin & Yang of Participation and Identity, Vision, Rotation, Leadership, Management Policy and Company Culture (Fig. 11.9). It is what it is! There is no simple solution to the context of multiple moving variables. The chaos theory is definitely not a solution as leaving any purpose to fate is opposite to what Cross-Training and this author stands for. If we want something, we need to make a plan and adjust that plan accordingly and on a continual basis to meet the ever changing environment. SOPOP is about preparing and empowering the individual to take control over his/her working environment and life. It is about creating a credible balance between input and output, thereby maximizing both long-term production and innovative development.

In chapter one, I discussed the seven rules of management. They were to:

1. constantly insure that the organization is *functionally and economically sound* through the effective production of goods and/or services by all ethical and sustainable means available,

2. frequently update and improve processes and operating structures within the organization through good *management practices and statistical controls,*

3. provide a *working climate that is mutually beneficial* to all stakeholders (employees, stockholders &customers) with vision and core values,

4. foster an *organizational culture with vision and dialog,* open communication channels between all stakeholders and partners (employees, union, leaders, stockholders, and customers),

5. endorse and *support a learning and flexible organization* using "Perpetual Motivation Positioning" (PMP: chapter 2) and PROCESS (chapter 7),

6. underwrite guidelines that foster the *health of the employees and good ethical behavior* in relation to one another, the company, its stockholders and customers,

SOPOP (Synergy of People, Objectives & Production)

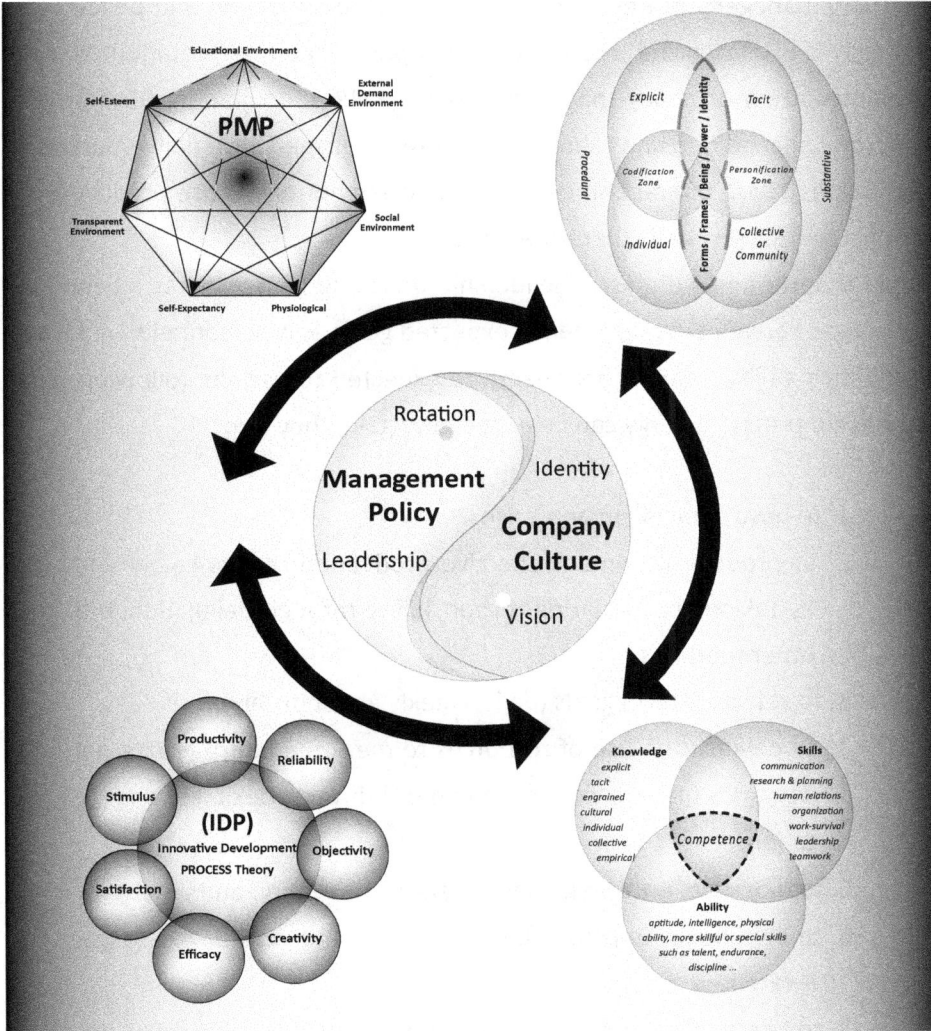

Fig. 11.9. Synergy of Objective, People, and Production is the interconnected elements of PMP, KSAC, IDP, Rotation, Management Policy, Vision, Company Culture and Leadership. There is no single approach which realizes all of this, but it is the collective actions of management and their leaders to stimulate these driving forces.

> 7. *root out departmental stagnation, greed enhances and other*
>
> *inconsistencies* in management.

Because synergy is a continually changing context, company culture needs to support this by being the glue that holds everything together. In the next chapter I will discuss the various components that make up company culture and how management needs to support this through action and policy. Paradoxically it is usually the inconsistencies in policy, the interpretation, and the implementation of policy that stifles vision, PMP and rotation. Strategy and structural change decisions should therefore be aligned with daily operational capabilities. Close interaction between management and those producing the product and/or service is therefore critical.

In chapter one, I discussed leadership traits and leadership as a pendulum in balance between management's expected goals and personnel's achievable productive ability. Leaders are therefore expected to use the following seven leadership traits if synergy can be expected. Again, they are:

1. to have a hands on approach,
2. to produce maximum effective production results safely and by taking and requiring responsibility through delegation and other methods,
3. to set short-term goals (daily, weekly and monthly),
4. to balance the use of resources to meet the internal/external demands (need based management) through flexibility and rotation,
5. to motivate, encourage participation, innovation and creativity,
6. to continually improve staff knowledge and workflow synergy, awareness, and
7. to practice open communication and reduce stresses and defense mechanisms.

Transformational Change According to Kotter

John P. Kotter (1996:1-20) discusses eight critical steps one should consider in regard to transformational change. Kotter goes further to state that almost 90% of transformational change efforts fail because they either take short cuts or 'slow the momentum and negating previous gains.' His eight steps for transforming an organization are:

1) Establish a Sense of Urgency; examine realities, crisis and opportunities,

2) Forming a Powerful Guiding Coalition; power to change, lead and motivate,

3) Creating a Vision; a vision which directs the change effort and strategies that support it,

4) Communicating a Vision; using all vehicles to communicate the vision and to teach new behavior through example,

5) Empowering others to Act on the Vision; eliminating hurdles that undermine vision and encourage risk taking, non traditional ideas, activities and actions,

6) Planning for and Creating Short-Term Wins; planning and creating for visible performance improvements, and recognizing employees for their efforts,

7) Consolidating Improvements and Producing Still More Change; change systems, structures and policies that don't fit, hire promote and develop employees that can implement change,

8) Institutionalizing New Approaches; articulate the inter connectedness between behavior and success and develop the means to ensure leadership development and succession.

Strategy, Purpose of Statement, Consistency in Management and Leadership are all traits we expect within a corporation; and, PMP balance, employee development, rotation, IDP, and corporate culture are usually overlooked. However, these are all contributing factors in a Cross-Training program which can make corporations competitive in changing your landscapes.

chapter **12** *Organizational Culture and Cross-Training*

According to Edgard Schein (2004) if managers are not conscious of the embedded cultures within an organization, those cultures will end up managing them. Moreover, managing situations, change efforts, individuals and teams can be a daunting task in themselves and present even more difficulties if the leader/manager is dependant upon changing unproductive engrained cultures. Bolman and Deal (2008:435-438) suggest that "both managers and leaders require high levels of personal artistry if they are to respond to today's challenges, ambiguities, and paradoxes."

It is important to remember that implementation and transformation of already established cultures within an environment requires a sustainable hands-on-approach with good leadership principles, cultural sensitiveness and a lot of time.

The first section of this book covered topics such as leadership principles and management roles, motivation, stress, personality, behavior, behavior promotion (AIDMA), workload and others.

The second section covered systems identification and understanding your workplace in the form of ergonomics, knowledge, process, SOPs, workflow, and landscape. However, managers face a leadership paradox as they have to maintain integrity and mission without making organizations rigid and intractable.

This section (section three) deals with change negotiation, learning and participation (individual, team, union and organization) at an individual and organizational level, including culture and union participation. It focuses on understanding organizational culture, union participation and how learning, cultural visions and images are part of the framework of change and a cross-training

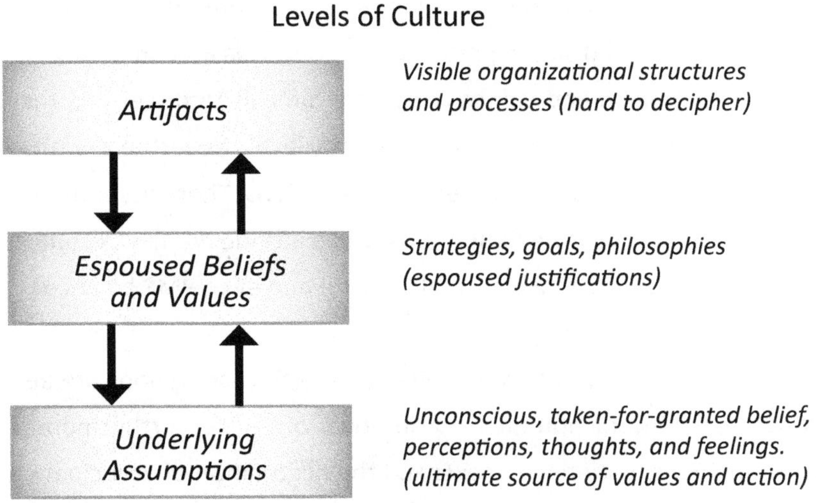
Levels of Culture
Artifacts
Visible organizational structures and processes (hard to decipher)
Espoused Beliefs and Values
Strategies, goals, philosophies (espoused justifications)
Underlying Assumptions
Unconscious, taken-for-granted belief, perceptions, thoughts, and feelings. (ultimate source of values and action)

Fig. 12.1. Reprinted with permission from Jossey-Bass (Wiley & Sons, Inc.) © E.H. Schein. Illustrates the three levels of culture.

environment. Today's working environment demands that organizational purpose needs to include ethically generated mechanisms in a mutually beneficial manner.

Edgard Schein (2004) believes that culture is one of the primary sources of resistance to change and we therefore need to understand organizational learning, development and planned change. If a leader is ignorant to the cultures embedded within the organization his/her leadership will be reduced significantly. Schein (2004:25-27) developed three levels of culture: Artifacts, Espoused Values and Basic Assumptions and Values (Fig. 12.1.) which are useful for the manager when interpreting group culture.

1. Artifacts. These are at the surface and can be easily discerned; however, hard to understand. Things like dress, structure and process.
2. Espoused Values. A level under Artifacts which include conscious strategies, goals and philosophies justifying one's actions.

3. Basic Assumptions and Values. These are the essence of culture and are represented by one's basic underlying assumptions and values which are difficult to discern as they primarily exist at the unconscious level. Nevertheless, they are very helpful in understanding actions. These assumptions are formed from dimensions which include human existence: nature, relationships, reality, truth and even PMP balance.

Naturally, learning tacit knowledge and basic assumptions are also formed through social interaction and rotation over one's life; furthermore, empirical data collected, situational contexts and the negotiation of participation, reifica-

The Yin & Yang of Learning and Identity

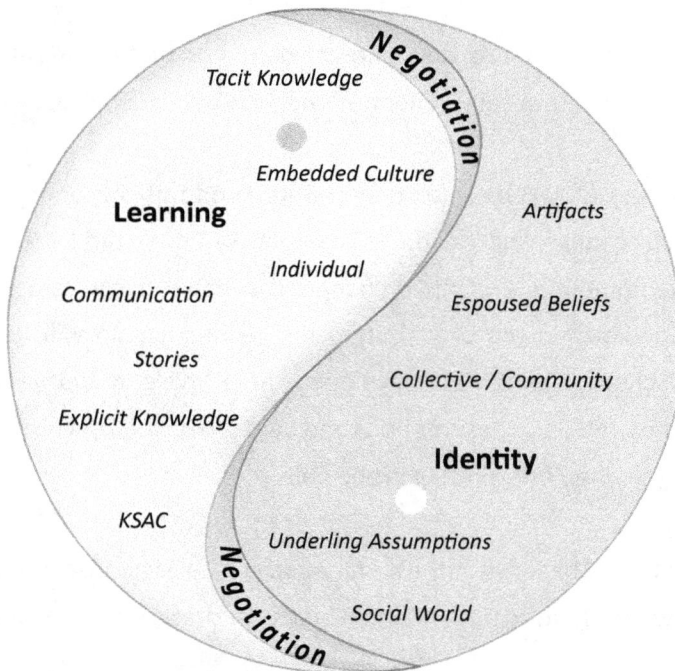

Fig. 12.2. Shows the Yin & Yang of Learning and Identity. The willingness of the individual and perceptions or assumptions that he/she has in regard to any changes in his/her identity as a result of learning are continually negotiated. Naturally, failure or the perception of failure in any context will have negative implications resulting in resistance or defense mechanisms being used.

tion and identity. The Yin & Yang complexity of learning and identity (Fig. 12.2) and 'it is what it is' helps the manager to create stories, images and scenarios to promote AIDMA (see chapter four). This also helps the manager to appreciate the conflict and tension caused during negotiation and the decisional process.

Organizational Culture, Value and Meaning

The internationalization process of negotiating individual, team and organizational culture, values and meaning is in a constant state of flux directly affecting one's identity and participation. The values are competing at all cultural levels.

> *"Briefly, a theory of social practice emphasizes the relational interdependency of agent and world, activity, meaning, cognition, learning, and knowing. It emphasizes the inherently socially negotiated character of meaning and the interested, concerned character of the thought and action of persons-in-activity. This view also claims that learning, thinking, and knowing are relations among people in activity in, with, and arising from socially and culturally structured world."* (Lave and Wenger, 1991: 50)

Therefore, understanding the negotiation of organizational culture within the individual, team and organization (separately and as a whole) will provide the leader and manager with more insight and afford him/her greater freedom to adjust the situational context, story, image, vision and/or tension to suit the required conformity.

Management by Cross-Training employs these aspects in a constellation of individual, team and organization which are negotiated through various types of learning (Fig. 12.3). Naturally for this to work the leader needs to insure that policy, vision, PMP balance, rotation, on-the-job-training, tacit, explicit and cultural learning programs support this effort.

Individual Negotiation

The individual parameters include a balanced PMP with the knowledge, skills, ability and competence to use one's identity to emerge from one's comfort zone by taking responsibility for actions, workload and control over one's changing environment. Naturally, frequent incremental small scale (one-to-one) training sessions along with rotation and action learning exercises (Revans; 1969) are instrumental in forging through boundaries and expanding one's comfort zone whilst at the same time embedding organizational meaning, values and culture as a part of daily routine.

Negotiation of Organizational Culture

Individual
- *PMP (x7)*
- *KSAC*
- *Identity*
- *Comfort Zone*
- *Responsibility*
- *Workload*
- *Control*

Learning

Negotiation

Organizational Culture, Values & Meaning

Negotiation

Learning   Negotiation   Negotiation   Learning

Team
Rotation •
Participation •
Adaptability •
Common Vision •
Belongingness •
Collectivity •
Process •

Organization
• Standard Operating Procedures • Ethics
• Behavior • Leadership • Participation
• Policy • Union • Management
• Meaning

Fig. 12.3. The illustration shows the complexity surrounding Organizational Culture, Values & Meaning. Here learning and cultural learning is continually negotiated to the situational context.

The leader applies all his learned communication and hands-on skills to ease the individual's negotiation of learning, participation, identity, and culture forward as pro-actively as possible by creating short-term goals and review of achieved milestone's. Keep in mind that individuals make up a team and teams an organization. The interaction of learning includes the key distinctions of knowledge (Fig. 12.3).

Team Negotiation

There is a duality of team negotiation which stems from tensions between a team's cultural identity and that of the individual. The team's identity can be diluted or even destabilized by the inclusion of individual's identity. Naturally, the team's cultural identity, whether proactive, reactive or complacent in nature, is therefore threatened as a result of cultural dilution caused by rotation of personnel in and out of the team. Here, the Competing Values Framework (Cameron & Quinn, 2005) also plays a role in the duality of team negotiation. However, one major goal of Cross-Training is achieving a number of IDP derivatives (objectivity, creativity, efficacy, and stimulus), and Synergy of People, Objectives and Production (SOPOP) and this cannot be achieved with changing team configurations and personnel on a continual basis.

Studies have shown that teams or groups without change tend to isolate themselves over time. Furthermore, competitive demands on their isolated teams lead to negative activities such as hindrances and other uncompetitive strategies towards other teams within the same company. Obviously competing cultures within the same team are not conducive to innovation and workflow and transparency.

Efforts need to be made to create a learning organizational culture of training, openness and rotation enabling individuals to break through boundaries and to excel in a variety of environments. These types of team environments help to engrain work values, efficacy, taking responsibility, social belonging, attitudes, and individual behavior. Rotation frames teamwork flexibility and openness by example.

Key Distinctions of Knowledge, Situational Learning Forms & Organizational Culture

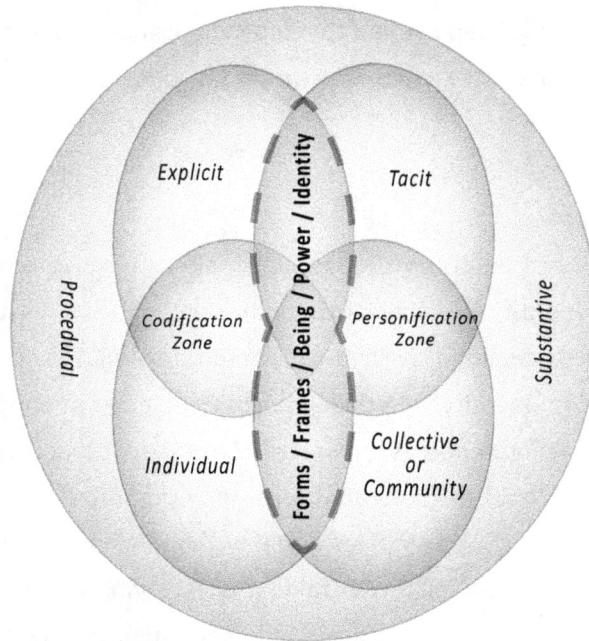

Fig. 12.4. Adapted from Allvesson's key distinctions of knowledge (Alversson, 2004: 45). Illustrates how the multi-dimensional transfer of knowledge (tacit and explicit) synergize with Organizational Culture, Values and Meaning. In Management by Cross-Training we achieve this through embedding additional duties (task forces, focus groups, individual educational matrixes, leadership and policy) into organizational culture.

The Key Distinction of Knowledge (Fig. 12.4.) illustrates the multi-dimensional transfer of knowledge from the individual to the community, and vice versa. Learning by incorporating this multi-dimensional approach in organizational culture is part and parcel what Cross-Training is about. The more time one can spend in negotiating and resolviong tensions between the individual, team and organizational policy the easier it is to embed new routines into the organizational culture. Leading individuals and teams through a mix of codification and personification duties, on an individual and team basis and in regard to assignments, workflow and process can only improve participation, identity, belongingness, and a common vision in organizational culture.

Organizational Negotiation

There is considerable negotiation at the organizational level. Here leaders, managers and unions, if they are represented, need to find the right mix of demands to be placed upon individuals and teams and to establish the type of culture to be sustained, changed or borne. Naturally, ethical standards with a mutually beneficial leadership style (managing and leading with respect, consistency, and flexibility when needed) and policy are critical if organizational culture is to benefit. Leaders and managers have to show by example what behaviors and standards are expected and that they too can participate in this program. Framing participation in the form of a hands-on-approach with good leadership principles and union representation and participation is vital to success. If leaders and managers cannot learn and rotate through their organization how can they expect individuals to do it?

Organizational negotiation is about reframing cultural artifacts (What images do the individual and teams have and who are they?); espoused beliefs (What are our goals, what is happening or about to happen? What do we value and what do we believe in?); and underlying assumptions (Are there socially significant aspects or beliefs that contradict themselves in actions or behaviors?) by implementing a long-term learning program that fosters the desired culture and create meaning. Management by Cross-Training is not a quick fix. As we have learned in the previous chapters, habit, attitude, behavior and change are engrained actions within individuals, teams and organizational cultures.

Teamwork, Belongingness & Communities of Practice

I have had the great fortune to play sports for over 26 years and the word Team or Team Building brings many vivid images and visions to memory. Culture is therefore what the individual, team, group or organization make it. One of the fundamental aspects of PMP is the Social Environment, which includes belongingness. Participation and belongingness are dualities of identity (see chapter ten). PMP asserts, what is believed in other motivational theories, that people have the need for affiliation. Therefore, if a person's belongingness and/or affiliation to a team and organizational culture are directly related to his/her identity, learning and motivation within the working environment.

Ordering or demanding specific situational output without meaning is just crazy. All participants need to believe in and identify with the program. Participating team members' should feel secure in their decision and this should be reinforced through organizational culture.

We have already established that learning is meaning and identity framed in individual development and within a community or team. This is done task-by-task and individual-by-individual. Just like the foundation of a house (built brick-by-brick), a solid organizational culture and winning team is accomplished individual-by-individual. A team is not a team if all its functions are not in sync.

Team and Communities of Practice in Cross-Training can take various forms. Sometimes they take form from type-2 transformational change efforts where the organization has had to change in order to survive. They can also be formed from existing departments where Cross-Training is being implemented, or created from individually chosen personnel to act as a flexible, multi-tasking, and roaming back-up team as found at the local hospital in Malmö.

Generally, there are nine basic steps used in team creation (Fig. 12.5.) but I am sure you will come up with a few more yourselves. As you start to create teams and cross-functional department you will learn to adjust these nine areas to best suit the demands of your environment, objectives and organizational culture.

Although communication between all the stakeholders is last in the process of team building, it is also the first, and it is the most consistent and repetitive task that you will have. Teams are about identity, communication, trust, participation, responsibility and naturally, façade-breaking instruments. Nevertheless, communicating the various steps prior to actually doing it is a good way to create an image, a vision and to get feedback. Obviously, feedback will be both positive and negative, so if you cannot handle resistance then you might as well change careers and become a dictator instead. The key to proper communica-

Selection of Participants	Create Goals and Vision	Micro-Task & KASC Matching
Trainer & Trainee Scheduling	Rotation (Individual)	Team Spirit, Vision and Social World
Support and Coaching	Use of Resources Focus Groups, etc.	Communication Feedback and Adjustment

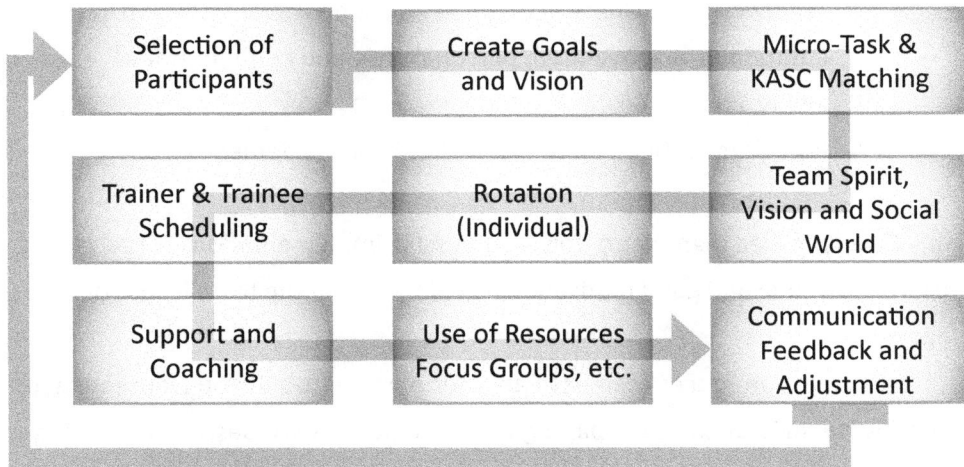

Fig. 12.5. This is the process that one follows when creating or renewing a team. This team building process can be used in both company and on the sports field. Many sports psychologists use it in their team dynamics programs. In order of progression it starts with the Selection of participants, establishing goals, and balancing micro-tasks or skills (KSAC), allocation or roles and training schedule (trainee/trainer) within the team, allocation of training rotations within the team, working personalities (working together), support for the team (coaching), effective use of resources, and communication between all stakeholders.

tion is to explain your message using images, stories, narratives and clear and concise terms in a variety of ways. If necessary you might have to adjust your goal, in the short term to appease any resistance and to harness support and trust.

Selection of participants

Selecting team members has a number of functions. Firstly, it provides the leader a tool to combat the complacency virus and problematic engrained behavior by diluting these traits. Secondly, it helps the leader to deal with personnel conflicts, between members or personality differences that cause overdue tension within the team. Four key factors in selecting your team members:

1. Job description; and educational constraints,
2. Working knowledge; their experience and problem-solving abilities (KSAC),

3. Teamwork; the ability to be open and supportive, action-ori-entation (pro-activeness), personal style and communicative ability, and

4. PMP Status; their ability to adapt to new the demands.

Clearly, other ingredients for a successful implementation will include a positive attitude and good motivational guidance from the team leader or man-ager.

The selection process can have another purpose too. If you want to create specific behavioral changes, pairing certain personality types to force change will help to breakdown group formations, whilst it forges new communication channels between other member participants. Obviously, as a department manager, this will be an additional agenda to help you to manage certain situ-ations.

Establishing goals

Creating goals in alignment with an individual's PMP Self-Expectancy levels isim-portant. One of the leadership traits mentioned earlier in the book spoke about setting achievable short-term goals (daily, weekly and monthly). Even if they are small goals, this is a vital tool in leadership, motivation, and team building. Un-derstanding the purpose and being able to identify with these goals and one's own development helps to negotiate participation; therefore, it is important that the team leader establish these goals as soon as possible. Goals or objec-tives lead to milestone's and these milestone's lead to a future of adaptability, flexibility, and a transparent environment. For the individual team members, achieving these goals can become fulfilling and motivating.

Furthermore, goals provide direction and produce a feeling of belonging-ness (achieving something together), value (accomplishment) and importance (status and identity). Unsurprisingly, the team leader needs to insure that the participants know how to accomplish their goals. You cannot just command implementation of a goal without proper instruction. Goals also provide direc-tion and without this to strive for, many members may lose motivation. Keep all your goals as simple and achievable as possible, but not too easy, otherwise they will become ridiculous. Goal setting will be beneficial to the team and will prove to be an integral part of your dynamics.

Micro-Task and KSAC Matching (Educational Environment Design)

The educational design phase focuses on the individual, type of duties to be performed (mental, physical, social, etc.), and KSAC needed for the position [Registered & Certified Positions (RCP), Specialized Positions (SP), and Industrial Non-certified Positions (INP)]. I sometimes call this the apprenticeship stage as individuals have not yet gained the necessary tacit and/or explicit knowledge from the one-to-one sessions. Training and rotation should begin with familiar working environments first and progressing onto more challenging environments/situation as time progresses. Before training outside of your initial groups, consistency in routine and knowledge is required. Members should not leave their areas of responsibility until they can display the minimum required quality assurance standards set by the department and position.

Clearly, as soon as this is achieved, personnel should be rotated and multi-tasked in other positions both laterally and vertically. Codification and QA/QC procedures should be applied as an instrument to monitor progress.

Allocation or Roles and Tutoring Schedule within the Team

Structure, structure and structure, without which, we would have the "Chaos Theory" at work in Cross-Training. It is essential that you assign roles for the trainer, trainee, and team leader with objectives, expectations, purpose, and a vision for all parties involved. As Cross-Training progresses and the participants rotate to various positions, their roles will reverse. Their role will change from being the trainer in one specific task to the trainee in another. This is achieved by assigning various tasks to each individual participant. The participant responsible for a specifically assigned task will also be responsible for training that position. Similarly, if more than one person is assigned (as in most cases), the same position, this will give them an opportunity to discuss or to design a lesson for that specific task together. Usually, one follows the workflow and all SOPs and directives connected to the specific tasks within the specified workflow.

Sometimes, employees resist and elect not to participate in the training program either, because they cannot accomplish the tasks physically or psychologically. Usually, this is due to imbalances in their PMP (self-expectancy self-esteem environments) and/or not believing in the purpose and vision. In these cases, you should design your program using the resistors to design lessons around their positions and to assign them as trainers for their specific positions. Others will rotate-in and -out for that specific training; however, the trainer will remain stationary. That is, until they see the benefits of participation, or become redundant due to a lack of teamwork and KSAC within the landscape. In most cases resistors change their opinions once the program starts and they see how other teammates are benefiting; furthermore, acting as a trainer helps to boost morale reduce resistance.

The scheduling of rotation-task educational sections is done by the team leader. Each participant should be given the opportunity to teach various tasks. Logically, the team leader will supervise and guide the participants in preparing their individual training sessions. Initially this becomes quite a task in itself, however, once completed and filed, all future training for each specific task becomes consistent. Keep in mind, the Standard Operating Procedures (SOPs) are the basis for the task education and should always be the instrument used. How the task SOP is presented or taught is, of course, up to the trainer but they have to give assurance that they have taught the specific objective and the trainee must also reassure that he/she has been taught and can fulfill the requirements of the task or position.

If there is a conflict on the SOP or the process being taught, the team leader will need to resolve it as soon as possible and see to it that the SOP is updated. If the conflict is in regard to how the result of the actual SOP task is achieved, the team leader should mediate and allow both the trainee and trainer to evaluate the pros and cons of each and to present their findings. Of course, the team leader will praise both the members for looking at the task in another light. Moreover, if an innovative solution is found for any given task, the two members should be rewarded in some way.

Scheduling should be during normal working hours and limited to three to eight hours per week. Solutions to scheduling are numerous; nevertheless, costing should always be considered. If extra personnel need to be used during a certain period, this should also be considered.

Allocation of Training Rotations within the Team

All positions rotate laterally within the team. The objective is to try to get as many of the participants trained in as many positions and tasks as possible. However, this is not always the case as some participants are more motivated than others and complete their internal team Cross-Training earlier. Once trained in at least three additional positions, for a 5 person team (two to three whole job descriptions within the same team), the team-leader selects two members to train vertically into his position. Naturally, the team-leader is the trainer. Similarly, the team leader receives lateral training with another parallel team leader where the trainer/trainee roles between the two team-leaders move back and forth (Fig. 12.6.). As a reward for completing their internal rotations, the team-leader can assign additional training outside of the team with other lateral or vertical teams. This serves many motivational purposes and is instrumental in the success of the program.

It is always important to keep in mind that Cross-Training is a multi-tasking tool, which allows for employee development and flexibility.

Working with Personalities (Working Together)

The team leader's role is of the utmost importance in Cross-Training as he/she provides the motivation and impetus to develop by balancing PMP and extending the individual's comfort zone. It is wise to remember that not all team leaders are equipped with the right skills to lead and motivate. They too should take part in a cross-training program with other leaders and supervisors. Knowledge transference occurs at all levels of the organization and is not limited to the first two levels.

It is vital to the success of any team that leaders not only understand their

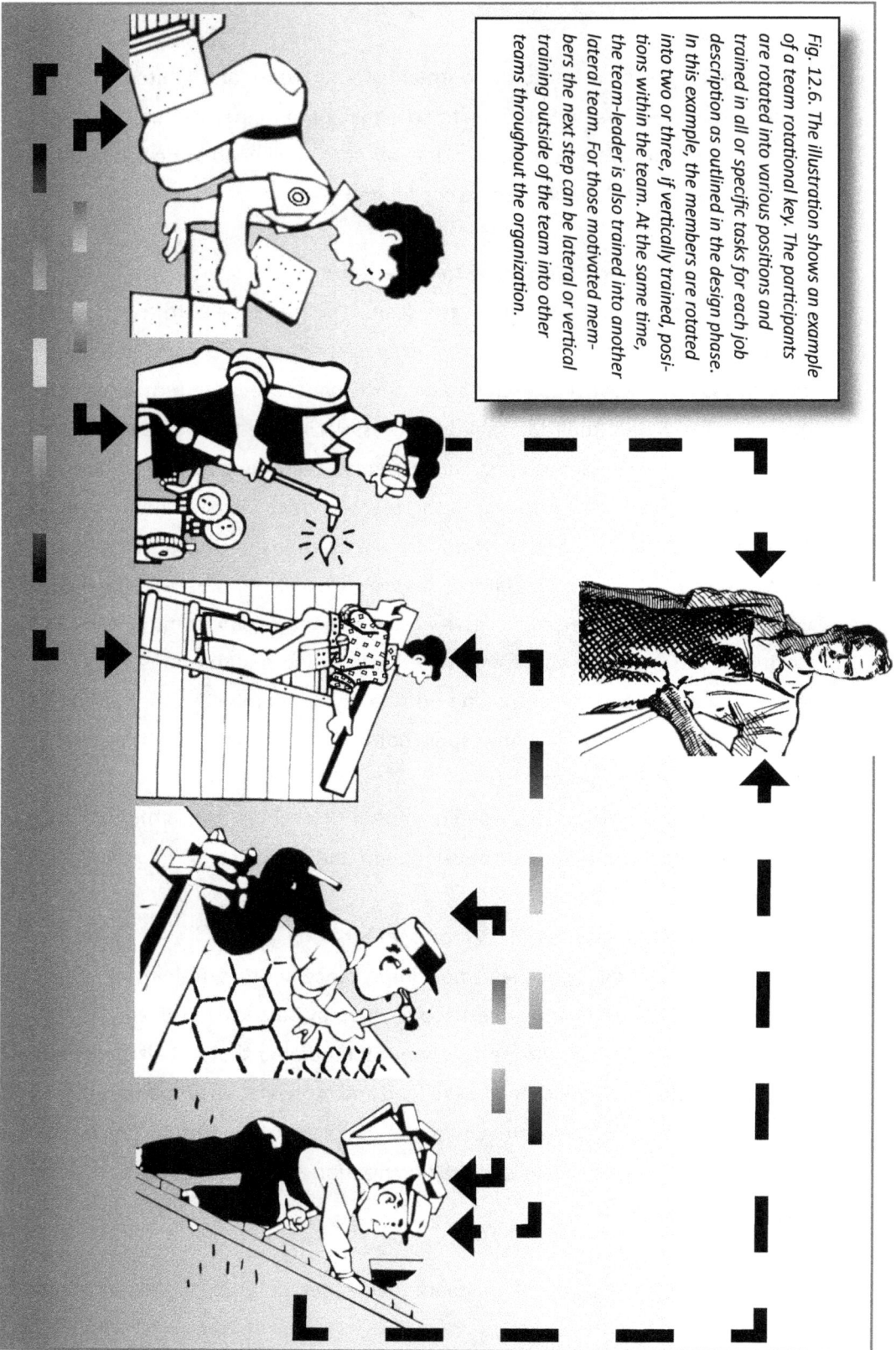

Fig. 12.6. The illustration shows an example of a team rotational key. The participants are rotated into various positions and trained in all or specific tasks for each job description as outlined in the design phase. In this example, the members are rotated into two or three, if vertically trained, positions within the team. At the same time, the team-leader is also trained into another lateral team. For those motivated members the next step can be lateral or vertical training outside of the team into other teams throughout the organization.

colleagues and know how to work together, but they should know their own PMP balances and KSAC too. Establishing goals and using communication skills to manage conflict is vital to team dynamics, participation and personalities working together (Fig. 12.7.).

Support for the Team

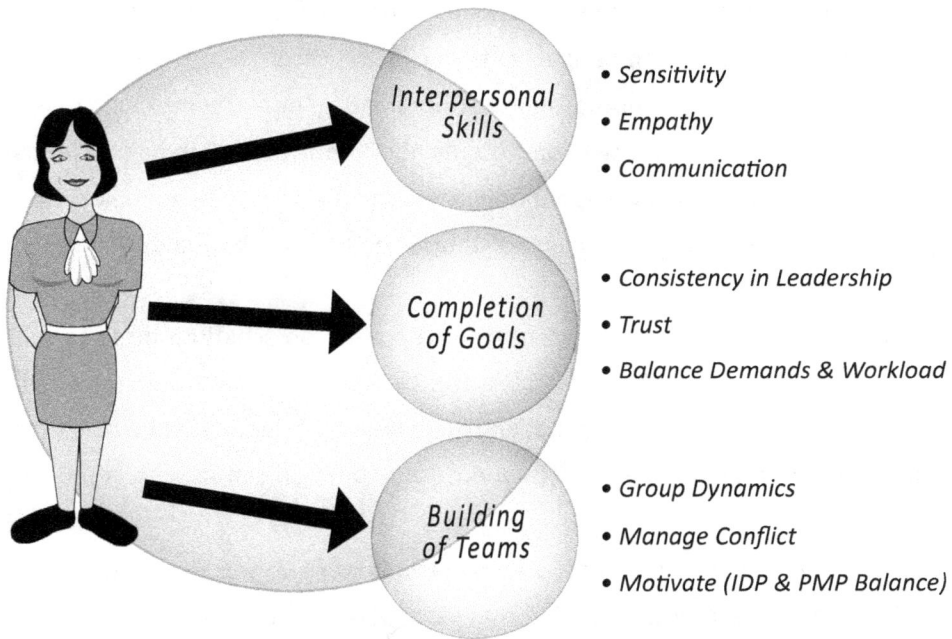

Interpersonal Skills

- *Sensitivity*
- *Empathy*
- *Communication*

Completion of Goals

- *Consistency in Leadership*
- *Trust*
- *Balance Demands & Workload*

Building of Teams

- *Group Dynamics*
- *Manage Conflict*
- *Motivate (IDP & PMP Balance)*

Fig. 12.7. Organizational culture begins with management. A sympathetic environment provides emotional support and belongingness. Good communication and interpersonal skills provides impetus for transparency and a team environment. A hands-on-approach builds trust. Goal preparation, KSAC and achievement enhance self-esteem and satisfaction. All of these characteristics assist in balancing PMP.

An important ingredient for any individual or team is the support that they receive. A supportive behavior or supportiveness is the aspiration to help others. Naturally, it would be good if all members felt the same way about helping others and the team's success. This is a message that not only needs to be communicated repetitively but all personnel behind the scenes (staff, senior management and other stakeholders) should also take an active role in supporting the teams to succeed. There are four types of support usually found in motivated teams: emotional, informational, instrumental and evaluation. If the team can support each other with these in mind, success is almost assured.

Effective use of Resources

Effectively using resources is an important function in Cross-Training. This is especially learnt when scheduling and designing the educational and rotational phases. Implementing these schedules and rotations takes some doing especially if you're on a limited budget, as is usually the case.

However, many studies indicate that workload, in non-assembly line operations during an eight-hour workday, is only about four to four and a half hours. About half of the workday is spent doing other odd jobs, coffee and tea breaks, personal errands, and other imaginative tasks that the employee can find to do instead of work.

Realistically, ninety-five percent of workplaces can schedule three to four hours a week for Cross-Training. This is the ideal situation, however, many employees will emphatically deny that any extra time exists and insist on a replacement during Cross-Training. This is where your communication skills come into play!

Remember your flow chart should include various job descriptions and critical areas where bottle-necking may occur. Designing a process with these aspects in mind will help to alleviate too many adjustments during the implementation phase.

Communication between all stakeholders

Cross-Training should be seen and communicated as a means to an end and not as the final solution. It is not a threat to the existing infrastructure but instead a synergy builder and personal competency development tool. Communicating team identity is instrumental to motivation, but keep in mind that identification with the organization is as important.

The most important contribution that the team-leader can bring to the team is to insure that all communication channels are open. There should be an atmosphere of openness enabling the team members to speak up and voice the real issues. Whether positive or negative all should be addressed. A sympathetic ear can do wonders, however it is important that the participants understand that this is a goal that needs to be achieved and that we are going to do it together. If changes are needed, then so be it. The team needs to feel comfortable, knowing that someone is listening to their viewpoints and that a resolution is in the making.

All members need to be informed about goals, plans, priorities, progress, and feedback in regard to any changes or adjustments. Furthermore good work needs to be recognized.

Union Strategy & Partnership

Everyone is talking about union strategy and how the unions can renew themselves within the new world economy. An excellent book by Dr. Tony Huzzard, et al. (2005) called Strategic Unionism and Partnership: Boxing and Dancing is an ongoing dialogue between researchers and practitioners in eight European countries. Huzzard's book addresses the metaphor and this position of a social partnership for future survival extremely well.

Most people assume that management and union are on opposite and conflicting sides and with totally different objectives. In support of Huzzard's book, I argue that management and union are on the same side, that their objectives are actually the same, and that their leadership will achieve their objective. This partnership in leadership takes the form of a social and organizational cultural partnership and is the only possible solution for synergy and long-term success. Furthermore this partnership is solidified with a Cross-Training program. To support my argument, I would like to reflect on figure 12.8. 'The Yin & Yang of Management and Union.'

The objectives for each of the parties are not different at all. It is without question that if a company cannot produce its products or services to meet the

The Yin & Yang of Management and Union

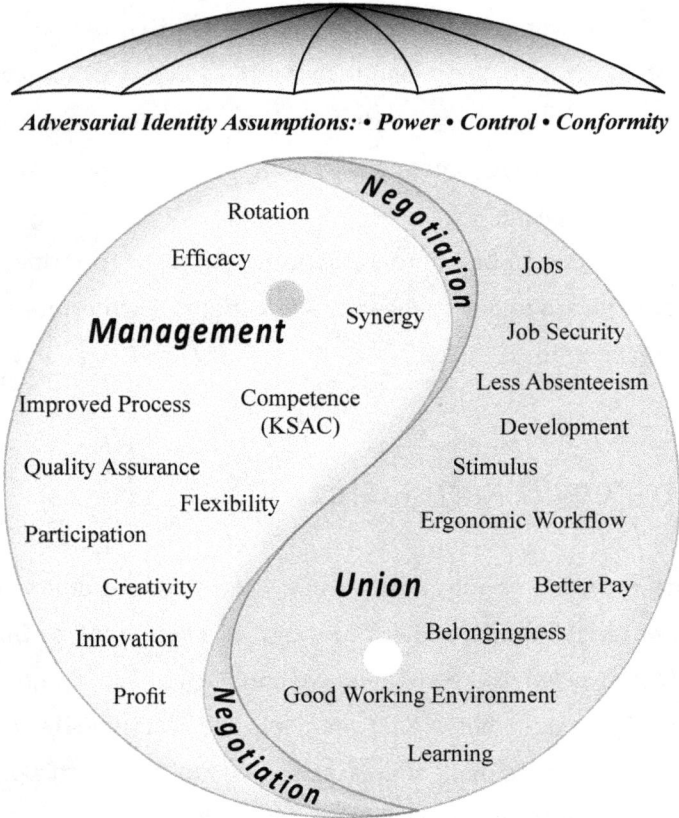

Adversarial Identity Assumptions: • Power • Control • Conformity

Rotation

Efficacy

Negotiation

Jobs

Management

Synergy

Job Security

Less Absenteeism

Improved Process

Competence
(KSAC)

Development

Quality Assurance

Stimulus

Flexibility

Ergonomic Workflow

Participation

Creativity

Union

Better Pay

Innovation

Belongingness

Profit

Negotiation

Good Working Environment

Learning

Fig. 12.8. The reification of management and union are obvious in this illustration as one sees the commonality on objectives. The fallacy that these are adversarial in nature, are only compounded by the ambiguity of commonality and the expected perceptions that each part entrenches. Here, the illustration clearly supports Huzzard's "Dancing" metaphor as the only proactive solution for all stakeholders.

needs of the customer and market (price, quality, time frame, etc.), the company will lose market share and eventually go out of business. The adversarial identity assumptions of power, control and conformity are abstractions and unrealistic perceptions or defense mechanisms used by stakeholders to justify anti-participatory decisions and/or behavior. The organization (all stakeholders: management, leaders, supervisors, and workers) and its culture need to solve these adversarial identity assumptions by realigning their objectives to their common goals. Job security and net profits are created by meeting the market forces and competition through a common organizational culture of sustained, creativity through innovation, flexibility, improved understanding of workflow process and KSAC.

Unions that have lost themselves in adversarial identity assumptions also lose sight of the overall benefits of goal commonality associated with the synergy of a partnership. I particularly found chapter two "Boxing and Dancing" (Huzzard et al, 2005) very informative as Huzzard draws correlations between union strategies used at various levels within organizations and the choices that were made within their own 'policy space,' based upon the power base of the union within the country and organization. Moreover, his research indicates that partnerships can operate at different levels of industrial relations processes and that they are sometimes connected; nevertheless, tensions 'boxing' may exist on one level whilst at the same time there is 'dancing' on another.

It is therefore the responsibility of management and union to participate in creating goal commonality through organizational culture using PMP and Cross-Training with mutual respect for individual and corporate development.

Section *4*

Economics & Star Employees

This section comprises just two chapters which deal with economic issues and V.I.P staff.

Chapter thirteen *The Economics of Cross-Training* focuses mainly on economic issues concerned with cost and benefit analysis. What factors and methods one might consider to use to monitor progress and to justify expenditures.

Chapter fourteen *Cross-Training Corporate Stars* concentrates on individual V.I.P.s or 'STAR' employees. Whether key personnel should be handled differently? The consequences surrounding rotation, participation, knowledge, and Cross-Training program within their domains.

chapter *13* *The Economics of Cross-Training*

The majority of this book has thus far focused on management and leadership skills required in the dynamics of a Cross-Training organization. However, it is important to understand that economic stability is a primary ingredient for sustainability. Unions, employees, customers and other stakeholders are dependant upon a positive balance sheet and the company is dependant upon them. This has been a Yin & Yang negotiation since the dawn of modern man. If you recollect, in the first chapter, one of the '7 Golden responsibilities of Management' was to manage a sound organization. This naturally implies to the financial stability of the company too.

Most people prefer to stay away from economics and accounting, but it is part and parcel of a good Cross-Training program and should be taken seriously even though some profit and loss calculations can be quite ambiguous. As the song goes, "money makes the world go round, the world go round, the world go round" so good fiscal policy (scrutiny of process, spending, budgets, etc.) and educated personnel make a Cross-training program go round. It is obvious that they both need one another. Without development, the individual will tire, lose interest and efficacy will deteriorate thereby affecting the organization—a compounding effect from the individual through to the bottom-line. Therefore it is important for all participants to understand the budgetary process and how budgets are created, cost-benefit analysis, the complacency gap, benchmarking benefits, competitive advantage versus competitive scope and direct costs related to training.

At the University of Lund's Medical Hospital, in Lund Sweden, a "Lean Health Care" program was instituted by the employees (Blomstedt, 2009: 4-6) in which forty nursing staff received additional training in Orthopedics, patient examination techniques, referral authority and ancillary services ordering capability (x-rays, blood-work, etc.). They realized by delegating some of the doctor's responsibilities, in regard to procedures and treatment of minor fractures, they could reduce a patient's total waiting time and free-up the doctor for more important tasks. The emergency room staff began by identifying and looking at their own routines, processes, and workflow and how they affected the patient's overall waiting time, while at the same time, maintaining quality care. Interestingly enough, after the nurses took over responsibilities for treatment and referrals to x-ray, they reduced the average waiting time for a patient referred by a doctor for an x-ray from 70 minutes to just 33 minutes. They also identified x-ray as one of the problems as it was located on another floor and not adjacent to the emergency room. By building an x-ray room adjacent to the emergency room they could reduce another 20 minutes off the patients' time to just 13 minutes. As a result, total patient time (entry to exit) was reduced from 4 hours to just 2 hours. Both the patients and the staff are subsequently very happy with the results.

Naturally, just like in Cross-Training, tasks and duties should be performed at the lowest entry level position possible. Maximizing and individual's KSAC is both stimulating and motivating for the individuals while at the same time alleviating bottle necking. The "Lean Health Care" approach at the University Hospital in Lund only confirms what US military medicine has been practicing for the last 40 years. Why it has taken so long for the civilian medical facilities to catch on beats me? Maybe it is due to money, power, old bureaucratic institutions doing what they have always done since the early 20th century, or all of the above. This is a direct economic savings to the patient, insurance companies, and community tax-payers. Treat the patient at the lowest possible level as quickly and efficiently as possible and in accordance with Cross-Training.

Another financial example of Cross-Training can be taken from (3)Screen, a screen printing company with 10 employees, in Malmö Sweden. Their Cross-Training focus was on employee flexibility, rotation, and workplace knowledge. Starting in 2006 and proceeding through 2008, the results where remarkable.

After the first year (2006-2007), their pre-tax profit increased by 14% on an 8.5% turnover increase. After the second year (2007-2008), their pre-tax profit increased by 323% on just an increase of 6.6% in turnover. Furthermore, their total absentee (sick) days dropped 61% from a high of 187 in 2007 to just 74 in 2008. Naturally, great credit can be given to the hands-on-approach shown by their C.E.O. Bengt Andersson.

Budgets

In most cases, corporate annual budgets are planned annually (fixed) but amended quarterly (rolling) and based upon a number of environmental pressures and demands:

1. Stock market (if listed), (legitimate and pressured quarterly results—can be misleading)
2. Stockholder dividends (legitimate and buffered or adjusted for strategic planning purposes)
3. Stakeholder bonuses (including management and sales bonuses—both legitimate reasonable payouts and those which are in excess and unethical),
4. Accounting purposes (trail balance and annual report, pre-tax profit, taxes other associated instruments), and
5. Zero-based (beginning each new cycle from zero, ground-up, critically reviewing all assumptions and proposed expenditures—this method takes a lot more time a effort from management) , and
6. Kaizen budgeting or continuous improvement process (requiring departments to continually, on an incremental basis, to reduce costs—additional attention or focus is given to those not achieving their goals).

In most cases companies start out with a master budget (Fig. 13.1). This master is the core of their budgeting process and it attempts to incorporate

Master Budget Flow Chart

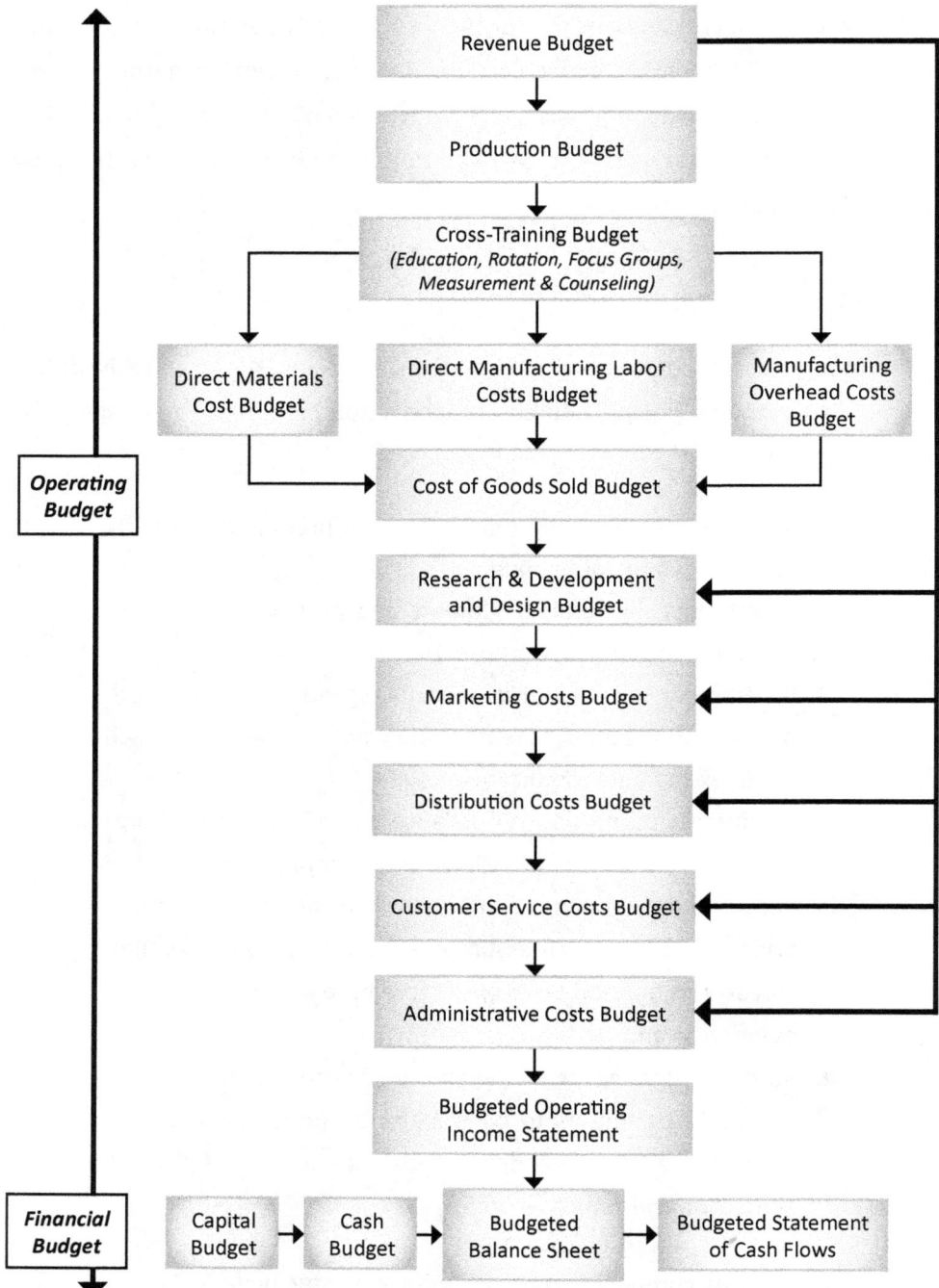

Fig. 13.1. Adapted from Charles T. Horngren, George Foster, and Srikant M. Datar, Cost Accounting (New York: prentice Hall, 2000) and shows Cross-Training incorporated into the budget flow of the core model.

the operating and financial budgets into one comprehensive picture. Not that I have included a Cross-Training into the flow chart.

Sometimes budgets are also construed around external forces or ad hoc situations which can arise in most companies. These can have positive and/or negative consequences for organizations. They include:

1. Cover short time spans (quarterly reporting, startups, new ventures, small adjustments, etc.),
2. Long-term perspective (new product development, research, new markets, etc.),
3. Specific projects (required resources for a specific project needed to improve efficiency such as new machinery, installation, etc.), and
4. Revenue based accounting (creating a plan based upon income revenue and expenditures).

As a Cross-Training budget includes individual change (understanding of the working environment, KSAC, behavioral conformity and competency development) and organizational change (strategic, culture, landscape, workflow and process) the calculations are problematic as they encompass most spectrums of an organizational environment. However, the flowing nine categories can be used as a good guide in your calculations:

1. Landscape, workflow and process analysis (initial design phase including evaluation and adjustment)
2. Information dissemination, feedback, adjustment and kick-off event,
3. Employee rotation (on-the-job-training, cost for effective time in rotation, actual salaries and other related costs accumulated during the rotational phases),
4. Specialized educational costing (internal & external training associated with additional or specialized education required

for a specific task or job description. This specialized education can be conducted both internally and/or externally within the organization),

5. Administrative fees (costs are the associated consulting,
   counseling and hourly management fees charged by the consultant),

6. Additional personnel (costs associated with the hiring of temporary personnel or overtime to alleviate scheduling or rotation hindrances to alleviate certain continuous assembly line
   positions and/or support personnel if needed),

7. Measurement fees (are costs related to the psychometric
   tests and/or the establishment of a base-point measurement
   for Cross-Training. At completion, a second measurement is
   taken and the differential analyzed psychometric testing and
   base point measurement fees),

8. Counseling sessions (generally four one hour sessions per
   individual—those with elevated stress and defense mechanisms normally require additional sessions),

9. Establishment of focus groups, task forces and special project
   teams (focus on routines, process, practices and more), and

10. Supervisor training (costs related to coaching and training
    supervisors and assisting them in institutionalizing the Cross-
    Training program into company culture).

Figure 13.2. Shows the complexity of this task and narrowing the parameters of
one's choices to evaluate cost and budgeting is not a clear cut as most accountants desire as it is somewhat ambiguous in nature. However, the actual costs,
listed on the left hand side, are somewhat obscure and harder to pinpoint.

The benefits listed on the right of the table have been discussed and linked
to Cross-Training, PMP, stress, competency development, and organizational
culture quite clearly throughout the preceding chapters. Nevertheless, cost to
benefit analysis, progress measurements, and comparisons are needed.

Cost of Cross-Training	Benefits of Cross-Training
1. Analysis and preparation costs for	1. Motivation (balanced PMP)
a. landscape analysis	2. Participation
b. workflow & process analysis	a. taking greater responsibility
2. Information dissemination & kick-off cost	b. job renewal
3. Employee rotation (OJT) costs	3. Identity
4. Specialized educational costs	a. subjectification (KSAC)
a. external education	b. belonging
5. Administrative fees	4. Synergy
a. consultants	a. workflow understanding
6. Additional personnel	b. flexibility
7. Measurement fees	5. Openness /Transparency
a. pre and post measurements	a. more interaction
b. analysis and presentation	b. improved communication
8. Counseling sessions	6. Less absenteeism
a. 4 sessions per participant	a. control over work place
9. Focus groups	b. less stress (can prioritize)
a. communication	7. Innovation & creativity
b. workflow	a. input improvement
c. maintenance & repairs	b. improved output
d. processes	9. Focus groups
e. safety and ergonomics	a. process improvement
10. Supervisor training	b. teamwork
a. seminars	10. Trained Supervisors / leaders
b. individual counseling	a. motivate to change
11. Time	b. improved support
12. Commitment	11. Efficacy
	a. improved process & workflow
	b. improved problem solving
	c. improved decision making

Fig. 13.2. Shows the associated costs and benefits of a Cross-Training program. It is important to keep in mind that creating a culture of participation, vision and identity is a long-term and continual process.

Cost-Benefit Analysis

A Cost Benefit Analysis is approaching and comparing this multi-dimensional program through a number of baseline measurements. An easy calculation is based upon dividing total financial benefits by total cost of the training.

A good example could be that of a Program that we did at Rexam. Rexam invest around $90,000 and during the initial analysis phase we strategically recommended and changed the workflow responsibilities for a neglected area within a department. The savings resulted in a savings of approximately $2.4 million. The Cost Benefit Ratio would be 2,400,000 / 90,000 = 26.77. An excellent ratio as averages usually range between 2.0 to 5.0.

Naturally, improved efficacy, turnaround time of new products and/or services, and flexibility are all competitive advantages that are hard to quantify.

Depending upon the agreed upon measurements—to be established between the organization and the consultant prior to the project start date—the baseline measurements should be taken prior to and during the first counseling sessions and repeated annually thereafter. There are four major measurement tools that can make up your battery. They are:

1. Psychometric assessments,
2. Benchmarking
3. PMP and Workload comparisons
4. Complacency gap Analysis

(1) Psychometric Testing as a Basis for Measurement

Psychometric testing is a well established non-financial tool which is used measure a person's psychological state prior to, during and implementation and is a good way to establish any psychological changes and patterns.

After the physical analysis, a psychological analysis of the department is a good way to establish a basis for measurement and the psychological wellbeing of the individuals involved. Psychological wellbeing constitutes: the employees capacity to function in a team environment, their ability to work under changing conditions, their ambition, energy, self-control and stress tolerance, amongst many others.

Testing has not always as easy as one might think, but recent developments in psychometric testing have improved and standardized measure emerged for Aptitude and Ability Tests, Personality and Behavioral Questionnaires, Appraisal and Development Measures and Career Guidance Tools. These tests are standardized measures that provide scores on hypothetical variables. Only tests used on a wide population basis can be called "standardized" and only these should be used. These tests provide you with a base measure of one or more

Psychometric Assessment - WPI Select

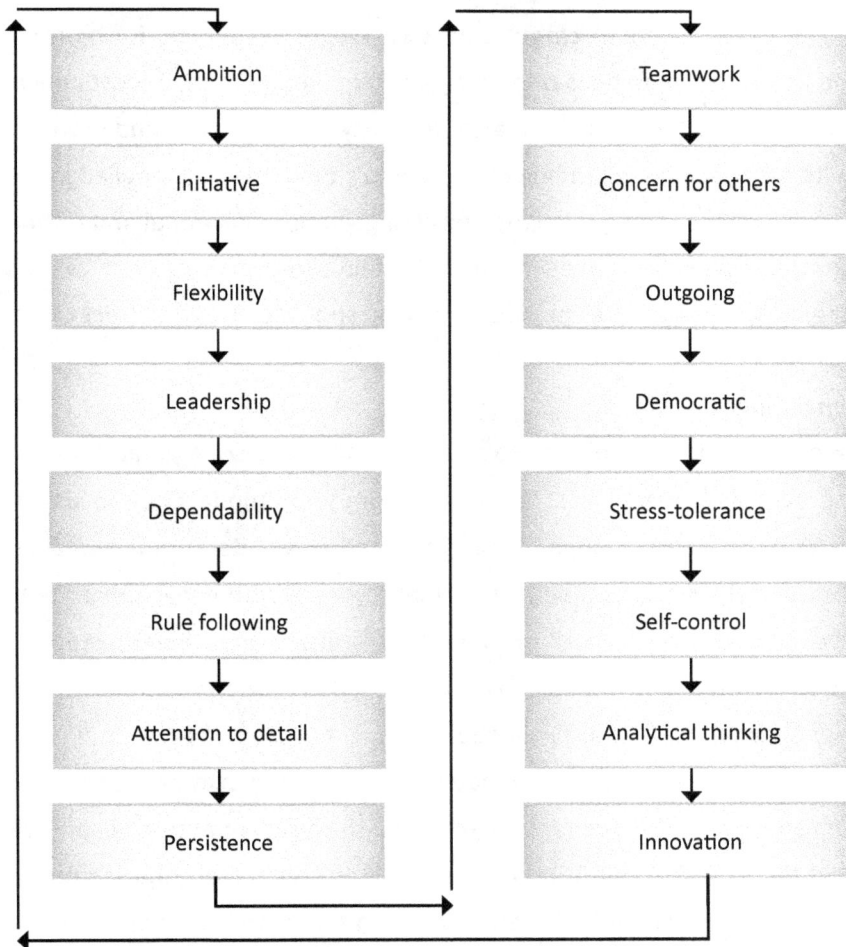

Ambition	Teamwork
Initiative	Concern for others
Flexibility	Outgoing
Leadership	Democratic
Dependability	Stress-tolerance
Rule following	Self-control
Attention to detail	Analytical thinking
Persistence	Innovation

Fig. 13.3. The Work Personality Index Select (WPI Select) is an example of one the tests that we use and is a work-oriented personality record that assesses the characteristics and tendencies that influence an individual's job performance. This test takes about 35 minutes to complete and consists of 153 items to be rated on a 5-point scale. These tests are used as a base measurement prior to team building and prior to Cross-Training. This test, along with a few others that I use, is repeated after both the lateral and vertical Cross-Training. Apart from the physical numbers, the second test provides us with a measurement of how the Cross-Training program fared.

facets of a person's behavior or personality. Modern Management Consulting & I use a number of tests to evaluate staff and managers and they prove to be very accurate and helpful in competency development and team building. An example of one of them is called the Work Personality Index Select (WPI) and measures 17 personality traits that directly relate to work performance (Fig. 13.3).

We use have literally hundreds of tests. They can be used to evaluate a large variety of aspect, see *www.mmc.st* or *www.cross-training.info* for more information and breadth on tests offered by us. Keep in mind that educational rotation and design can benefit from a competency measurement and will provide you with a better understanding of the group's fundamental knowledge. Naturally, certain measurements might well change your educational and rotational design to enable you to take advantage certain competencies or to avoid others. Logically, if deficiencies are identified you should strive to correct them.

(2) Benchmarking

Benchmarking is a tool used to analyze performance of organizational practices, processes and activities. There are a number of models that focus on the organization as a whole, departments, and business units from the smallest of processes to the most complex by comparing them with other similar entities or processes as a benchmark or point of reference. Large manufacturers like Rexam are always benchmarking by comparing their regional factories with one another by analyzing data, production figures, number of personnel per unit produced, etc. The use of benchmarking spans a vast platform and includes the Kaizen model of reducing budget costs, to the competitive advantage by Michael Porter (2004: 34-36) with his focus on the three generic strategies: overall cost of leadership, differentiation, and focus. You might be wondering why strategy, economics and benchmarking are in the same category. Well, it's because focus, differentiation and the cost of leadership are all interconnected and compared in order to solidify a competitive advantage. In Cross-Training we strive to inspire employees to participate in the vision and to take responsibility for understanding and adjusting their working environments to meet applicable challenges.

Traditionally, organizations measured performance at different times. In cross-training we do just that; however, after a certain point the bar needs to be raised and external benchmarking becomes very useful. If you recollect one of the leadership traits is to 'set short-term and achievable goals' and this is done through internal performance measurements and provides a good indication of achievements and speed. This however, does not mean that the organization is competitive in relation to external benchmarked measures. There are five basic benchmarking types:

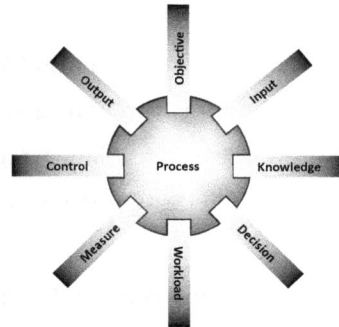

(Fig. 13.4) In Cross-Training benchmarking will include OIK-DW-MCO: objective, input, knowledge, decision, workload, measure, control, and output. The OIK-DW-MCO process method helps to identify task/ objective specifics by conforming data specific information into meaning and benchmarks.

1) Internal benchmarking (within the same organization and between similar production lines, processes, workflows),

2) Competitive benchmarking (organizational and production processes with competitors),

3) Functional benchmarking (similar processes within the same type of industry),

4) Generic benchmarking (operational processes or workflows between unrelated industries), and

5) Collaborative benchmarking (industry organizations and different countries and subsidiaries within a multinational corporation).

Usually there are a number of steps to be followed when benchmarking. If you recollect the chapter seven dealt with process (Fig. 13.4) and the employees' commitment to understanding 'OIK-DW-MCO.' Benchmarking is providing the ability to measure and compare with scope and definition. Individual and leaders need to determine measurement methods, unit specifications, indicators, data collection methods, analysis frequency of presentation procedures. Furthermore, they need to agree on how to analyze discrepancies and plan for corrections and whether adjustment and/or changes are needed. Naturally, responsibility for implementation, adjustment and other related duties need to be agreed upon.

(3) PMP and Workload Comparisons

Monitoring individual PMPs and Workload (task load index) is an excellent way to measure incremental improvements and changes. After baseline measurements are taken and the program started, Cross-Training will initially produce numbers lower than the baseline. However, as the new routines, OJT, rotations and understanding take form measurement results will continually improve as individuals become more confident, and in more than 95% of cases level off more than 25% above benchmarked baseline measurements. This dramatic increase directly affects participation, efficacy and output.

Baseline questions are provided in the appendix section of this book. It is important to remember that if you have decided to use these as measurement instruments they should be used as a baseline and prior to program start. If you recollect a workflow and workload change in Rexam produced an annual savings of more than $2,400,000.

(4) Complacency Gap Analysis

What are the economic consequences of lethargic complacent workforce? I am sure you will be able to come up with a number of examples. For legality reasons I will not mention the name of one of the top pharmaceutical, R&D, and manufactures in the word. Their research and development division hasn't come up with any significant advances in the last 12 years. It is not surprising that medicine costs to much. The question is, why the complacency? Chapter 14, will cover a relevant topic called Cross-Training Corporate Stars, but for now, let's focus on the why, how can we recognize it, and measure it. If you recollect, in the earlier chapters 1 & 4, I addressed the 'Positional Work-Cycle Stages' (Fig.13.5.). A fundamental flaw in management philosophy is stimulating and

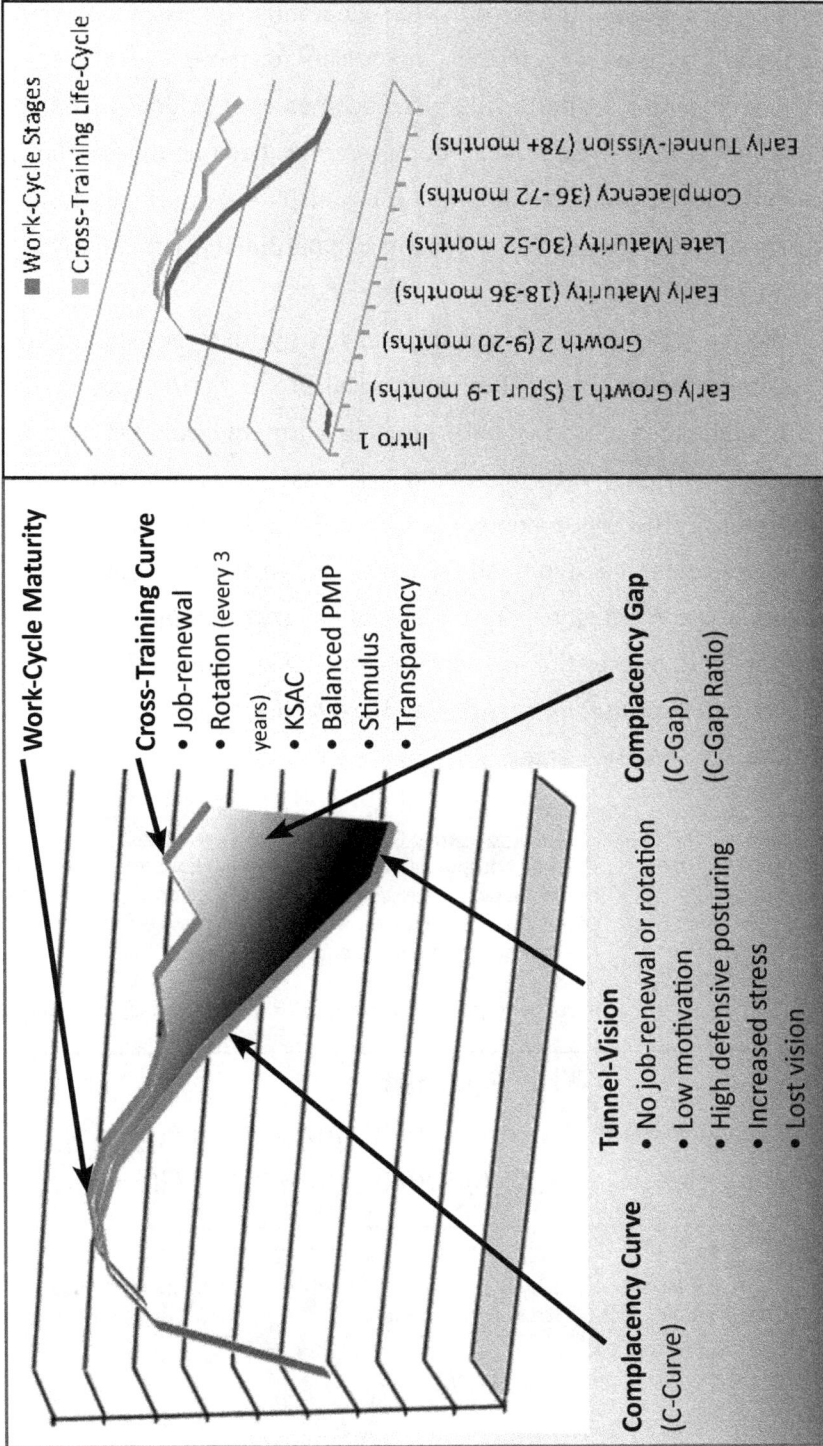

Work-Cycle Maturity

Cross-Training Curve
- Job-renewal
- Rotation (every 3 years)
- KSAC
- Balanced PMP
- Stimulus
- Transparency

Complacency Gap
(C-Gap)
(C-Gap Ratio)

Tunnel-Vision
- No job-renewal or rotation
- Low motivation
- High defensive posturing
- Increased stress
- Lost vision

Complacency Curve
(C-Curve)

■ Work-Cycle Stages
■ Cross-Training Life-Cycle

Intro 1
Early Growth 1 (Spur 1-9 months)
Growth 2 (9-20 months)
Early Maturity (18-36 months)
Late Maturity (30-52 months)
Complacency (36-72 months)
Early Tunnel-Vission (78+ months)

Fig. 4.6. Shows an example of the author's Complacency Gap Analysis. Based on a ratio between Output and Input divided by Motivation and Stress (O/I)/(M/S). Behavioral analysis in relation to measures of output and input is an important step in managing employees as it can assist the leader/manager in rotational and task assignments thereby preventing the complacency virus from infecting individual team members and overall motivation.

renewing employee participation. Far too often, a paradigm between long-term industrial workers (those working in the same facility for more 15 – 30 years) and research facilities and higher academics becomes very evident if change and stimulus is not part of the equation. Comfort zones become more defined and emerge into opaque walled boundaries. The transparency normally associated with openness tends to become defensive as a natural mechanism to hide the lack of stimulus.

The complacency gap analysis naturally looks at the differential between organizational benchmarks (internal and historical production/service statistics) and the baseline for each individual. Annual assessment levels will indicate change. As the complacency virus takes hold individual assessment scores will continue to decrease. This is not a one or two time decrease but depends with time (over the 3-7 years). Keep in mind that this is a management and leadership tool to monitor and adjust routines, job-renewal, and rotations and is not an instrument used to hire or fire an individual employee. Measurements are used in coaching and counseling sessions and are to assist the leader in this matter (Fig. 4.7.). The measures are:

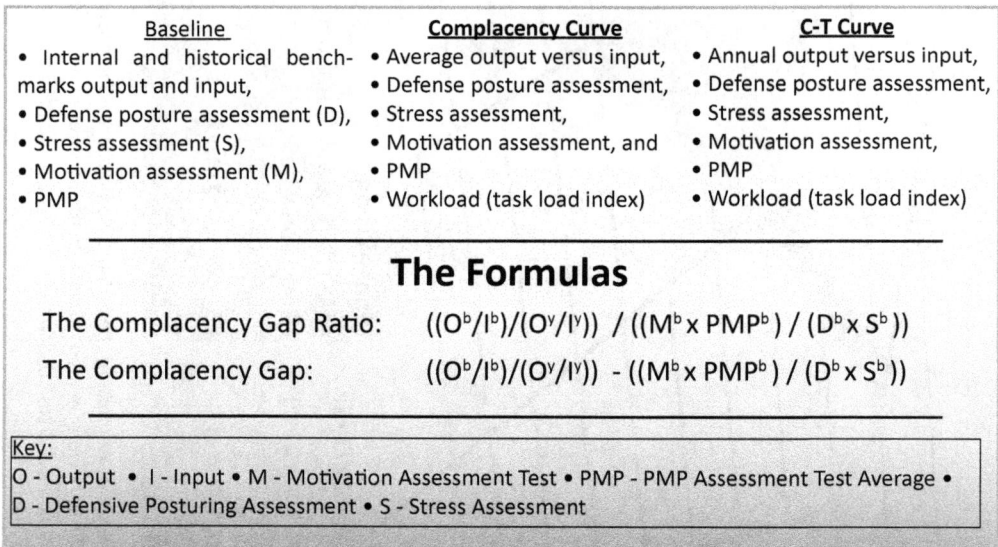

Baseline	Complacency Curve	C-T Curve
• Internal and historical benchmarks output and input,	• Average output versus input,	• Annual output versus input,
• Defense posture assessment (D),	• Defense posture assessment,	• Defense posture assessment,
• Stress assessment (S),	• Stress assessment,	• Stress assessment,
• Motivation assessment (M),	• Motivation assessment, and	• Motivation assessment,
• PMP	• PMP	• PMP
	• Workload (task load index)	• Workload (task load index)

The Formulas

The Complacency Gap Ratio: $((O^b/I^b)/(O^y/I^y)) \,/\, ((M^b \times PMP^b) \,/\, (D^b \times S^b))$

The Complacency Gap: $((O^b/I^b)/(O^y/I^y)) \,-\, ((M^b \times PMP^b) \,/\, (D^b \times S^b))$

Key:
O - Output • I - Input • M - Motivation Assessment Test • PMP - PMP Assessment Test Average • D - Defensive Posturing Assessment • S - Stress Assessment

Fig. 4.7. Shows the formulas used in measuring complacency.

chapter **14** *Cross-Training Corporate Stars*

Throughout this book I have stressed the importance of a balanced PMP, consistency in management and leadership, participation, identity and understanding ones working environment as a part of the organizational culture. However, a large question still remains. What do we do with corporate stars and should we have a rotational program for them? How do we handle vital or strategic areas when one or two people hold a monopoly of knowledge in a specific area? What do we do if they are unwilling to participate? Should we handle them differently from others within the organization? This chapter will discuss these issues in relation to the objectives surrounding Management by Cross-Training.

In order to take a stand, maybe a good place to start is using the metaphor 'organism' to describe an organization and its function (Morgan, 1996). If we look at Wikipedia's reference to an organism it states,

> *"In at least some form, all organisms are capable of response to stimuli, reproduction, growth and development, and maintenance of homeostasis as a stable whole. An organism may either be unicellular (single-celled) or be composed of, as in humans, many billions of cells grouped into specialized tissues and organs. The term multi-cellular (many-celled) describes any organism made up of more than one cell."* (http://en.wikipedia.org/wiki/Organism)

In this case the individual would be an organism and the organ the organization. Naturally, organizations are made up of many individuals all working towards the same vision of a strong sustainable corporation—a mutually beneficial association or one can even acknowledge an agreement. All employees within this organization have in someway or form a part in the drive towards a common goal. From the cleaner who cleans at two o'clock in the morning, and sees to it that coworkers arrive to a comfortable, clean and healthy working environment. To the receptionists, clerical staff, accounting personnel, sales personnel, machinists, warehouse, production personnel, and many others whom contribute to the functioning of that 'organ's purpose.' Each has a different function, individualistic approach, personality, and behavioral patterns built into their own PMP make-up—but what is remarkable—is that with good leadership, policies that are consistent and supporting, and a solid 'organ' culture they're all committed participants in the 'organ's purpose.'

Special treatment of an individual is therefore inconsistent with this methodology as all individuals are participating to some extent in the purpose. Do not get you feather's in a ruffle if you think I am trying to advocate a socialist platform. Politics, socialism, capitalism, or any other 'ism' is irrelevant as it's about maximizing participation, efficacy and doing one's best. Cross-Training is about a mutually beneficial agreement, a fundamental cornerstone to the democratic legal system of the west. Rewarding excellent performance is good and it should be utilized to its fullest; however, it can become a double ended sword if not management properly. Any inconsistencies can be de-motivating to other contributors within the function as they have helped to pave the way in achieving the specific goals or milestones.

I am sure you have noticed that I am against bonus structures that cannot benefit the 'organ' as a whole. However, this does not make me blind to the fact that some individuals strive to work harder, produce more product or better service, create ideas and innovations, or even contribute to the greater good of the organizational culture.

Bonuses and other remunerations as rewards for good work are extremely important; however, maybe we should reevaluate our approach to insure that we can maximize the return of the motivational bonus to insure that the investment can produce a greater return with maximum benefit to the 'organ'.

A good example is Scandinavian Enskilda Bank (SEB). Right in the middle of the financial crisis their directors are proposing bonuses for themselves. In difficult times everyone is forced to tighten their belts. Here is an inconsistency in management. Do what I say but not what I do. Maybe, instead of paying the top one hundred directors a hefty bonus or giving them preferred stock options at lower than market price annually, they should reconsider their ethical position. Some argue that if they don't pay bonuses then they will lose that specific individual. If they leave based upon an inconsistent bonus then they are not part of the team, are not team players, find it hard to identify with organizational culture, and will most probably leave if they get a better paycheck somewhere else anyway. I believe in individual bonus schemes that reward exceptional, out of the ordinary, effort like innovations, creativity, efficacy improvements, and the like.

As most senior corporate staff are on contract, their contracts usually specify bonuses if the corporation meets its objectives and/or improves pre-tax profit. However, this can also lead to quarterly management tactics and harm the organization in the long-term. Instead, senior management should be paid properly and according to their responsibilities and purpose and senior corporate bonus should be abolished totally. Unfortunately, this will most likely never happen so maybe an 80/20 bonus split is more applicable. 80% to the employee collective, who helped achieve the result, and 20% to the executive/s. Naturally, as process starts with the individual, the return on investment or benefit to the organ as a whole is far greater. Obviously, a positive pre-tax bottom line performance (one, two or three year period) is also a criteria and not based upon quarterly figures. This way all employees will benefit from the bottom line and all would be willing to participate to a greater extent. The 'we and them' scenario would also diminish. Understanding process, workflow, focus groups, and IDP will become more realistic, easier to implement, and with a purpose.

Some theoreticians suggest that intellectuals or corporate stars should be treated differently, with autonomy, and that they should have the flexibility to set their own course and workload. The reason they claim, is that their working routines are sort of ambiguous in relation to corporate policy and culture, and that they should therefore be handled from a distance and differently. I disagree totally with this approach. EVERYONE within the organization should have the ability to work with as much autonomy, delegation, and participation as possible. The whole purpose of Cross-Training is to create greater understanding of the workplace. This understanding in itself creates control over one's environment. This control is naturally related to having the ability to make decisions in relation to one's working environment, to change process, and workflow in order to improve output and minimize input, raw materials, etc. If this isn't autonomy, I don't know what it.

I had a professor that once implied that only intellectuals could self-actualize. Naturally, I believe that this was a lot of bullocks. Everyone has the ability to self-actualize. No matter what your status, station or position. If your PMP is in balance you will feel great. You will have control over your situation and be able to forge new paths. Self-actualization is 'situational well-being' in which one finds oneself in balance. This balance always be situational as the environment changes. It is up the leader and manager to maximize situational circumstances where all individuals feel in control, motivated and willing.

Rotations and rotating key personnel on the other hand are a little ambiguous. Sometimes in research facilities, like pharmaceutical research, key researches are needed to innovate. Their unique competencies and drive are usually a competitive advantage for the 'organ's purpose;' however, they too need extra stimulus from time to time. These can be provided through lateral rotations, additional projects, and injection of other methods and processes from within the organization and externally. Therefore, I argue that rotations for these types of jobs are just as vital. Many would argue that it is too costly to rotate key individuals as they are needed to do a critical task, supervise, make decisions or implement critical changes in strategy or routine. I stand firm in my belief that short-term rotations (one, two or three month) annually will produce greater benefits in the long-term. Sometimes these types of positions can also be prone the complacency virus and tunnel vision, and therefore a rotational period can have a stimulating effect. Take for example the major pharmaceutical company

I mentioned earlier in the book who hasn't produced a major new drug in the last 12 years. Rotation and the costs related therewith are minuscule, and anyone of the three rotations types discussed earlier in the book, short-term, long-term and roaming, are well suited to about 99.9% of job descriptions.

It is obvious that high security areas and other related industries are subjected to different participation rules. In these situations transfer of knowledge and routines are confined to close-quarter parameters; however, this does not change basic system procedural functions.

If for some odd reason you are confronted with the refusal to rotate, a system of rotations into the areas vulnerable area are called for instead. Refusal is usually a defense mechanism and has a lot to do with individual perception of control and dependency. These boundary-walls need to be reduced otherwise the 'organ' can become too dependent upon an individual, vulnerable due to illness, and even subjected to unrealistic demands. Assimilating knowledge by means of focus groups, process evaluations and SOP codification programs could be a good course of action to reduce dependencies and minimizing risk.

No matter how significant or insignificant you might think a position might be, it is extremely important that leaders and managers are consistent in their ability to make everyone feel that they are vital, necessary to the function of the organization, its identity, and its culture. Cross-Training is about empowering individuals to participate in the understanding of their workplaces and to identify with the organization as a whole. All employees should be treated as you would want to be treated.

Section **5**

Appendix
Glossary
Bibliography
Index

251

Appendix

The appendix section includes a number of assessment tests, a group communication and dynamics socio-gram, and a process assignment guide.

The assessments are as follows:

Appendix A – Motivation Assessment

Appendix B – Stress Assessment

Appendix C – Defense Posture Assessment

Appendix D – PMP Assessment

Appendix E – Group Communication and Dynamics Socio-gram

Appendix F – Process Assignment Guide

Assessment Guidelines

Always fill in the appropriate name, job description and current date (Fig A.1.).

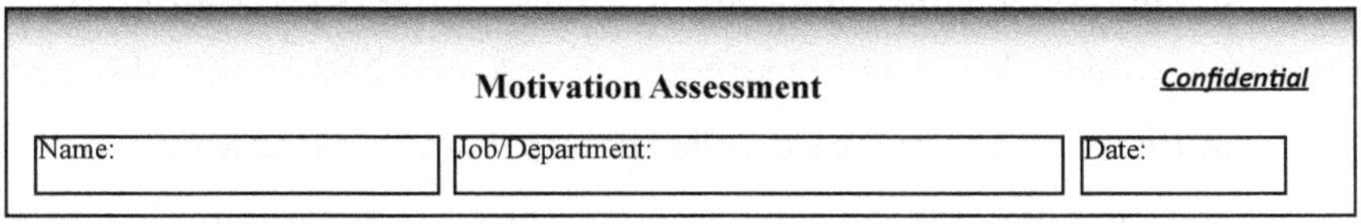

Motivation Assessment		*Confidential*
Name:	Job/Department:	Date:

Fig. A.1.

Insure that the assessed fills in the "X" along the line adjacent to the questions (Fig. A.2.). Notice that the numbers, above the boxes, are not on the actual assessment tests. The reason for this is that we do not want to unduly influence the test taker. The assessor will have to count the squares when adding up the

Fig. A.2.

total; however, to make the adding easier, you will notice that after the 10 box the line is slightly elevated. It is important to remember to fill whether the test is a baseline, annual or other measure (Fig. A.3.). The boxes will help you with order when analyzing changes and statistical models and the complacency virus.

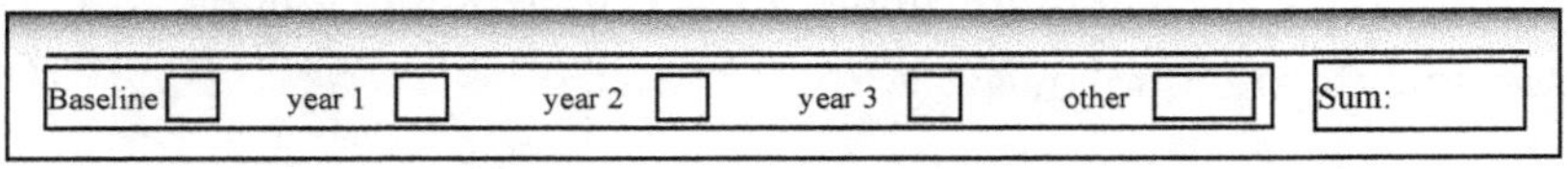

| Baseline ☐ | year 1 ☐ | year 2 ☐ | year 3 ☐ | other ☐ | Sum: |

Fig. A.3.

The Assessment Procedure

The assessment test is filled in by the individual being assessed. Usually the assessed can complete the test within the allotted 25 minutes. Before starting make sure that they fill in their name, job description and current date. The assessor should mark, at the bottom of the page, whether the purpose of the test is Baseline, a yearly follow-up or other.

The leader or manager can either choose to counsel the assessed directly after completion or schedule another time later in the week. If more than one assessment is taken (motivation, stress, defense, and PMP), then the assessor can add up the scores of one test while the assessed is taking another. If more than one test is taken during the same session, it is recommended that you schedule another time for discussion and counseling of the assessment tests. An additional counseling tool can be that the leader/manager assesses the individual using the same assessment test but giving the leader's/manager's opinion. The two assessments (the one take by the individual and the one taken by the leader/manager in regard to the individual) can be compared and contrasted during the next counseling session.

Using the counseling techniques discussed earlier in the book, take your time to discuss the assessment test. If you are to be a consistent trustworthy leader you should be as honest about your comments. Use examples, narratives and stories to discuss points. N.B.: Never try to correct someone else's problem area if you have the same problem area if you cannot admit that you are working on the problem area yourself. If this is the case then you should discuss how you are tackling your problem area. Set goals, plan a course of action and practical instruments (mechanisms and/or suggestions on how to remind oneself of a specific behavior or the corrections thereto). Keep in mind that if leaders/managers are not aware of their on assessments it will be difficult for them to help others.

Appendix A - Motivation Assessment

Motivation Assessment is a quick subjective overview of an individual's general motivation. This should not be confused with PMP status. PMP is an indication tool used to provide the leader or manager with information in regard to which motivational indicators are affecting or sustaining individual motivation.

Scoring the Assessment

The Motivation Assessment, opposite, is calculated by adding up the scores for each of the 20 questions. Each question has a possible score ranging between: 1 to 20. The maximum potential score is therefore 20 x 20 = 400. However it is not reasonable to assume that anyone receiving scores lower than 30 or higher than 370 and in those circumstances one should retake the assessment.

General Score Assessment:

0 – 30	retake test
31 – 100	low motivation (make a plan)
101 – 200	average motivation
201 – 300	motivated
301 – 370	highly motivated
371 – 400	retake test

Motivation Assessment

Name:	Job/Department:	Date:

Place an "X" in the appropriate box which best represents how you feel.

1. I have control over my work load and my extra curricular activities.

Very Little — Very High

2. I receive support for my opinions and ideas at work.

Very Little — Very High

3. My work is stimulating and interesting.

Very Little — Very High

4. I am proud of the organization that I work for.

Very Little — Very High

5. I have the respect of my colleagues and supervisor/boss.

Very Little — Very High

6. My job description provides me the possibility to advance and develop within the organization.

Very Little — Very High

7. I can affect change and make decisions related to my job tasks.

Very Little — Very High

8. I am proud of the department that I work in.

Very Little — Very High

9. I feel part of a team that respects and care for one another.

Very Little — Very High

10. My pay and benefits are in line with my job description.

Very Little — Very High

11. My job description and responsibilities are clear to me.

Very Little — Very High

12. I like to take responsibility for tasks or projects at work.

Very Little — Very High

13. I feel confident about my workplace knowledge and understanding.

Very Little — Very High

14. I feel needed and important at work.

Very Little — Very High

15. I feel that my input and suggestions are welcome.

Very Little — Very High

16. My colleagues come to me for advice and help often.

Very Little — Very High

17. I like to participate in new assignments or focus groups.

Very Little — Very High

18. I believe the work that I am doing is important.

Very Little — Very High

19. I see criticism from my supervisor as positive and constructive.

Very Little — Very High

20. I like to tell my friend about my work.

Very Little — Very High

Baseline ☐	year 1 ☐	year 2 ☐	year 3 ☐	other ☐	Sum:

Appendix B - Stress Assessment

The Stress Assessment is a quick subjective overview of an individual's general stress condition. This can have an impact on PMP status. They are interconnected as a PMP imbalance between the educational, demand and self-expectancy environment will cause stress. Furthermore, the chapter 3 highlights many other stress signals that leaders and managers should be aware of. Diligently observing, adjusting situational demands and expectations to lesson the impact of regression or other adverse behaviors through diligent communication, monitoring and signal awareness is key in motivation and leadership.

Scoring the Assessment

The Stress Assessment, opposite, is calculated by adding up the scores for each of the 20 questions. Each question has a possible score ranging between: 1 to 20. The maximum potential score is therefore 20 x 20 = 400. However it is not reasonable to assume that anyone receiving scores lower than 30 or higher than 370 and in those circumstances one should retake the assessment.

General Score Assessment:

0 – 30	retake test
31 – 60	very low stress (make a plan to prevent complacency and distress)
61 – 100	low stress
101 – 200	average stress "Eustress"
201 – 300	stressed (adjust workload and counsel)
301 – 370	highly stressed (make a plan, adjust demands, etc.)
371 – 400	retake test

Stress Assessment

Name:	Job/Department:	Date:

Place an "X" in the appropriate box which best represents how you feel.

1. No balance between job demands and the allotted time to accomplish tasks.
    Very Little ———————————————————— Very High

2. Poor leadership. No support, feedback or information.
    Very Little ———————————————————— Very High

3. I am unable to use my competence and experience at work.
    Very Little ———————————————————— Very High

4. I am not allowed to give my opinion at work.
    Very Little ———————————————————— Very High

5. Poor balance between taking responsibility, authority to make decisions and resources.
    Very Little ———————————————————— Very High

6. Unclear goals and a lack of organizational vision.
    Very Little ———————————————————— Very High

7. Poor reward systems (lack of recognition and appreciation for a job well done).
    Very Little ———————————————————— Very High

8. Lack of ability to vent complaints.
    Very Little ———————————————————— Very High

9. Lack of relief when under pressure, having angry outbursts, mood swings or overly negative.
    Very Little ———————————————————— Very High

10. Many simple and monotone tasks.
    Very Little ———————————————————— Very High

11. Many conflicts, poor teamwork, harassment, and name calling.
    Very Little ———————————————————— Very High

12. Shift work and irregular working times.
    Very Little ———————————————————— Very High

13. Poor environmental conditions, inadequate lighting, uncomfortable tasks, etc.
    Very Little ———————————————————— Very High

14. Violence, threat of violence or perceived threat.
    Very Little ———————————————————— Very High

15. Too much responsibility for others.
    Very Little ———————————————————— Very High

16. Insecure working environment (too much change, layoffs, etc.)
    Very Little ———————————————————— Very High

17. Tasks that are in conflict with my own personal values.
    Very Little ———————————————————— Very High

18. Poor justice and inconsistent and unfair treatment of personnel, etc.
    Very Little ———————————————————— Very High

19. Frequent headaches, teeth grinding, tiredness, and worrying.
    Very Little ———————————————————— Very High

20. Having difficulties in concentrating, forgetfulness, often restless and anxious.
    Very Little ———————————————————— Very High

Baseline ☐	year 1 ☐	year 2 ☐	year 3 ☐	other ☐	Sum:

Appendix C - Defense Posturing Assessment

The Defense Posture Assessment is a quick subjective overview of an individual's general defensive nature which can affect teamwork, communication and participation. This can have an impact on PMP status. They are interconnected as a defensive posture can arise from PMP imbalances in all of the seven variables: self-expectancy, physiological, external demand, social, educational, transparent and self-esteem environments.

Furthermore, the chapter 3 highlights many other defense mechanisms that leaders and managers should be aware of. Diligently observing, adjusting situational needs, demands, and expectations to lesson the impact of regression or other adverse behaviors through diligent action. Break these boundaries and minimize or fix, if possible, the imbalances causing the defensive posturing.

Scoring the Assessment

The Defense Posturing Assessment, opposite, is calculated by adding up the scores for each of the 20 questions. Each question has a possible score ranging between: 1 to 20. The maximum potential score is therefore 20 x 20 = 400. However it is not reasonable to assume that anyone receiving scores lower than 30 or higher than 370 and in those circumstances one should retake the assessment.

General Score Assessment:

0 – 30	retake test
31 – 100	low defense posturing (open for change, teamwork, etc.)
101 – 200	average defensive posturing (open for change and team work with some reservations)
201 – 300	defensive (adjust PMP variables, work assignments and counsel)
301 – 370	highly defensive (counseling, re-assign, radical adjusts, etc.)
371 – 400	retake test

Defensive Posture Assessment

Name:	Job/Department:	Date:

Place an "X" in the appropriate box which best represents how you feel.

1. I tend to lose my patience and blame others very quickly.
   Very Little — Very Often

2. Everyone seems to be against me, so I have to defend myself often.
   Very Little — Very Often

3. I tend to have very long, drawn out replies when rationalizing.
   Very Little — Very Often

4. I often feel sorry for myself.
   Very Little — Very Often

5. I tend to teach and preach to others.
   Very Little — Very Often

6. I don't like change situations and others say that I am inflexible.
   Very Little — Very Often

7. I find it difficult to agree with others and become cynical and sarcastic.
   Very Little — Very Often

8. I like to make jokes about other people.
   Very Little — Very Often

9. I find it hard to concentrate when others talk to me and I tend to block them out.
   Very Little — Very Often

10. Others believe that I am eccentric (an oddball), but I believe that I am unique or special.
    Very Little — Very Often

11. I am addicted to alcohol (drink more than five drinks daily), medicine or sex
    Very Little — Very Often

12. I go to attack often (I believe that attack is the best defense).
    Very Little — Very Often

13. I am overly nice and amenable.
    Very Little — Very Often

14. I sometimes spontaneously play dumb or crazy.
    Very Little — Very Often

15. People say that I tend to blame others for things that have happened to me.
    Very Little — Very Often

16. I find it hard to forgive others for what they have done.
    Very Little — Very Often

17. I sometimes feel really bad and end up having a mishap or even injuring myself by accident.
    Very Little — Very Often

18. For some odd reason, I am frequently telling others that "I know" and to "leave me alone."
    Very Little — Very Often

19. People say that I tend to joke and brush-off serious matters.
    Very Little — Very Often

20. I tend to intellectualize things too much.
    Very Little — Very Often

Baseline ☐	year 1 ☐	year 2 ☐	year 3 ☐	other ☐	Sum:

Appendix D – PMP Assessment

The PMP Assessment is a quick subjective overview of an individual's motivational position in regard to the seven variables. The interconnectedness of stress, defensive posturing and general motivation is without question and has been show within this book. The nature of this assessment is to monitor an individual's position, establish as plan of action in regard to imbalances and to set personal and organizational goals in line with individual capabilities. It should be obvious by now that when deficiencies are noted in an individual's PMP efforts should be taken to correct them. The leader's/manager's responsibility is to maximize the employee's potential, efficacy, participation and contribution to organizational objectives.

Management by Cross-Training is about creating an organizational environment which fosters development, growth, innovation, creativity, transparency, and a competitive advantage in a mutually beneficial, economically sound, and sustainable setting. PMP assessment is just a small piece of the puzzle and the collective can only be truly competitive if the cells and organs which make up the organism fully function.

The PMP assessment can be used annually or semi-annually. Counseling sessions following the assessment should be constructive and focused on development of the individual's PMP variables.

Scoring the Assessment

The assessment is divided into seven sections representing the seven PMP variables with seven questions for each variable; however, the self-expectancy environment has eight questions instead of seven. This brings the total number of questions to 50.

All questions in each section are added up and divided by either "28" or "32." This number is then placed into the box and market on the PMP diagram on the last page. The maximum potential score for each section after the calculations are done is 5. The goal is to achieve an average of 5 for all of the PMP variables.

General Score Assessment:

1 Clearly a **problematic PMP** and efforts should be made to counsel and assist the individual as soon as possible. Team work and overall participation will be very poor. An ethical management trait would be to repair what has gone wrong. An unethical approach would be to get rid of the problem.

2 **Low PMP** but not catastrophic. With good leadership and communication skills you'll be ale to turn things around; however, it will take dedication from all parties.

3 An **average minus PMP** might fall into this category. Spread across the spectrum of PMP variables the leader/manager will have to coach the individual into identify issues of imbalance and to create a plan to raise the averages.

4 An **average plus PMP** might fall into this category. The individual's PMP variables are pretty high and are good and equilibrium exists. However, coaching is still required to raise the bar. The assessed is a good worker, participates in change and is a good team player.

5 An **excellent PMP** will have an average of 5 for all variables. These individuals are usually the driving forces (20% doing 80% of the collective's share of work). They usually, are creative and innovative and always willing to change as needed. The key is to keep them generating ideas, innovative solutions and continually on the move so to prevent complacency from setting in though lack of stimulus.

PMP Assessment (Page 1 of 4)   *Confidential*

| Name: | Job/Department: | Date: |

Place an "**X**" *in the appropriate box which best represents how you feel.*

Educational Environmental

1. I have the practical (tacit) knowledge necessary to be good at my job.
    Very little — Absolutely

2. I have the formal technical (explicit or OJT) knowledge necessary to be good my job.
    Very little — Absolutely

3. I have the skills to communicate and negotiate situations around my job description.
    Very little — Absolutely

4. I have ability to think outside of the box, innovate, and create new ideas at work.
    Not at all — Absolutely

5. I understand the workflow of goods/services before, in, and after my position.
    Not at all — Absolutely

6. I can discuss all processes within my job description and working environment.
    No at all — Absolutely

7. I feel that my knowledge (KSAC) is improving on a weekly basis.
    Seldom — Very often

Educational Environment Total:(   ) / 28 = (   )

External Demand Environment

8. I feel it is easy to accomplish the tasks asked of me.
    Very little — Very often

9. I feel that my workload is in balance with the demands.
    Very little — Very often

10. I feel that my teammates do their fair share.
    Very little — Very often

11. I feel that my partner/teammates/boss place too much responsibility on me.
    Absolutely — Not at all

12. I feel that my boss has unrealistic demands and requires too much.
    Absolutely — Not at all

13. There is a conflict with processes and workflow at work.
    Absolutely — Not at all

14. I have very little time to complete my tasks properly.
    Always short of time — All the time I need

External Demand Environment Total: (   ) / 28 = (   )

PMP Assessment (Page 2 of 4)

| Name: | Job/Department: | Date: |

*Place an "**X**" in the appropriate box which best represents how you feel.*

Social Environment

15. I like to participate in new assignments and/or focus groups.

Very little — Very often

16. I like to take responsibility for my teammates at work.

Very little — Very often

17. I feel like my working colleagues are like a second family to me.

Absolutely not — All the time

18. I have good relations with my partner at home.

Very little — Very good

19. I feel welcome and look forward to coming to work. We often go out together after work.

Very little — Very often

20. It feels good to belong to the organization.

Very little — Very often

21. I feel that my teammates do their fair share at work and they are my best friends.

Very little — Very often

Social Environment Total: (   ) / 28 = (   )

Physiological Environment

22. The workload at work makes me irritable or gives me a bad temper.

Very little — Very often

23. I am a little over weight / underweight and that my clothes don't fit anymore.

No at all — Absolutely

24. After work I go home stressed and/or in pain.

Never — Very Often

25. I live a healthy lifestyle (good food, lots of exercise, and a healthy relationship).

Sometimes — All the time

26. I feel that the working conditions at work are safe.

Dangerous — Very Safe

27. I feel threatened at work/home/somewhere else. (PTSD/Violence/other)

Never — Often

28. I have more bills at home than income.

Very seldom — All the time

Physiological Environment Total: (   ) / 28 = (   )

PMP Assessment (Page 3 of 4)   *Confidential*

Name: Job/Department: Date:

Place an "X" in the appropriate box which best represents how you feel.

Self-Expectancy

29. I have a good balance between my private life and work.

    Very little ——————————————— *Very often*

30. I have time for my hobby/ies every week.

    Very little ——————————————— *Very often*

31. I have achieved many of my personal goals over the years.

    Very few ——————————————— *Almost all*

32. I am able to establish goals at work and make plans on how to achieve them.

    Very little ——————————————— *Very often*

33. I enjoy new challenges and a changing environment.

    Absolutely not ——————————————— *Often*

34. I get a lot of satisfaction from my work.

    Very little ——————————————— *Very satisfied*

35. I feel appreciated by my partner/boss/collective.

    Very little ——————————————— *Very often*

36. My pay and benefits are in line with my job description.

    Really underpaid ——————————————— *Very good*

Self-Expectancy Environment Total: (   ) / **32** = (   )

Transparent Environment

37. I feel that it is easy to voice problems as work.

    Very difficult ——————————————— *Very easy*

38. I trust my teammates/boss/partner.

    Very Little ——————————————— *Very much*

39. I feel that I can communicate openly with my boss.

    Very bad ——————————————— *Very good*

40. I feel a little isolated at work and feel that I am not part of the team.

    All the time ——————————————— *Absolutely not*

41. I try to accept people for you they are and not what others think they should be.

    Very seldom ——————————————— *All the time*

42. I can talk to my partner (at home) about any-thing.

    Very Little ——————————————— *Absolutely everything*

43. I usually look into the eyes of people when I talk to them.

    Very seldom ——————————————— *Very often*

Transparent Environment Total: (   ) / **28** = (   )

PMP Assessment (Page 4 of 4)

Name:	Job/Department:	Date:

Place an "X" in the appropriate box which best represents how you feel.

Self-Esteem

44. I can identify with my work and organization.

Very Little — Very Often

45. I have a good image about balance myself, my private life and my work.

Poor — Absolutely

46. I feel good about myself and my knowledge.

Very Little — Very much so

47. I see criticism from my supervisor as positive and constructive.

Absolutely not — Very much so

48. My colleagues come to me for advice and help often.

Very Little — Very Often

49. I like to tell my friends about my work and about the company.

Very Little — Very Often

50. I believe the work that I am doing is important.

Not important — Very much so

Self-Esteem Environment Total: (   ) / 28 = (   )

Baseline ☐   year 1 ☐   year 2 ☐   year 3 ☐   other ☐

PMP Score Diagram

1 - Problematic PMP

2 - Low PMP

3 - Average-minus PMP

4 - Average-plus PMP

5 - Excellent PMP

Appendix E – Group Communication & Dynamics Sociogram

Name:

Name:

Name:

Name:

Name:

Name:

Analysis Symbols:

/ Communicating

> Active Listener

< Poor Listener

X Conflict Shy

D Defensive

General Comments:				
Positive	Participatory	Stubborn	Accepting	Open
Negative	Reserved	Dominating	Questioning	Closed
Creative	Passive	Warm	Aggressive	Serious
Idea Rich	Active	Cold	Isolationist	Relaxed
Leader	Spontaneous	Logical	Formal	Nervous
Follower	Controlled	Methodical	Informal	Tense

Appendix F – Process Assignment Guide

Objective Define the goal:
who is going to do it?
what is going to be accomplished?
when is the mechanism triggered in the process
how is it dependant upon situational environment and
          workflow (draw a workflow diagram)

Input Define actual inputs:
who is responsible?
what are the inputs?
          electrical, mechanical, physical, psychological, raw materials
when are the triggers for each input phase realized ?
how do the inputs used and can they be used in anther more effective manner?

Knowledge Define the knowledge resources needed:
who is responsible for knowing?
what is needed for knowledge?
when is the knowledge used?
how can the knowledge be improved upon?

Decision Define the decisions that need to be made.
who makes the decisions?
what decisions are to be made?
when are the decisions made?
how are the decisions made (machine or man and what parameters)

Workload Define the process demands.
who will be affected by the workload demand?
what are the realistic demand capabilities of the man or machine
when has workload reached its maximum (speed, errors, quality)?
how are we going to minimize effort?

Process Assignment Guide

Is a leadership and participation tool used to help employees understand and improve their working routines.

It is most effective as an assignment for focus groups, task force, and team work activities and can cover any working environment from process to landscape.

Measure Define the measures.
who, man or machine, will measure the produced product or service?
what aspects should and are to me measured?
          electrical, mechanical, physical, psychological, raw materials (input/output)
when and at what critical points should and are we measuring?
how are we going to measure Input/output?
               (time, length, volume, weight, space, use of raw materials, etc.)
               (sensors, task workload index, errors, effort, frustration, stress)?

Control Define the controls.
who will be responsible for controlling?
               (input, knowledge, decision, workload, and measures)
what controls are necessary to insure quality and effectivity?
when and how often should these controls be taken?
how are the controls going to me recorded, analyzed and presented?

Output Define the outputs.
who will interpret the output?
what output aspects should be considered?
               (objective, inputs and output, cost, cost reduction, time, implementation, etc.)
when should output be accomplished?
how was the output produced?
               (did we have synergy, on time, adequate use of raw materials, service, product, etc.)

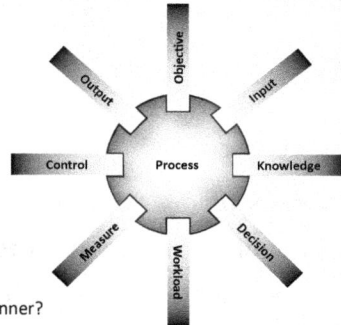

Glossary

Brainstorming is a decision-making and problem-solving technique used by individuals, groups or teams to improve creativity, innovation and spontaneity. This encouragement tool helps to produce the ability to think outside of the box by proposing alternative solutions, with or without concern for reality or company tradition.

Codification is putting personalized tacit information into explicit. Codifying.

Cognitive Model is a rational thought process.

Cog's Ladder is based on the work written in 1972 by George Charrier, an employee Procter and Gamble. The original document was created to help group managers to better understand the dynamics of group work in order to improve efficiency. It was adopted into the US Naval and Air Force Academy's leadership program in the 1980's and has also spread to other businesses. It focuses on five team-building steps that are necessary for small teams to work efficiently together. They are: the polite stage, the why we're here stage, the power stage, the cooperation stage and the esprit stage.

Common Morality is the body of moral rules governing normal ethical behavior positively and negatively. Individuals, groups, and teams form their own common morality rules both within and out of acceptable norms.

Complacency Gap Analysis is the analysis between baseline assessments for input, output, motivation, PMP, stress and defensive posturing. The analysis is completed on an annual basis to prevent complacency from taking hold.

Complacency Virus is a condition where an individual moves through a number of positional work life cycles and ends up with tunnel syndrome. The body of moral rules governing normal ethical behavior positively and negatively.

Corporate Social Performance is a commonly used term for corporations trying to respond to social issues rather than following normal ethical standards. In many cases corporations with a poor social performance will lower their social responsibilities, in comparison to those at home, when operating internationally.

Cost Points in Cross-Training. Employee Rotation costs are the employees' actual salaries and other related costs accumulated during the rotational phases. **Special Education** costs are all the costs associated with additional or specialized education required for a specific task or job description. This specialized education can be conducted both internally and/or externally within the organization. **Administrative** costs are the associated consulting, counseling and hourly management fees charged by the consultant. **Additional Personnel** costs are the costs associated with the hiring of temporary personnel to alleviate scheduling or rotation hindrances. **Measurement** costs are the psychometric tests and/or the establishment of a base-point measurement for Cross-Training. At completion, a second measurement is taken and the differential analyzed. A bonus cost factor can be included if certain agreed upon measurements are achieved.

Cross-Functional Team consists of a group of people with various (different) functional experts/competencies working towards a common goal.

Cross-Training is a lateral and vertical internal development tool used to train, motivate and develop an organization's culture to be flexible, learn and innovate.

Decision Tree is a tool used to break down complex problems into smaller manageable parts.

Division of Work is the breakdown of a large complex task into smaller more controllable tasks so that individuals become responsible for a limited amount of activities rather than the whole task itself.

ERG Theory. Alderfer believed that needs existed in only three categories: ***Existence needs*** (basic needs as addressed by Maslow plus the fundamental needs in the workplace such as basic benefits, coffee etc.)*,* ***Relatedness needs*** (the social company or interpersonal relations) and lastly, ***Growth needs*** (creativity, personal development and productive influence over the process).

Ethical Management is the result of a mutually beneficial environment for the supplier, worker and customer. A well-managed, socially and ethically responsible company will insure that they manage resources (employees and suppliers) in a mutually beneficial way, consistently and reliably, with a social and ethical platform. The consumer, knowing this, will inevitably benefit by knowing that they have contributed to an ethical working environment. This will lead to further brand loyalty, market share. The development of the employee and supplier will subsequently lead to a competitive situation. Keep in mind that competitiveness is not always price but also, loyalty, market share and innovation provide long-term stability.

Façades the front or outer appearance shown by a person, team, group or organization. These can be both deceptive and genuine. Also known as boundaries and are created by individuals as defense mechanisms to protect themselves.

Foundation Management is an ethical and socially responsible management philosophy, created by the author, with a primary focus on the management and development of its employee resources.

Group Dynamics or group culture is a group process that refers synergy and the understanding and acceptance of each individual's behavior within the group. The group leader (or facilitator) will usually have a strong influence on the group due to his or her role in the shaping and structure of the group including the group's communication, patterns of influence, patterns of dominance, social and task balancing factors, the level of effectiveness expected and achieved and how conflict is handled.

Hawthorne Effect was a study by Elton Mayo that showed that workers who received special attention would perform better.

Herzberg's Motivational Theory stems from his two-factor theory, which suggests that work satisfaction and dissatisfaction arise from two different sets of factors.

Innovative Development Process (IDP) is the product of Perpetual Motivation Positioning (PMP) and seven derivatives (productivity, reliability, objectivity, creativity, efficacy, satisfaction and stimulus).

Job Description is a written description of a job's title, duties, responsibilities, and to whom one reports (reporting into the position and reporting to).

Job Enrichment is commonly known as the combining of several activities from a vertical cross section of the organization in one job. This increase in job depth provides the employee with greater autonomy, flexibility and responsibility.

Knowledge is ambiguous and can include tacit and explicit knowledge, skills, abilities and competence or understanding.

Management is the process of leading an organization to achieve its goals by planning and organizing the resources.

Maslow's Hierarchy of Needs belongs to the Content theorists of motivation and claims that people are motivated to meet five types of needs in a hierarchal order. The lowest need needs to be fulfilled before you can move onto the next level.

McClelland's & Atkinson's Theories on Motivation. McClelland found that how well individuals are motivated depended upon a strong need for achievement and the desire to succeed or excel in competitive situations. Atkinson's model suggests that performance and behavior are related to the strength of the need and that the anticipation of achieving the goal, along with the incentive value, are the driving forces behind motivation.

Moral a concern with or relation to human behavior and the distinction between what is considered good and bad or right and wrong.

Morale is the degree of mental confidence, esprit de corps, self-esteem, spirit and heart that a person or group displays. Morale directly affects the level of motivation.

Motivation is an individual or team's ambition, desire and drive to induce an inspired change.

Perpetual Motivation Positioning (PMP) is a theory that to motivate an individual or team you will need to continually monitor and change the motivating variables. Theory of Perpetual Motivation Positioning (PMP) is based upon seven fluid variables facing the individual and the specific situation. As the circumstances change, so does the ability to achieve all seven variables. The individual's motivational level increases with each of the motivational criteria. These criteria are achieved either subconsciously (with a manager's help) or consciously through personal goal setting. PMP provides the impetus to IDP through stimulus (motivation) and this in turn increases total performance.

Physical Department Review includes the Environmental Demands, Environmental Needs, Strengths and Weaknesses. The **Environmental Demands** are internal and external demands placed upon the department to produce. The **Environmental Needs** or the resources needed to accomplish the demands. The **Strengths** are the areas in which the department is efficient and competitive whilst the **Weaknesses** are the areas in which the department lack in both efficacy and competitiveness.

Positional Work Life Cycle. A set of stages: *Intro 1, Intro 2-6 weeks,* Early Growth (Spur 1-9 months), Maximum Growth (6-12 months), Growth 2 (9-20 months), Late Growth (18-24 months) ,Early Maturity (18-36 months), Maturity (24-36 months), Late Maturity (30-52 months), Complacency (36 -72 months), Stagnation (54-96 months), Early Tunnel-Vision (78+ months), and Tunnel-Vision (96+ months)

Process Theories of Motivation focus on the thought processes made by the individual and the various decisions on how to behave concerning their degree of performance, specific role and/or degree of responsibility.

Quality Check-Points are the various check points with and operational task. All tasks should be fitted with a quality assurance and quality control step to insure that the tasks are accomplished in the same manner.

Quarterly Management has its focus on profit and short-term results dictated by the stock market. This leads to number-function management where employees are functional units on a spread sheet.

Scientific Management Theory was created between 1890 to 1930 by Fredrick Taylor and others to show that the best methods for performing any task, selecting, motivating and training of workers could be designed and proven scientifically.

Selecting Team Members is done in the following three steps: 1) Job description and educational constraints which are Registered & Certified Positions (RCP), Specialized Positions (SP), and Industrial Non-certified Positions (INP) , and Non-certified Positions (NP), 2) Working knowledge is their experience and problem-solving abilities, 3) Team work is their ability to be open, supportive, action-orientation (pro-activeness), personal style, and communicative capability.

Team Building Process can be used in both company and on the sports field. Many sports psychologists use it in their team dynamics programs. In order of progression it starts with the Selection of participants, establishing goals, and balancing micro-tasks or skills (Educational Design), allocation or roles and tutoring schedule (trainee/trainer) within the team, allocation of training rotations within the team, working personalities (working together), support for the team (coaching), effective use of resources, and communication between all stakeholders.

Theory X according to McGregor, a traditional motivation theorist, that work is distasteful to employees and that they must be motivated by force, money or praise.

Theory Y according to McGregor, a traditional motivation theorist, that people are inherently motivated to work and want to do a good job.

Total Quality Management (TQM) is a strategic commitment to improve quality through a combination of statistical methods and innovation leading to increased productivity and lower costs.

Tuckman's Stages is a 4-stage group decision making process model: ***Forming*** (pretending to get on or get along with others); ***Storming*** (letting down the politeness barrier and getting onto the issues at hand, even if tempers can flare up); ***Norming*** (getting used to each other and developing trust and productivity); ***Performing*** (working as a group to achieve a common goal in a highly efficient and cooperative manner). A fifth stage has subsequently been added called the ***Adjourning*** (team functionality). Naturally, if distrust persists the group can never pass the Norming stage.

Bibliography

Alversson, Mats. (2004), *"Knowledge Work and Knowledge-Intensive Firms."* New York: Oxford University Press. Pages 17-40.

Alversson, Mats. (2004), *"Knowledge Work and Knowledge-Intensive Firms."* New York: Oxford University Press. Pages 70-97.

Alversson, Mats. (2004), *"Knowledge Work and Knowledge-Intensive Firms."* New York: Oxford University Press. Pages 188-220.

Alderfer, C.P. (1969), *"An Empirical Test of a New Theory of Human Needs,"* Organizational and Human Needs." New York: Free Press, 142-175.

Alderfer, C.P. (1972), *"Existence, Relatedness, and Growth: Human Needs in Organizational Settings"* New York: Free Press.

Atkinson, John W. and Birch, David. (1978), *"An Introduction to Motivation."* rev. ed. New York: Van Nostrand Reinhold.

Atkinson, John W. (1983), *"Personality, Motivation and Action."* Selected Papers. New York: Praeger: 174-188.

Belbin, Meredith R. (1981 & 2003), *"Management Teams - Why They Succeed or Fail."* London: Butterworth Heinemann.

Belbin, Meredith R. (1997), *"Changing the Way We Work."* London: Butterworth Heinemann.

Blomstedt, Åsa. (2009) "Effectivity when nurses take larger responsibility for fractures." *Vårdfacket*. Nr. 3., 3/2009- Pages 4-6.

Bolman, Lee G. and Deal, Terrence E. (2008) *"Reframing Organizations: Artistry, Choice, and Leadership."* San Francisco: Jossey-Bass. 527 Pages.

Bolt, Laurance G. (1999) *"The TAO of Abundance: Eight Ancient Principles for Abundant Living."* New York: Pengiun Compass. 353 Pages.

Boyd, David and Chinyio, Ezekiel. (2006), "Understanding the Construction Client." Oxford: Blackwelll Publishing Ltd. Page 65 (The Johari-Window).

Breckler, Steven J. (1984), "Empirical validation of affect, behavior, and cognition as distinct components of attitude." *Journal of Personality and Social Psychology*. Issue 47. Pages 1191-1205.

Breckler, Steven J. and Wiggins, E. (1991), "Cognitive responses in persuasion: Affective and evaluative determinants." *Journal of Experimental Social Psychology*. Issue 27. Pages 180-200.

Brun, Emmanuelle and Milczarek, Malgorzata. (2007) *"Expert forecast on emerging psychosocial risks related to occupational safety and health."* European Agency for Safety and Health at Work: Luxembourg 2007, 127 pages.

Burke, Warner and Litwin, George. (1992) "The Burke-Litwin Model" *Journal of Management*: Vol 18. No. 3.

Calhoun, Wick W. and Stanton, Leon Lu. (1993) *"Individual learning nutures J.P. Morgan."* Personnel Journal. Santa Monica: Nov. Vol. 72, Iss. 11; pages 49-53.

Cameron, Kim S. and Quinn, Robert E. (2005) "Diagnosing and Changing Organizational Culture: Based on the Competing Values Framework." San Francisco: Jossey-Bass. Pages 256.

Campbell, Andrew and Nash, Laura L. (1992) *"A Sense of Mission: Defining Direction for the Large Corporation."* (International Management Series. London: Addison Wesley Publishing Company. Pages 317.

Cassitto, Maria; Fattorini, Emanuela; Giliolo, Renato; and Rengo, Chiara. (2003) *"Psychological Harassment at Work,"* World Health Organization. Geneva: Protecting Workers' Health Series No. 4 , 1-40.

Dr. van Cauter, Eve and Copinschi, George. (1998) *"Endocrine Rhythms: Roles of the Sleep-Wake Cycle, the Circadian Clock & the Environment: Diagnostic & Therapeutic Implications 40th International Henri-Pierre Kolts (Hormine Research, 3-4)"* Switzerland: S. Karger AG.

Cheraskin, Lisa and Campion, Michael A. (1996) *"Study clarifies job-rotation benefits."* Personnel Journal. Nov 1996. Vol. 75, Issue 11; pg. 31 (6 pages).

Cote, James E. and Levin, Charles (2002) *"Identity Formation, agency, and culture: A social psychological synthesis."* Mahwah, NJ: Lawrence Erlbaum Associates.

Davenport Thomas H. and Prusak, Laurence. (1998) "Working Knowledge: How organizations manage what they know." Harvard Business School Press. Pages 199.

Davenport Thomas H. (1992) "Process Innovation: Reengineering Work Through Information Technology." Boston: Harvard Business School Press. Pages 352.

Deci, Edward L. and Ryan, Richard M. (1985) *"Intrinsic Motivation and Self-determination in Human Behavior."* New York: Planum.

Duffy, Tom. (1997) *"Cross-training at work."* Network World. Framingham: Dec. 15, 1997. Vol 14, Iss. 50; pg. 53, 1 page.

Eastman, C.I., Hoese, E.K., Youngstedt, S.D. and Liu. Li. (1995) *"Phase-shifting human circadian rhythms with exercise during the night shift."* Physiol Behav. 1995;58:1287-1291.

European Agency for Safety and Health at Work. (2002) *"Working on Stress."* EU-OSHA Magazine 5, 2002, 32 pages

Fairhurst, Gail T. and Sarr, Robert A. (1996) "The Art of Framing: Managing the Language of Leadership." San Francisco: Jossey-Bass. Pages 207.

Flemming, Peter & Spicer Andre (2003) "Working at a Cynical Distance: Implications for Power, Subjectivity & Resistance." *Organization*; 10; 157-179.

Forsyth, D.R. (2006) *"Group Dynamics."* 4th Edition. Belmont. CA: Thomson Wadsworth, 2006.

Foucault, Michel. (2001) "Fearless Speech," Chapter ! In Fearless Speech. Los Angeles: Semiotext (e). Pages 128.

French, Wendell L. and Bell, Cecil H. Jr. (1984) *"Organizational Development: Behavioral Science Interventions for Organization Improvement."* 3rd ed. Englewood Cliffs, N.J.: Prentice Hall, 1984, pp. 54-62.

French, J. P. R. Jr., and Raven, B. (1960). The bases of social power. In D. Cartwright and A. Zander (eds.), *Group dynamics* (pp. 607-623). New York: Harper and Row.

Freud, Anna. (1937). *"Ego and mechanisms of defense."* London: The Hogarth Press & Institute of Psychoanalysis.

Freud, Sigmund. (1923) *"The Ego and the Id."* London: The Hogarth Press Ltd. London.

Freud, Sigmund. (1949) *"The Ego and the Id."* London: The Hogarth Press Ltd. London.

Funk, Jeffery L. (1988) *"How Does Japan Do It?"* Production. Cincinnati: Aug 1988. Vol. 100, Iss. 8; pg. 57, 6 pages.

Galbraith, J. D. and Kates, A. (2002) *Designing dynamic organizations.* New York: AMACOM.

Guglielmino, Lucy M. and Guglielmino, Paul J. (2007) *"Productivity in the workplace: The role of self-directed learning and the implications for human resource management."* International Journal of Human Resources Development and Management. Geneva. Vol. 8 Issue 4; page 293.

Van Gundy, Arthur B. (2007) *"Getting to Innovation: How asking the right questions generates the great ideas your company needs."* New York: AMACOM. Pages 270.

Hammer, Michael and Champy James. (2003) *"Reengineering the Corporation: A Manifesto for Business Revolution."* New York: Harper Collins. Pages 272.

Hanners, Angela C. (1999) *"Organizational factors that influence absence."* Huntsville: The University of Alabama in Hunstville, 1999, 37 pages.

Hart, S. G. & Staveland, L. E. (1988) *"Development of a multi-dimensional workload rating scale: Results of emperical and theoretical research."* In P.A. Hancock / N. Meshkati (Eds.), *Human Mental Workload*. Amsterdam. The Netherlands: Elsevier.

Henderson, Chris J. and Cemohous, Cindy. (1994) *"Ergonomics: A business approach."* Professional Safety. Park Ridge: jan 1994. Vol. 39, Iss. 1; pg 27, 5 pages.

Herzberg, Fredrick; Mausner, Bernard and Synderman, Barbara. (1959) *"The Motivation to Work."* New York: John Wiley & Sons.

Herzberg, Fredrick. (1966) *"Work and the Nature of Man."* New York: World Publishing.

Herzberg, Fredrick. (1968) *"One more Time: How do You Motivate Employees?"* Harvard Business Review 46, no 1 (January-February 1968):53-62.

Hoff, Ron. (1992). *"I Can See You Naked."* Kansas City: Andrews and McMeel.

Holmes, Thomas and Rahe, Richard. (1967). *"The Social Readjustment Rating Scale."* J Psychosom Res. 1967 Aug; 11(2):213-8

Hofstede, G. (1980) "Culture's Consequences: International Differences inWork-Related Values, Sage: London.

Hoc, Jean-Michel & Debernard, Serge. (2002). *"Respective demands of task and function allocation on human-machine cooperation design: a psychological approach."* Connection Science, Vol. 14, No. 4, 2002, pages 283-295.

Huse, Edgar F. and Cummings, Thomas G. (1985). *"Organizational Development and Change,"* 3rd ed. St Paul, Minnesota: West. Page 20.

Huzzard, T., Gregory, D., and Scott, R. (2005) *"Strategic Unionism and Partnership: Boxing or Dancing?"* London: Palgrave Macmillan. p384.

Ilmarine, Harma; Rutenfranz, Knauth P. and Hanninen, J. (1998). *"Physical training intervention in female shift workers. I. The effects of intervention on fitness, fatigue, sleep, and psychosomatic symptoms."* Ergonimics. 1998; 31:39-50.

Ilmarine, Harma; Rutenfranz, Knauth P. and Hanninen, J. (1998). *"Physical training intervention in female shift workers. II. The effects of intervention on the circadiam rhythms on alertness, short-term memory, and body temperature."* Ergonomics. 1998; 31:51-63.

Jorgenson, D.W. and Griliches, Z. (1999). *"The Explanation of Productivity Change."* Review of Economic Studies. 34(99): p249-283.

Kanter, Rosbeth Moss. (1983) *"The Change Masters."* New York: Simon & Schuster.

Kaplan, Robert and Norton David P. (1996). *"The Balanced Scorecard: Translating Strategy into Action."* Boston: MA. Harvard Business School Press, Pages 322.

Klein, Gary A.; Orasanu, J. and Zsambok, C.E. (1993). *"Decision Making in Action: Models and Methods."* Ablex Publishing Co., Norwwod, NJ. 1993.

Klein, Gary A. (1998). *"Sources of Power. How People Make Decisions."* MIT Press, Cambridge, MA. Pages 1-30.

Kleiner, Art. (2003). "Who Really matters: The Core Group Theory of Power, Privilege and Success." London: Nicholas Brealey Publishing Ltd. Pages 292.

Kotter, John, P. (1996) Leading Change: Why Transformation Efforts Fail." *Harvard Business Review on Change*. Boston: Harvard Business School Press. Pages 1-20.

von Krogh, Georg, Ichijo, Kazuo and Nonaka, Ikujiro. (2000). "Enabling Knowledge Creation: How to Unlock the Mystery of Tacit Knowledge and Release the Power of Innovation." Oxford University Press: Oxford. 292 Pages.

Lave, Jean and Wenger, Etienne. (1991) "Situated learning: Legitimate peripheral participation." Cambridge: Cambridge University Press. Pages 139.

Lazarus, Richard. (2002). *"From psychological stress to the emotions: a history of changing outlooks."* Annual Review of Psychology 44: 1-22

Locke, Edwin A. and Latham, Gary P. (2002). *"Building a practically useful theory of goal-setting and task motivation: A 35-year odyssey."* American Psychologist. 57, 701-717.

Maddux, Robert B. and Wingfield, Barb. (2003). *"Team Building."* Boston: Course Technology.

Magrath, Allan J. (1989). *"Eight Strategies Engender Teamwork Between Functions."* Marketing news. Chicago: Jun 19, 1989. Vol. 23, Iss. 13; pg. 12, 2 pages.

Malhotra, Y. (1998). *"Tools@work: Deciphering the knowledge management hype."* Journal for Quality and Participation, special issue on Learning and Information Management, 21(4):58-60.

Marguiles, Newton and Raia, Anthony P. (1984) *"The Politics of Organizational Development and Change."* Training and Development Journal 38, no.8, August: pages 20-23.

McCune, Jenny C. (1994). *"On the train gang."* Management Review. New York: Oct. 1994. Vol. 83, Iss. 10; pg. 57, 4 pages.

Maslow, Abraham, H. (1970). *"Motivation and Personality."* 2nd ed. New York: Harper & Row.

Mayo, Elton. (1953). *"The Human Problems of an Industrial Civilization."* New York: Macmillan.

McClelland, David. (1961). *"The Achieving Society."* Princeton, N.J.: Van Nostrand Reinhold.

McClelland, David. (1962). *"Business Drive and National Achievement."* Harvard Business Review 40, no 4 (July-August 1962): 99-112.

McClelland, David. (1965). *"Toward a Theory of Motive Acquisition."* American Psychologist 20, no 5 (May 1965): 321-333.

McGregor, Douglas. (1960). *"The Human Side of Enterprise."* New York: McGraw Hill.

McGregor, Douglas. (1967). *"The Professional Manager."* New York: McGraw Hill.

McGregor, Eugene B. Jr. (1991). "Strategic Management of Human Knowledge, Skills, and Abilities: Workforce Decision Making in the Post-Industrial Era." San Francisco: Jossey-Bass Publishers. Pages 348.

Messmer, Max. (1992). "Cross-Discipline Training: A Strategic Method to Do More with Less." *Management Review.* New York: May, Vol. 81, Iss. 5; pg. 26, 3 pages.

Michelsen, Clive. (2007). *"Cross-Training: Theory, Design & Implementation."* Charleston, South Carolina: BookSurge.

Minor, Marianne. (1995). *"Coaching for Development."* Boston, MA: Thomson Learning/Course Technology.

Mintzberg, Henry, Ahlstrand, Bruce and Lampel, Joseph. (1998) *"Strategy Safari: The complete guide through the wilds of strategic management."* Glasgow, U.K.: Prentice Hall. Pages 233-262.

Morgan, Gareth. (1996) *"Images of Organization."* 2nd Ed. London: Sage Publications. Pages 485.

Nadler, David A. and Lawler, Edward E. III. (1977) *"Motivation—a Diagnostic Approach."* In Richard Hackman, Edward Lawler III, and Lyman Porter, eds., *"Perspectives on Behavior in Organizations."* New York: McGraw-Hill, page 27.

Nadler, David A. (1981). *"Managing Organizational Change: An Integrative Perspective."* Journal of Applied Behavioral Science 17, no. 2 (April-May-June): 191-211.

Nadler, David and Tushman, Michael. (1988) "Strategic Organization Design: Concepts, tools, & process." Glenview, IL.: Scott Foresman.

Nonaka, Ikujiro and Takeuchi, Hirotaka. (1995). "The Knowledge-Creating Company: How Japanese Companies Create the Dynamics of Innovation." Oxford University Press: Oxford, Pages 284.

Odiorne, George S. (1979). *"MBO II."* Belmont California: Feron Pitman.

Palmer, I., Dunford, R. and Akin, G. (2009) *"Managing Organizational Change: A multiple perspectives approach."* Boston: McGrawHillIrwin. Pages 413.

Pascale, Richard T. and Athos, Anthony G. (1981). *"The Art of Japanese Management."* New York: Simon & Schuster.

Porter, Michael E. (1998). *"Competitive Advantage: Creating and Sustaining Superior Performance."* The Free Press (Simon & Schuster): New York, Pages 557.

Porter, Michael E. (1998). *"Competitive Strategy."* The Free Press (Simon & Schuster): New York, Pages 396.

Porter, Michael E. (2008). *"Porter on Competition."* Harvard Business School Publishing: Boston, Pages 21-38.

Prahalad, C.K. and Hammel, Gary. (1996). *"Competing for the Future."* Harvard Business School Press: Boston, pages 357.

Prahalad, C. K. and Krishnan, M.S. (2008). *"The New Age of Innovation: Driving Co-created Value Through Global Networks."* McGraw-Hill: New York, Pages 304. Business Process, 44-79; Efficiency and Flexibility, 174-203; Dynamic reconfiguration of talent, 204-233; Essence of innovation, 234-266.

Price, Allan. (2008). "Human Resource Management in a Business Context." Thomsan Learning: London, 745 pages.

Prendergast, Canice and Topel, Robert H. (1996). *"Favoritism in organizations."* The Journal of Political Economics. Chicago: October. Vol. 104., Iss. 5; pages. 958-979.

Rahe, Richard H. (1978). *"Life Changes and illness studies: past history and future directions."* J Human Stress 4 (1): 3-15.

Roan, Shari (2008). *"Sleep deprived pay the price for shift work."* Los Angeles (Staff Writer): Los Angeles Times, March 24th.

Roberts, John. (2004). *"The Modern Firm: Organizational Design for Performance and Growth."* Oxford: Oxford University Press, 318 pages.

Rolland, C.; Prakash, N. and Benjamen, A. (1999). *"A Multi-Model View of Process Modelling."* Requirements Engineering. Volume 4, no. 4, Springer-Verlag, London.

Santalo-Mediavilla, Jaun Ph.D. (2002). (Dissertation) *"Two essays on applied economics of organizations."* Chicago: The University press of Chicago, 144 pages (AAT 3060261).

Schein, Edgar H. (1980). *"Organizational Psychology,"* 3rd ed. Englewood Cliffs, N.J.:Prentice Hall, 1980, pp.243-247.

Schein, Edgar H. (2004). *"Organizational Culture and Leadership."*San Francisco: Jossey-Bass; 3rd. ed. 437p.

Schön, D.A. (1973). *"Beyond the Stable State. Public and private learning in a changing society."* Harmondsworth: Penguin.

Selyle, Hans. (1950). *"Diseases of adaptation."* Wisconsin Medical Journal 49 (6): 515-6.

Senge, P.M. (1990). *"The Fifth Discipline. The art and practice of the learning organization."* London: Random House.

Shutz, W. (1958). *"FIRO: A Three-Dimensional Theory of Interpersonal Behavior."* New York: Holt, Rinehart & Winston.

Stetenfeld, Beth. (1995). *"Cross paths" Credit Union Management."* Madison: January, Vol. 18, Iss. 1; pg. 41, 3 pgs.

Straub, Joseph T. (1991). *"Cross-training: Blend Ability with Flexibility."* Supervisory Management. Saranac Lake: may 1991. Vol. 36, Iss. 5; pg. 11.

Synder, Joanne and Nethersole-Chong, Denise. (1999). *"Is cross-training medical/surgical RNs to ICU the answer?"* Nursing Management. Chicago: February, Vol. 30, Iss. 2; pages. 58-61.

Tampoe, Mahen. (1993). *Motivating Knowledge—The Challenge for the 1990s."* Pergamon Press Ltd.: London. Long Range Planning. Vol 26, No. 3, pages 49-55.

Todd, P. and Gigerenzer, G. (2001). *"Putting Naturalistic Decision Making into the Adaptive Toolbox."* Journal of Behavioral Decision Making: Vol. 14, 353-384.

Tuckman, B. (1965). *"Development sequence in small groups."* Psychological bulletin 63:384-399.

van Reeth, Olivier. (1988). *"Sleep and Circadian Disturbances in Shift Work: Strategies for their Management."* International Journal of Experimental and Clinical Endocrinology: Hormone Research; 49: 158-162.

Volokh, Eugene. (2003). *"The Mechanisms of the Slippery Slope."* Harvard Law Review: 116 (4); pages 1026-1137.

Warr, P., Editor. (1984). *"Sources and Management of Excessive Job Stress and Burnout."* Psychology at Work. New York: Pengiun Books, 1984 (pp.188-223).

Easterby-Smith, M.; Burgoyne, J. and Araujo, L.; Editors. (1999). *"Organizational Learning and the Learning Organization."* London.

Weber, Max. (1947). *"The Theory of Social and Economic Organizations."* Talcott Parsons, ed. A.M. Henderson and Parsons, trans. (New York: Free Press.

Wendell, L.., Bell, C.H. Jr., Zawacki, R..A. (2005) *"Organization Development and Transformation: Managing Effective Change"* 6th ed. Boston: McGrawHillIrwin. Pages 506.

Wenger, Etienne; McDermot, Richard; and Snyder William M. (2002) "Cultivating Communities of Practice" Harvard Business School Press. P. 283.

Wenger, Etienne. (1998) "Communities of Practice: Learning, Meaning and Identity. " Cambridge: Cambridge University Press. Pages 318.

Willmott, Hugh & Contu, Alessia. (2003). *"Re-Embedding Situatedness: The Importance of Power Relations in Learning Theory."* Organization Science: Volume 14, No. 3, May-June, pages 283-296.

Williamson, A.M. and Fèyer, Anne-Marie. (2000). *"Moderate sleep deprivation produces impairments in cognitive and motor performance equivalent to legally prescribed levels of alcohol intoxication."* Occupational and Environmental Medicine: 2000; 57:649-655 (October).

Wittgenstein, Ludvig. (2000). *"Ian Heaton, John M. Wittgenstein and Psychoanalysis."* Cambridge: Icon Boolks Ltd., page 18.

Wolf, Murray B. (2007). *"Faster Construction Projects with CPM Scheduling."* New York: McGraw-Hill, pages 3-33.

Xie, Bin & Salvendy, Gavriel. (2000) *"Preview and reappraisal of modelling and predicting mental workload in single- and multi-task environments."* Work and Stress: Vol. 14, No. 1, pages 74-90

"Sales Training: Effective Steps to Increase Sales -Part 2." Small Business Report. New York: Jan 1986. Vol. 11, Iss. 1; pg. 85, 4 pages.

"Why People Behave the Way They Do," Darden School Case UVA/OB/183. Charlottesville, Virginia: Darden Graduate Business School Foundation. Charlottesville, 1986.

"Webster's New World Dictionary of the American Language," Second College Edition. Simon & Schuster.

Index

Symbols

A

B

M

T

U

V

W